PROPHETIC TRADITIONS IN ISLAM

On the Authority of the Family of the Prophet

PROPHETIC TRADITIONS IN ISLAM

On the Authority of the Family of the Prophet

Shaykh Fadhlalla Haeri

Zahra Publications

First published in 1986
Distributed & Re-published by the Muhammadi Trust UK 2016
PO Box 50764
Wierda Park 0149
Centurion
South Africa
Email: zp@sfhfoundation.com
Website: www.sfhfoundation.com/
www.zahrapublication.com

© 2015 Shaykh Fadhlalla Haeri

All rights reserved. Except for brief quotations in critical articles or reviews, no part of this book may be reproduced or utilized in any form or by any means, electronic or mechanical, without permission in writing from the publisher.

Designed and typeset in South Africa by Book Lingo
Cover Design by Mizpah Marketing Concepts
Artwork and ebook design by Abdal Latif Whiteman
Project Management by Quintessence Publishing

Set in 11,5 point on 15 point, Garamond
Printed and bound in USA by Lightning Source

ISBN (Printed Version) – Paperback: 978-1-919826-92-9

Table of Contents

Book Description	i
About the Author	ii
Editor's Note	iii
Preface	iv
Preface to the English Edition	v
Foreword by Professor Seyyed Hossein Nasr	vi
Introduction by Sayyid Bahr al-'Ulum	vii
I: OUR SYSTEM OF BELIEF	**1**
Belief in Allah	**1**
The Way of Oneness	1
Islam	6
Faith	9
Fear of Allah and carefulness in one's behavior (*taqwa*)	13
Trust in Allah	17
Reflection	20
Sincerity and Devotion	22
Justice	23
Having a good opinion of Allah	27
The Trial and the Test	29
Contentment with Allah's Decree and One's Own Destiny	32

Belief in the Last Day and the Place of Return	36
Remembrance of death	41
The *Barzakh*, or matters pertaining to the time spent in the grave before the Day of Resurrection	45
The Place of Assembly of the Day of Resurrection	49
The Garden and the Fire	51
Belief in Prophethood	**53**
Creation's Need of the Prophets and Messengers	53
The Mission of the Seal of the Prophets	57
The Life Story of the Prophet Muhammad	61
Belief in Imamate	**65**
Necessity of the existence of the Imam after the Prophet	65
Necessity of Obedience to the Imam after the Prophet	69
The Family of the Prophet	73
The Commander of the Faithful, Imam `Ali ibn Abi Taalib	78
Imam al-Hasan ibn `Ali ibn Abi Taalib	82
Imam al-Husayn ibn `Ali ibn Abi Taalib	86
Imam `Ali ibn al-Husayn	90
Imam Muhammad ibn `Ali al-Baaqir	94
Imam Ja`far ibn Muhammad al-Saadiq	98
Imam Musa ibn Ja`far al-Kaazim	102
Imam `Ali ibn Musa al-Rida	105
Imam Muhammad ibn `Ali al-Jawaad	108
Imam `Ali ibn Muhammad al-Haadi	112

Imam al-Hasan ibn `Ali al-`Askari	113
Imam Muhammad ibn al-Hasan al-Mahdi	117
Imam al-Mahdi	118
The Importance of the Learned (*al-`ulama*) during the period of the Mahdi's occultations	123
II: OUR WAY OF WORSHIP	**126**
Prayer *(salaat)*	**126**
The Obligatory Prayers at the Appointed Times	126
Prayer in the Night	131
Remembrance of Allah	133
Supplicatory prayer (*du`aa*)	136
The Conditions of Prayer	140
Humility	141
Fear and Turning to Allah for Forgiveness	143
Different Kinds of Wrong Actions	150
Recitation of the Qur'an	151
Fasting *(sawm)*	**157**
Pilgrimage *(hajj)*	**161**
Purification or Poor-Rate Tax *(zakaat and khums)*	**166**
Zakaat	166
Khums	170
Struggle in The Way Of Allah *(Jihad)* **and Enjoining Good and Forbidding Evil** *(Al-Amr Bi Al-Ma`Ruf Wa-Al-Nahian Al-Munkar)*	**174**
Struggle in The Way of Allah	174

Enjoining Good and Forbidding Evil	179
III: BEHAVIOR AND COURTESY IN ISLAM	**183**
Human Values	**183**
The Struggle against the Self	183
The Intellect	183
The Heart	187
Knowledge of the Self	189
The Faults of the Self	194
Self-Reckoning and Vigilence over the Self	196
Keeping Watch	201
Controlling the Passions	203
Withdrawel from Society and Solitude	207
Purification and Cleanliness	209
Noble Behavior	**213**
Good Character	213
Forbearance	215
Forgiveness	219
Modesty	221
Virtue	223
Humility	224
Generosity	227
Preference for Others	230
Fear amd Hope	232
Patience	236

Doing Without	239
Good Actions towards Others	244
Contentment	246
Trust	249
The Keeping of Secrets	251
Kindness taowards Parents	253

Maintaining Family Ties and the Courtesies of Social Intercourse   255

The Education of Children	255
Maintaining Good Family Relations	257
The Courtesies of Marriage and what is Obligatory for the two Spouses	260
The Duties of the Wife and the Rights of the Husband over his Wife	267
The Courtesies of Social Relations	268
Greeting People with the Greeting of 'Peace'	272
Shaking Hands and Kissing	275
The Courtesies of Sitting	278
The Courtesies of Asking Permission	280
The Giving of Gifts	282
The Adoption of Brothers	283
Respect for Elders	287
The Rights of the Neighbor	289
Helping the Believers	292
Love of Men who are Righteous	295

Visiting Each Other	297
Kindness and Compassion towards People	299
Accompanying the Corpse to the Grave	301
Visiting the Sick	303
Keeping Company with People and Assisting them	304

Vices and Blameworthy Behavior and Characteristics 307

Vices	307
Oppression	307
Miserliness	310
Lying	312
Hypocrisy	315
Anger	317
Backbiting	320
Defamation or Slander	324
Dissemblance	325
Flattery	328
Blameworthy Behavior	329
Pride	329
Vanity	332
Love and Greed for this World	335
Luxury	339
Play and Idle Sport	341
Greed and Covetousness	343
Envy	345

Blameworthy Characteristics	347
Hopelessness and Despair	347
Excessive Hope	349
Love of Reputation	352
Disdain of Others	354
Heedlessness	355
Obligation	358
Bibliography	**360**

Book Description
TRANSLATED BY
Asadullah adh-Dhaakir Yate

This collection of verses from the Qur'an and traditions from the Prophet Muhammad (may the peace and blessings of Allah be upon him and his family) and the Imams is unique for it makes available for the first time in English a comprehensive selection of Islamic teachings arranged according to topics that deal with belief and worship as well as the social and spiritual values which Islam upholds.

Prophetic Traditions in Islam — On the Authority of the Family of the Prophet contains a wealth of wisdom, knowledge and inspiration for all who seek to know more about Islam and the process of refining one's character and conduct. Taking as its source the gnosis and science transmitted by Allah on the tongue of the Prophet Muhammad, it presents fundamentals of the legal parameters and spiritual truths of Islam.

From [this book] one can learn a great deal about the Islamic concept of God and prophecy, of worship and virtue, of the character of the Shi'ite Imams and even of early Islamic history. Furthermore, one can also learn much about the human state, its origin and end, and the meaning of terrestrial existence and our role here on earth. The book therefore addresses itself not only to the lovers of the Ahl al-Bayt and all Muslims, but in fact to all human beings, whatever their background may be, as long as they are attracted to the world of the Spirit and are in quest of meaning in their transient lives here on earth.

from the foreword by Seyyed Hossein Nasr

About the Author

Shaykh Fadhlalla Haeri is a spiritual philosopher and writer whose role as a teacher grew naturally out of his own quest for self-fulfillment. Since childhood he has been attracted to scientific investigation and intellectual pursuit. After a stint in industry and consulting, he embarked on teaching, writing and meditating.

His awareness of global realpolitik compelled him to seek a truth that would reconcile the past with the present, the East and West. His discovery affirms that One Cosmic Reality is the source behind all known and unknown states.

Shaykh Haeri's unifying perspective emphasizes practical, actionable knowledge of self-transformation. It provides a natural bridge between different approaches to spirituality, offering common ground of higher knowledge for various religions, sects and secular outlooks. With a lifetime's experience of contemplation, research, and insights, he shares what it means to live in the light of the Absolute in a relative world and maintains that spiritual awakening is potentially available to all.

Editor's Note

While it is customary to include invocations of peace and blessings upon the Prophet Muhammad and his family whenever his name is mentioned, these have not been included in the text for reasons of space. Nonetheless such prayers are implicit in the mention of his name and we trust the reader will naturally invoke Allah's blessings upon the Prophet and his family.

Any commentary on the traditions appears in italics.

It may be of interest to the reader to note from the full title of one of the primary sources of *hadith* for this collection – *al-Muhajjah al-Bayda' fi Tahdhib al-Ihya'* by Muhammad ibn al-Murtada al-Fayd al-Kashani – that it owes much to Abu Hamid al-Ghazzali's opus *Ihya' `Ulum al-Din*. Al-Kashani based his own work on the format of the *Ihya'*, confirming its contents from the perspective of the Ahl al-Bayt. This means that while the chains of transmission (*asanid*) may differ the *hadith* are largely the same or similar in content.

The beloved Prophet Muhammad (may peace and blessings be upon him) is referred to interchangebly as the Prophet, the Prophet of Allah, the Messenger and the Messenger of Allah. Due reference is intended in all cases.

The Holy Qur'an is referred to interchangebly as the Book, the Book of Wisdom, the Holy Book and the Noble Book.

Imam `Ali is also referred to as `Ali and due reference is accurate in both formats.

Imam al-Sadiq is also referred to as Al-Sadiq and due reference is accurate in both formats.

☼ The sun symbol within the book, indicates all the Qua'ranic verses.

Preface

Praise belongs to Allah, Who has taught us what we did not know, and praises and blessings be upon the seal of the prophets and messengers, Muhammad, the Messenger from the Lord of the Worlds, on his blessed and fortunate family, and on the chosen of his companions and whoever follows him and his correct path of behavior until the final day.

I present this book as a concise manual containing the fundamentals of the legal parameters and spiritual truths of Islam – taking as its source the gnosis and science transmitted by Allah on the tongue of Muhammad; I present it to whoever desires the path of success and prosperity in this world and in the world to come after death.

In this age, man is experiencing tremendously rapid shifts in culture, and is subject to much emotional and psychological disturbance. This results in a hurried, even frenzied mode of existence, a feeling of contraction in the breast and submission to the superficial and material. The best way out of this crisis is to return to a religion which contains a legal framework, a method of worship and a system of correct behavior and morality. I have sought to make this work concise in an attempt to be of the utmost benefit to both the scholar and the ordinary man.

I have laid particular emphasis on knowledge of the self, directives for the guidance of the intellect and refinement of behavior, and on those things which increase courtesy and unify one's intentions towards Allah. Also emphasized are those actions which enable the sincere to renounce the love of this world, to adorn themselves with praiseworthy qualities and to achieve illumination of the heart – for whoever knows his self knows his Lord. Through Islam, the slave recognizes and adopts good manners, lives his life according to the prophetic pattern, travels the path of worship and affirms His Oneness.

I ask Allah that He show us His mercy and His unbounded infinite justice; that He enable us to have mastery over the desires of the self and whatever leads it astray; that He crown our efforts with excellence and prosperity in this world and make them bear fruit in the next world, for 'whoever is blind in this world, will also be blind in the hereafter, and more erring from the way' [Qur'an 17:72].

Praise and thanks belong to the Sole God, the One, the Unique, the One on Whom all depend, Who neither begets nor is begotten, and none is like unto Him.

I would like to thank sincerely all my brother believers who encouraged me and took part in the production of this work, in particular Hujjat al-Islam wa-al-Muslimin Doctor Sayyid Muhammad Bahr al-Ulum, for his encouragement and direction and his concern for the accuracy and correctness of the text. I would also like to express my gratitude to Doctor Jasim Husayn for his suggestions, for planning the form of the index and for researching many of the traditions. Similarly, I owe special thanks to Muhyi al-Din al-Khatib, who brought together and checked the book – my thanks together with my prayers for his health and blessings in this world and the next. Finally, I would mention all those brothers and sisters who participated in the production of this book.

I would like to conclude by begging forgiveness of the reader for any mistakes or shortcomings in this work, and I ask of the Creator that He grant me, my parents and all believing men and women, forgiveness. I seek forgiveness of Allah, there being no other god but Allah, the Beneficent, the Merciful, the One Who gives and maintains life, and I turn to Him in repentance. There is no success except by Allah, the Sublime, the Mighty, and I ask for praise and blessings on our lord Muhammad and on his Family.

Shaykh Fadhlalla Haeri

Preface to the English Edition

Our *Din* is based on preoccupation with the knowledge of Allah, following the Prophet's path. As Muslims we are privileged to have the glorious Qur'an and the life and conduct of the Prophet Muhammad. While the Qur'an is an ever-fresh source of inspiration, the Prophetic way was its human manifestation.

In this volume I have endeavored to select what I considered most appropriate and useful from the Prophetic teachings, as narrated by the Prophet's household. Brevity and the transformative potential of these *ahadith* have been the guidelines. The source books of these teachings are easily available as they continue to be published as part of the Ahl al-Bayt traditions and teachings. However, there was a need for an easily accessible collection in English, and this we have undertaken to make available for the seeker.

Thanks are due to Muna Bilgrami for preparing this English edition for publication and to Luqman Ali Ansari for his help in checking the translation.

I request the reader to ponder upon these gems and to see how the divinely revealed truth manifests in the existential and transactional life.

Shaykh Fadhlalla Haeri

November 1999

Foreword
In the Name of God,
the Infinitely Good, the All-Merciful

The collection of the sayings or traditions of the Blessed Prophet of Islam, known as *Hadith*, constitutes an ocean of wisdom and is the source, along with the Noble Qur'an, of all that is authentically Islamic. These *Hadiths* were transmitted by numerous sources and assembled by Sunni and Shi'ite scholars of *Hadith*, or *muhaddithun*, with great care and deliberation into collections of which a number gained canonical authority in the Sunni as well as the Shi'ite world. Although the content of most of the *ahadith* or traditions is the same in both worlds, the Shi'ite emphasize the significance of the family of God's last messenger or Ahl al-Bayt in the transmission of the words of the Blessed Prophet over all other lines. The Ithna `Ashari collections contain, moreover, sayings of the twelve Shi'ite Imams as well, although a clear distinction is made between prophetic *hadith* (*hadith nabawi*) and the sayings of an Imam (*hadith walawi*).

To understand why these collections such as al-Kulayni's *al-Kafi* contain also the sayings of the Imams, it must be understood that according to Twelve-Imam Shi'ite doctrine, the Muhammadan Light (*al-nur al-Muhammadi*) also flows in the being of the twelve Imams, starting with `Ali ibn Abi Taalib and ending with the Mahdi – upon all of whom be peace. Therefore, although the revelation came to an end with the Blessed Prophet Muhammad – upon whom be blessings and peace – who is therefore called the ' seal of the prophets', the spiritual and esoteric function of the Blessed Prophet (*walayah*) continued within the being of the Imams who were also inheritors of the Blessed Prophet's religious authority without, of course, possessing his prophetic power and function. The sayings of the Imams, therefore, are seen by Shi'ite as an extension of those of the Blessed Prophet and in many cases a commentary upon them, and they play a basic role in their religious life coming in importance only after the Noble Qur'an and prophetic *Hadith*. Moreover, many of the sayings of the Imams have also played a very important role in the Sunni world. The *Nahj al-Balaghah*, containing the sermons and sayings of `Ali, is in fact as well known in the Sunni world as in the Shi'ite. It might be said that the sayings of the Imams belong to the whole of the Islamic world, providing a vast treasury of wisdom dealing with both the outer and inner life of Muslims as well as with metaphysics, cosmology, psychology and eschatology.

Until now, however, much of this treasury has remained hidden from those not acquainted with Arabic and Persian and certainly from those whose knowledge of Islam is based only on sources in the English language. The present work is the first to deal with major aspects of Islam by drawing from this treasury along with the Noble Qur'an and prophetic *Hadith*. It provides a view of Islam on the basis of the vision of those attached to the Ahl al-Bayt and also as seen by the Ahl al-Bayt. The author, who hails from a well-known family of religious scholars from Iraq and Iran and who, having spent many years in the West, is well acquainted with present day spiritual needs of Western people and the best manner to present Islam to them, has chosen, judiciously, verses from the Noble Qur'an as well as traditions of the Blessed Prophets and the Imams to illustrate various aspects of Islam.

The book is organized in such a manner as to lead from a discussion of Islamic doctrines concerning God, the Blessed Prophet and the Imams, to the ritual aspects of the religion and finally to the spiritual struggle to refine one's character through the acquisition of virtue and removal of blameworthy traits. This last section concerns itself with issues that are very similar to those dealt with by the Sufis and reveals the close nexus between the inner dimension of Shi`ism and Sufism. But above all the book reveals the universality of the teachings of the Imams which belong not only to all Muslims, but, like the spiritual message of the Noble Qur'an and prophetic *Hadith*, to the whole of humanity.

Shaykh Fadhlalla Haeri is to be commended for his conceiving of the structure of the work and the selection of verses and sayings to illustrate each subject, as is the translator for rendering an original Arabic that is often condensed and abstruse into simple and clear English. The result is a work which introduces the English speaking reader for the first time to the world of the wisdom left by the Imams of the Ahl al-Bayt. The Noble Qur'an and much of the prophetic *Hadith* are of course already available in English, but even in their case, the author has brought a new dimension to bear upon the subject by revealing how those basic sources of Islam are seen by the Ahl al-Bayt and how the sayings of the Imams are integrated into their message.

From the pages that follow one can learn a great deal about the Islamic concept of God and prophecy, of worship and virtue, of the character of the Shi'ite Imams and even of early Islamic history. Furthermore, one can also learn much about the human state, its origin and end, and the meaning of terrestrial existence and our role here on earth. The book therefore addresses itself not only to the lovers of the Ahl al-Bayt and all Muslims, but in fact to all human beings, whatever their background may be, as long as they are attracted to the world of the Spirit and are in quest of meaning in their transient lives here on earth. Shaykh Fadhlalla Haeri's book is therefore an important addition to Islamic literature as well as to religious literature in general in the English language. We congratulate him on the fruits of his efforts and pray that this book will bring about a better understanding of Islam in the West and also draw many hearts and minds closer to God.

Seyyed Hossein Nasr
Bethesda, Maryland
Rajab 1420 AH.
November 1999

Introduction

In the Name of Allah, the Beneficent, the Merciful

Praise belongs to Allah, the Lord of all the worlds. His peace and blessings be upon the Master of all creatures, Muhammad, prince of messengers, on his family, the elite and the fortunate, leaders of guidance and lamps in the darkness, on his companions, and whoever follows him in the performance of good deeds to the Last Day.

I present to the reader in general, and to those wishing to drink from the purest sources of prophetic tradition in particular, a new book of distinctive character and methodology. The reader and the researcher may take from it material to quench their thirst for knowledge of their faith, and may find in it guidance for this life, so fraught with deceit, destructive ideas and conditions hostile to noble conduct.

The source material and background of this work

The prophetic pattern of behavior, known as the *sunnah*, is one of the two major sources of Islam – the other being the Qur'an. All the laws necessary for the establishment of human society are derived from these two sources, and indeed, the whole pattern of exemplary human behavior may be obtained from them. Much importance has been attached to the recording of prophetic traditions (*ahadith*, sing. *hadith*[1]) and to presenting them in such a way as to benefit the *ummah* (the Muslim community)

---

1   The term *hadith* is nevertheless more commonly used in English to denote the plural.

whether it be in the domain of politics, law, social behavior or moral conduct.

The first person to attach importance to the collecting of prophetic traditions was Imam `Ali ibn Abi Taalib. Adhafir al-Sirafi has described how he once saw al-Hakam ibn `Uyaynah question Abu Ja`far Muhammad ibn `Ali al-Baaqir. The latter was feeling averse to him and they fell to arguing over something. Abu Ja`far then sent his son to go and get the book of `Ali. He took out a great rolled up scroll and opened it, examining it until he had found the explanation of the matter in dispute. Abu Ja`far then said, 'This is the hand of `Ali and the dictation of the Messenger of Allah.' Then he went up to al-Hakam, saying, 'Go with Miqdad and transmit it as you wish to the right and the left, for by Allah, you will certainly not find more sure knowledge amongst people which has been revealed through the words of Jibril (Gabriel).'

The first person actually to write down the *hadith* was the Prophet's servant, Abu Rafi`, who later kept company with Imam `Ali, the Commander of the Faithful and became his treasurer and secretary in Kufa, He wrote the book *al-Sunan wa-al Ahkam wa-al-Qadaya*, ascribing his chain of transmission to the Commander of the Faithful, in the various chapters on prayer, fasting, pilgrimage, purification, tax and legal affairs.[2]

The leading scholars of *hadith* made great efforts to collect and arrange the prophetic traditions; those belonging to the school of the Family of the Prophet were very painstaking in this field, relying on the Twelve Imams for guidance as a valid source of narration because of their relation to the Messenger. Other sources of transmission were subject to the investigation of their content and chain of narration (*isnad*): if the chain was

---

2   See *Ta'sis al-Shi'ite li-`Ulum al-Islam*, by al-Seyyid Hasan al-Sadi, pp. 279-80.

sound or trustworthy, then it was accepted, and if not, then it was rejected.

The result of the importance attached to the collection of *hadith* is that various valuable sources of material sprang up from the different Islamic schools of thought; these sources are relied upon by all scholars and researchers, who use them and refer to them whenever necessary.

In the Twelve Imam school, four books are of note:

- *al-Kafi*, by Muhammad Ya`qub ibn Ishaq al-Kulayni al-Razi Abu Ja`far, d. 329 AH. 16,019 *hadith* attributed to the Family of the Prophet are mentioned in it.

- *Man la Yahduruhu al-Faqih*, by Muhammad ibn `Ali ibn Babawayh al-Qummi Abu Ja`far, d. 381 AH. This book contains 9,044 *hadith* on law and prophetic behavior narrated by the Family of the Prophet.

- *Tahdhib al-Ahkam*, by Muhammad ibn al-Hasan ibn `Ali al-Tusi Abu Ja`far, d. 460 AH. 3,590 *hadith* are contained in this work, arranged into 393 chapters.

- *al-Istibsar fi Ahadith al-Ahkam*, by Abu Ja`far al-Tusi, who has been mentioned above. In it he has collected 5,511 *hadith* and arranged them into chapters on jurisprudence, worship and commercial transactions.

Thereafter came the leading scholars of the Twelve Imam school in the tenth century. Those specializing in the science of *hadith* wrote books which contained all the *hadith* narrated by the Family of the Prophet, including those recorded in the four books mentioned above. They became an important source in the field of *hadith* science and are listed below:

- *Bihar al-Anwar bi al-Ahadith al-Marwiyyah `an al-Nabi wa-al-A'immah min Alihi al-Athar*, by Muhammad Baaqir ibn Muhammad ibn al-Maqsud `Ali al-Majlisi, d. 1110 AH. This book has been printed in 26 volumes.

- *al-Wafi*, by Muhammad ibn Murtada ibn Mahmud, known as Muhsin al-Fayd al-Kashani. This has been reprinted several times and consists of 14 volumes which contain the fundamental principles and ramifications of the prophetic law.

- *Mustadrak Wasa'il al-Shi'ite*, by al-Husayn ibn Muhammad al-Nuri Abu Muhammad, d. 1320 AH. Printed in several volumes, this work expands considerably on *Wasa'il al-Shi'ite*.

To these we may add the collections of *hadith* from the scholars of the four schools (all of which have been printed several times and been subject to scholarly commentary), the most eminent among them being the following:

- *al-Muwatta'*, by Malik ibn Anas al-Asbahi, the Imam of the Maliki school, d. 179 AH.

- *al-Masnad*, by Ahmad ibn Muhammad ibn Hanbal Abu `Abd Allah, d. 241 AH, from whose name the Hanbali school is derived.

- *Sahih al-Bukhari*, by Muhammad ibn Isma`il ibn Ibrahim Abu `Abd Allah al-Bukhari, d. 256 AH.

- *Sahih Muslim*, by Muslim ibn al-Hujaj ibn Muslim al-Qushayri Abu al-Hasan, d. 261 AH.

A number of voluminous works on the same subject appeared after these four books, the most significant being the following:

- *al-Mustadrak*, by Muhammad ibn `Abd Allah al-Naysapuri, known as Ibn al-Biya`d. 405 AH.

- *al-Sunan al-Kubra*, by Ahmad ibn al-Husayn ibn 'Ali al-Bayhaqi Abu Bakr, d. 458 AH.

- *Kanz al-'Ummal*, by 'Ala' al-Din 'Ali ibn Husam al-Din, known as al-Muttaqi al-Hindi, d. 975 AH.

Yet the scholars of *hadith* have not restricted their efforts to mere recording, classification and arranging of the *hadith*, but have also produced work on a wide range of social, moral and philosophical topics, the more important of which are the following:

- *Tanbih al-Khatir wa Nuzhat al-Nazir*, by Abu al-Husayn Daram ibn Abi al-Fawaris 'Isa al-Harithi, d. 650 AH.

- *Irshad al-Qulub*, by al-Hasan ibn Abi al-Hasan al-Daylami, a leading scholar of the seventh century AH. This book is arranged into 55 chapters on philosophy, wisdom, instruction and counsel.

- *Makarim al-Akhlaq*, by Abu Mansur al-Hasan ibn al-Shaykh Amin al-Din Abi 'Ali al-Fadl ibn al-Hasan al-Tabrasi, one of the eminent scholars of the sixth century AH.

It is against this fertile background of literature that we may return to the present book, *'Prophetic Traditions – On the Authority of the Family of the Prophet.'* On reading this work we realize that the compiler has followed those who preceded him, believing it to be the best. He has given the texts of the *hadith* and while he had investigated the depth of meaning contained therein he has not involved himself in lengthy commentary or explanation, which might have led to obscurity and obstructed the goal of such a book. This goal may be defined as an awareness of the relevance of the *hadith*; application of the *hadith* helps man towards the perfection of his humanity and faith, and to bear the responsibility of the prophetic message entrusted to him by Allah. In his capacity as vicegerent on earth, man must aim to establish a just society founded on mutual love and respect.

This work is characterized by four qualities: firstly, it contains collections of *hadith* pertaining to belief and to the formation of character. Particular emphasis on the part of the compiler is given to the education of man: by applying the teachings of the Messenger and the Imams of guidance, a person may become a healthy member of society and thereby establish the social order desired by Allah – for perfection engenders perfection, and someone who lacks something is in no position to give that thing to others. Secondly, in making his choice of *hadith*, which describe the various qualities of human perfection, the compiler has relied mostly upon those *hadith* which are connected to a practical application in life; moreover, his arrangement of the *hadith* according to subject matter lends support to his educational designs and constructive purpose. Thirdly, the author has lived in the West and has understood its negative aspects. Realizing that Western society is undergoing a moral and educational crisis, he has discovered that all spiritual values have been lost to the alluring culture of materialism, hollow in substance but filled with pomp and marked by a misleading superficial gloss. He is able, by his choice of *hadith*, to connect with the spirit of western man, who is only resisting the guidance of Islam because of his distrust and confusion. Finally, the enemies of Islam have tried to distort the truth of Islam and its call to a perfect social order by exaggerating certain of its aspects in order to alienate the ignorant – it is to such people that this work presents a sane and comprehensible outline of Islam, valid for this and all ages.

In addition to the above-mentioned characteristics, this work is distinguished by the fact that the *hadith* in the book awaken a spirit of earnestness, and encourage the reader to action. Moreover, the trustworthiness of the material is confirmed by the chains of transmission which accompany the *hadith* (not included in the text for lack of space, but available in the references). When we examine the sources relied upon by the compiler in his selection of *hadith*, we find that the majority are from among the most important and trustworthy collections. The authors of these collections are from an elite of scholars and jurists, who are deemed to be completely acceptable according to the principles of veracity and authenticity; it is on these people that the researchers rely when producing their studies in this field. These sources are also readily available being recently – or still – in print.

Thus in assessing this work we recognize that it contains an important body of wisdom which is of a real and relevant nature when relied upon and applied to one's own situation. We hope that it will be an effective means of reaching the compiler's goal.

A few notes on the compiler are necessary to throw light on his character and the influences which caused him to immerse himself in the current of spirituality – a current which has become a distinguishing feature of all aspects of his life.

Shaykh Fadhlalla is the son of the late Shaykh Ahmad ibn al-Shaykh Muhammad Husayn ibn al-Shaykh Zayn al-`Abideen. His family, renowned for its knowledge and excellence since the end of the twelfth century AH, has been associated with the holy town of Karbala in Iraq, and other areas of Iraq, India and Iran.

The first of this family to achieve renown was Hujjat al-Islam al-Shaykh Zayn al-`Abideen ibn Muslim al-Mazandarani al-Ha'iri, who was born in Mazandaran in 1229 AH., where he studied with the outstanding scholars of his birthplace. In 1250 AH he moved to Iraq, alternating between Karbala and Najaf, where he studied in the religious institutions and learned from the leading scholars. He settled in Karbala in 1262 AH where he spent his time teaching, receiving people, leading the prayers and taking decisions on matters of jurisprudence[3], achieving his greatest renown as an eminent jurist, Imam of the shrine of Imam Husayn, and as a guide for the people in their religious affairs. The late Hujjat al-Sayyid Muhsin al-Amin has described him as 'Shaykh of the jurists and legislators, and unique among religious guides'.[4]

He left several works for posterity, among them *Sharh Shara`i`al-Islam*, also known as *Zinat al-`Ibad fi al-Fiqh*, commented on by other scholars of repute, like Shaykh `Abd al-Karim Ha'iri Yazdi; *Dakhirat al-Ma`ad fi Takalif al-`Ibad*, a legal manual for his followers, arranged in the form of questions and answers and translated and printed many times in Arabic, Persian and Urdu; commentaries on other scholarly texts, including *Hawashi `ala Kitab Masalik al-Ifham Sharh Shara`i` al-Ahkam*, by al-Shahid al-Thani, d. 965 AH; and a book on the Principles of Religion.

Shaykh Zayn al-`Abideen sent Mulla Qadir Husayn to Bombay in 1873 CE in order to strengthen Islam and organize the Shi`iahs there. He played a leading role in the separation of the Khwaja Twelver Shi'ites and the Isma`ilis in 1901 CE. He also sent Sayyid `Abd al-Husayn al-Mar`ashi Shushtari to Zanzibar in 1885 CE, to spread Islam and serve the Shi'ite communities there. Shaykh Zayn al-`Abideen died in 1309 AH in Karbala and was buried near the Bab al-Hajat graveyard, in the shrine of Imam Husayn. To this day he is accorded special distinction by his descendants.

After his death, his eldest son Shaykh Muhammad Husayn took his place as leader of the Friday prayers and teacher in the religious institutions of Karbala. His followers came from those

---

3 My reference: *A`yan al-Shi'ite*, by al-Sayyid Muhsin al-Amin, p. 168/7, and *al-Dhari`ah ila Tasanif al-Shi'ite*, Aghabozorg al-Tehrani, 92/12.
4 Al-Sayyid Muhsin al-Amin, op. cit. p. 167/7.

areas in which his father had been known, and people would refer to him when seeking legal decisions. The late Sayyid Muhsin al-Amin described him as 'a knowledgeable scholar, a man of excellence, a friend and a leader after the death of his father'[5].

Shaykh Muhammad Husayn remained in Karbala until his death in 1340 AH, whereupon his eldest son, Shaykh Ahmad – and the father of the compiler of this book – took his place and became known for his excellence, knowledge, piety and scrupulousness. He became the prayer leader in the same place that both his father and grandfather had led the congregation, namely, in the shrine of Imam Husayn.

As a growing number of believers would consult him in matters of religion, and would follow his legal decisions, he made a commentary on the 'Manual of Laws' written by his father, explaining any points of difference and elucidating those particularly complicated points of law which demanded new legal judgments. He was also interested in the sciences of astronomy, chemistry and astrology, and founded a thriving library in Karbala for the works of such sciences and other branches of knowledge. He died there in 1957 at the age of 80, and was buried in accordance with his will in a *wadi* which has since become the public cemetery of Karbala, rather than with the rest of his forbears within the compound of the shrine.

The late Shaykh Ahmad left six sons, of whom the youngest is Shaykh Fadhlalla. He chose to study modern academic subjects, thus departing from the family tradition of studying in religious institutions. Having attained the position of the second most distinguished pupil of sciences in Iraq for his grade, he left to study at a university in England, after which he became an engineer in the Iraq Petroleum Company in 1960. In 1966 he moved to Beirut where he opened an industrial and petroleum

---

5   ibid. p. 26/6.

consultancy, and practiced in this professional capacity until 1975, the year of the outbreak of civil war in Lebanon. Because of the conditions governing his sphere of work, he began to move between Europe, America and Asia. During this period he was able to pursue his quest for self-knowledge and to rediscover the relevance the *Din al-Islam* to our much confused present age, until, by the late seventies, he broke off his commercial and engineering activities to devote himself unreservedly to uncovering and sharing the essential and transformative teachings of Islam . He thus embarked upon a period of intense activity, spending of his wealth and energy to enable seekers to discover Islam and to live it, and to this end he established a religious educational trust and publishing house. The trust ran a full-time residential school, opened for Westerners to learn Islam, as well as a correspondence course. While travelling and teaching extensively in Europe and America, he also travelled in the East, working with devoted people in Pakistan and India to establish schools, clinics and orphanages for the Muslims.

Many of his talks have been turned into books , in addition to which he has written several others, both in English and Arabic, among them: five commentaries on selected *surahs* of the Qur'an, *Beginning's End, The Journey of the Universe, Decree and Destiny, The Journey of the Self, Elements of Islam, Elements of Sufism* and others.

After this short description of the life and work of Shaykh Fadhlalla al-Haeri[6], it should not be forgotten that works such as these have a profound influence on the formation of a Muslim's character, by strengthening and preparing him for his role in propagating the beliefs and behavior demanded by Islam – a role which must be undertaken by every Muslim who is

---

6   The name al-Haeri (al-Ha'iri) refers to the area surrounding the grave of Imam Husayn in Karbala.

seriously concerned with the state of his religion and the *Ummah* of Muslims.

In conclusion, I would like to call upon Allah to grant success to all who are working for the establishment of Islam and who are striving with sincerity and devotion to make its noble aims a reality.

Muhammad al-Sayyid Ali Bahr al-`Ulum
London
15 Sha`ban 1405 AH
6 May 1985

I: Our System of Belief

BELIEF IN ALLAH

The Way of Oneness

Allah, may He be exalted, says in the Qur'an:

☼ Say: He, Allah is One. Allah is He upon Whom all depend. He begets not, nor is He begotten. And none is like unto Him. (112:1-4)

☼ All praise is due to Allah, the Lord of the worlds. The Beneficent, the Merciful. Master of the Day of Judgment. Thee do we serve and Thee do we beseech for help. (1:1-5)

☼ Allah is He besides Whom there is no god, the Ever-living, the Self-subsisting, by Whom all subsist; slumber does not overtake Him nor sleep. Whatever is in the heavens and whatever is in the earth is His; who is he that can intercede with Him but by His permission? He knows what is before them and what is behind them, and they cannot comprehend anything of His knowledge except what He pleases. His knowledge extends over the heavens and the earth, and the preservation of them both tires Him not, and He is the Most High, the Great. (2:255)

☼ Say: O followers of the Book! Come to a fair agreement between us and you, that we shall not serve any but Allah and [that] we shall not associate aught with Him, and [that] some of us shall not take others for lords besides Allah. (3:64)

☼ And your god is one God! There is no god but He; He is the Beneficent the Merciful. (2:163)

☼ If there had been in them [the Heavens and the earth] any gods except Allah, they would both have certainly been in a state of disorder. (21:22)

☼ ...They were enjoined that they should serve one God only, there is no god but He. (9:31)

☼ Those who believe and do not mix up their faith with iniquity, those are the ones who shall have security and they are the ones who go aright. (6:82)

☼ Is there any doubt about Allah, the Maker of the Heavens and the earth? (14:10)

The Messenger of Allah has said, 'Truly Allah resembles no "thing" and no "thing" resembles Him; everything which enters one's imagination concerning Him is a misinterpretation.'[7]

It is related from Imam `Ali that he heard the Messenger of Allah say, 'Truly Allah has said, "For one to whom I have granted belief in My Oneness, there is no other reward than the Garden".'[8]

'Whoever says "There is no god except Allah" with sincere belief will enter the garden, his sincerity being that "no god except Allah" safeguards him from what Allah has forbidden.'[9]

Imam `Ali has narrated that the Messenger of Allah said, 'Whoever dies and has not associated any partners whatsoever with Allah will enter Paradise – be his deeds good or bad.'[10]

7	al-Kaashaani, al-Muhajjah al-Bayda', I,219.
8	al-Ṣaduq, al-Tawhid, 18-30.
9	ibid.
10	ibid

Needless to say, this cannot be interpreted as a license to perform bad deeds, as long as one believes in the Oneness of God. Rather, it indicates, on the one hand, that sincerity of belief implies and produces a fundamental orientation towards the good; and, on the other hand, that all human actions are grasped as relativities in the dazzling light of the Divine Oneness.

It is related by al-Saadiq that the Messenger of Allah has said, 'The best of worship is the phrase "There is no god except Allah".'[11]

It is also related by him that Gabriel came to the Messenger of Allah and said, 'O Muhammad, whoever of your *ummah* says "There is no god except Allah, Him alone, Him alone, Him alone", will be content.'[12]

It is related on the authority of Imam `Ali that the Messenger of Allah said, 'Allah has said that, "The words 'no god except Allah' are My fortress: whoever enters it gains protection from My torment".'[13]

A Bedouin (a nomadic tribesman of the desert) came to the Prophet and said, 'O Messenger, teach me something amazing in the realm of knowledge!' The Messenger replied, 'What have you achieved regarding the basis of knowledge that you ask about the amazing within this realm?' The Bedouin then asked, 'What is the basis of knowledge, O Messenger of Allah?' He replied, 'That you know Allah in truth.' The Bedouin asked, 'What is true knowledge of Allah?' The Messenger replied, 'That you know Him without making a companion with other-than-Him, without making a likeness, without setting up rivals with Him; that you know He is unique, the One, the Outward, the Inward, the First, the Last; that there is none comparable to Him

---

11	ibid.
12	ibid.
13	ibid.

and there is no equal to Him: this is true knowledge of Him.'[14]

Imam `Ali has said, 'Praise belongs to Allah, Who cannot be perceived by touch nor by any investigation by means of the physical faculties. He cannot be understood by the five senses, and imagination cannot grasp Him. Anything sensed, felt or touched by the hand is created (and is therefore not the Creator). Allah is Sublime, the Powerful: whatever is desired by Him comes into existence.'[15]

Imam `Ali was asked, 'How do you know your Lord?' He replied, 'By the way in which the action one intends is cancelled, and by the way one's designs and resolutions are not realized. When I endeavor to do something, He comes between me and my endeavor; when I have decided to do something, the Decree and the Destiny act against my decision; thus have I understood that the organizer of my affairs is other than me.'[16]

He also said in his last instructions to his son, Hasan, 'Know, my son, that had there been a partner with your Lord, then surely His messengers would have come to you and you would have seen the signs of His dominion and power; you would thus have come to know His actions and His attributes. He is the only God, just as He has described Himself; there is no rival to Him in His dominion, and He will never be caused to perish.'[17]

A Bedouin came up to Imam `Ali and asked him if he thought that Allah is one. 'O Bedouin,' he replied, 'the statement that Allah is one has four divisions [of meaning]: two of them may not be applied to Allah, may He be exalted, and two are valid. As for the two which are not applicable, the first is when "one"

---

14   al-Tabarsi, *Mishkaat al-Anwaar*, 10.
15   *al-Tawhid*, 60.
16   *al-Muhajjah al-Bayda'*, II, 208.
17   Imam `Ali, *Nahj al-Balaghah*, III, 559; *al-Muhajjah al-Bayda'*, I, 213.

refers to the question of number – and this is not permissible since that which has no second cannot be considered in terms of number. You realize, then, that he who says, "He is the third in the trinity", is committing *kufr* (i.e. covering up reality). The second is the statement, "He is One from amongst mankind", meaning one of a kind, or genre. This is not permissible, as it is tantamount to *tashbih* (likening Him to His creation) – may our Lord be glorified above this. As for the two which are valid when applied to Him; first there is the statement "He is One", meaning that He has no likeness amongst things (in creation) – such is our Lord; the second is the statement "He is Oneness in concept", meaning that He cannot be divided in existence, nor by the intellect or imagination – thus is our Lord.'[18]

Imam `Ali, on whom be peace, delivered a discourse one day after the afternoon prayer: 'Praise belongs to Allah, Who will never die and Whose wonders will never cease. Each day He is active in creation, producing amazing manifestations, which were non-existent previously. Praise belongs to Allah, Who does not give birth to anyone lest there be a partner in His glory; Who has not been born Himself lest He be (like all creation which was born into this world) doomed to die. Praise belongs to Him who the imagination of man cannot perceive, but rather can arrive only at a shadow-like comparison of Him, and Whom vision cannot contain. He has no ending to His beginning nor limits to His remoteness; He has been preceded by neither time nor space, and is unaffected by increase or decrease; He cannot be described in terms of place, matter or space. When the prophets were asked about Him, they did not describe Him by ascribing limits or deficiencies to Him, but rather described Him according to His actions, and guided men to Him by His signs.'[19]

---

18 Al-Saduq, *al-Khisaal*, I, 2.
19 *al-Tawhid*, 31-32.

Islam

Allah, may He be exalted, says in His Book of wisdom, the Qur'an:

☼ Surely the [true] religion with Allah is Islam. (3:19)

☼ And whoever desires a religion other than Islam, it shall not be accepted from him. (3:85)

☼ This day have I perfected for you your religion and completed My favor on you and chosen for you Islam as a religion. (5:3)

A man of the Khath`am tribe asked the Messenger of Allah what was considered best in Islam. 'Faith in Islam', the Messenger replied, 'followed by respect for one's family, enjoining good and forbidding evil.' When the man asked him what Allah hated most, he said, 'Associating partners with Allah, breaking off relations with one's family, enjoining evil and forbidding good.'[20]

The Messenger of Allah said, 'Truly Allah will help this religion by means of a corrupt man.'[21] And elsewhere, 'Two qualities are not to be found in a Muslim: miserliness and bad behaviour.'[22]

Talking about Islam, Imam `Ali said, 'Islam is surrender, and surrender is certainty; certainty is belief, and belief is affirmation, affirmation is execution [of one's duty], and execution is virtuous action.'[23]

'There is no honor higher than Islam and no character more noble than that which has *taqwa* (respect and fear of Allah

---

20   *Mishkaat al-Anwaar*, 49.
21   al-Kaashaani, *al-Haqaa'iq fi Mahasin al-Akhlaq*, 51.
22   *al-Khisaal*, I, 75.
23   *Nahj al-Balaghah*, IV, 685 & 744.

in one's actions), and there is no refuge more secure than scrupulousness and self-restraint.'[24]

'Truly this religion of ours is the religion of Allah: He has chosen it for Himself, fashioned it for Himself and granted it to the best of His creation; He has set up the Pillars of its support on His love; He has brought other religions low by His power; He has abased all other faiths by His sublimity, humiliated its enemies by His nobility, and has defeated those who challenged it by His victorious strength. He has destroyed the pillars of falsehood by erecting the pillars of His religion, and has given the thirsty to drink from His fountain.'[25]

'Praise belongs to Allah, Who has laid down the laws of Islam and has made application of these laws easy for the one who takes them as the source of his life's actions; Who has raised high its pillars over those who would try to overcome it, and has made it a place of security for whoever adheres to it, a place of peace for whoever enters it, a proof for whoever speaks by it, a witness for whoever disputes with another by it, a light for whoever seeks light by it, an understanding for whoever uses his intellect, a meaning for whoever reflects, a sign for whoever seeks to perceive, knowledge for whoever intends an action, a lesson for whoever takes counsel and acts by it, and a release (from the torment of the fire) for whoever gives in charity.'[26]

'Thus He has sent Muhammad, may peace be upon him, in truth to bring His slaves from worshipping idols towards worshipping Him, and from obeying Satan to obeying Him; he has explained these matters and has established the laws by means of the Qur'an so that the slaves may know their Lord if they had been ignorant of Him, that they may establish themselves firmly

---

24   ibid.
25   ibid., II, 453; I, 253; II, 318.
26   ibid.

in Him if they had been denying Him, and to strengthen their faith if they had been rejecting Him. He has manifested His glory to them through His Book and has shown them a measure of His power, yet without their having seen Him. He has struck fear into them by His force.'[27]

Imam al-Baaqir has said, 'Islam has been established on five principles: prayer, purification through giving away one's wealth, pilgrimage, fasting and governance by the laws of Allah.' He was then asked which of these things was the best. He replied, 'Governance by the laws of Allah. It is the key to all things, and the governor is the guide to them.' Then he was asked what followed next, so he said, 'Prayer, for truly the Messenger of Allah has said, "Prayer is the pillar of your religion". Next in order of excellence is the giving of one's wealth, since he [the Messenger] has mentioned these two matters together, and has mentioned prayer first. The Messenger of Allah has said, "One's wrong actions are effaced through the giving away of one's wealth".'

Imam al-Baaqir proceeded to the next principle, in order of excellence: 'Pilgrimage to the house [of Allah, i.e. the Ka`bah] is incumbent upon men for the sake of Allah, upon everyone who is able to undertake the journey; and whoever disbelieves, then surely Allah is Self-sufficient, above any need of the worlds.' He was then asked, 'How is it that fasting is the last of all these matters?' He replied, 'Prayer, the giving away of wealth, pilgrimage and governance by Islam cannot be replaced by anything if they are not put into practice; yet fasting, if missed, shortened or excused by your travelling, is made up for by a corresponding number of days. Moreover, this deficiency is corrected through giving away charity to the needy, in which case you have nothing else to make up; nothing, however, can make

---

27   ibid.

up for the other four practices.'[28]

Sulayman ibn Khalid related that Imam al-Baaqir said, 'Shall I not teach you about the root and branches of Islam and the peak and crown of the matter? The root is prayer and its branches are purification by giving away one's wealth; the crown of the affair is *jihad* (struggle undertaken in serving Allah by whatever action).'[29]

It is related from Imam al-Saadiq that the Messenger of Allah said, 'Islam is naked: its clothes are modesty and its beauty is dignity in manners; its nobility is good actions and its foundation is prudence. Everything possesses a foundation and the foundation of Islam is love of me and of my family.'[30]

Faith

Allah has said in the Qur'an:

☼ Surely [as for] those who believe and do good, they shall have gardens [of Paradise]. (85:11)

☼ Allah will exalt those of you who believe, and those who are given knowledge, in high degrees. (58:11)

☼ Except such as repent and believe and do good, these shall enter the Garden. (19:60)

☼ And they say: we believe in Allah and in the Apostle and we obey. (24:47)

☼ Allah, there is no god but He; and upon Allah, then, let the believers rely. (64:13)

☼ [As for] those who believe and do good, a good final

---

28   al-Kulyani, *al-Kafi*, II, 19 & 46.
29   ibid.
30   ibid.

state will be theirs and a goodly return. (13:29)

☼ Successful indeed are the believers, who are humble in their prayers and who keep aloof from what is vain. (23:1-3).

The Messenger of Allah has said, 'Faith is a compact undertaken by the heart, an expression of this on the tongue and the putting into action of the fundamentals [of Islam].'[31]

'The fruits of faith are three: loving for the sake of Allah, hating for the sake of Allah, and the feeling of modesty in front of Allah, may He be exalted.'[32]

'There are three things which, if practised, perfect the qualities of one's faith: first, if one is content, one is not led to wrong action and falsehood; second, if one becomes angry, then his anger does not divert him from the truth; and third, if one has the power, one does not take over that which does not belong to him.'[33]

The Messenger has said, 'Above the highest station of faith is a special rank, and whoever has obtained this has obtained the goal, and is victorious. It is the rank of those whose inner thoughts are only directed to righteousness, so they are not worried if these thoughts become known and they do not fear punishment if they remain hidden.'[34]

'Whoever is made happy by his good actions and is saddened by his bad ones is a believer.'[35]

'There are over seventy gates to faith: the largest is the

---

31 al-'Inaathi, *Adab al-Nafs,* II, 151-152.
32 ibid.
33 ibid.
34 ibid.
35 *al-Khisaal,* I, 47.

witnessing that there is no god except Allah and the smallest is the removing of an obstacle from the path.'[36] The Messenger of Allah was asked, 'Which people possess the best faith?' He replied, 'Those whose hands are the most generous.'[37]

'Whoever assists the poor man and deals fairly with people of his own accord, is truly a believer.'[38]

It is related on the authority of Imam `Ali that the Messenger of Allah said, 'Whoever washes himself in the prescribed manner before prayer, prays correctly, purifies himself by paying out part of his wealth, controls his anger and his tongue, seeks forgiveness for his wrong actions and gives advice to his family, has perfected true faith, and the gates of heaven are open to him.'[39]

And Imam `Ali said, 'Faith is based on four pillars: patience, certainty, striving to perform what one believes in and justice.'[40]

'The best thing that one may request of Allah is belief in Him and His Messenger, and striving in His way, for this is the height of Islam.'[41]

'A man's faith indicates his good actions, and his good actions indicate faith, and through faith knowledge prospers.'[42]

Imam `Ali has said, 'Faith is that you prefer the truth (though it harms you) to the lie which benefits you; truth is that there is no excess in your speech in respect to your actions (that you say what you do not do), and that you fear and respect Allah when

---

36	*Mishkaat al-Anwaar*, 40.
37	ibid.
38	*al-Khisaal*, I, 47.
39	al-Tabarsi, 39.
40	*Nahj*, IV, 663; I, 265; II, 334.
41	ibid.
42	ibid.

reporting the speech of others.'⁴³

Describing the qualities of the believer, Imam `Ali has said, 'A believer's serenity is in his face, his sadness is in his heart, the most expansive thing is his heart and the most humble his self (his personality). He dislikes high rank and hates reputation. Great is his concern for the hereafter, and he avoids idle talk about others; he occupies his time fruitfully, is grateful to Allah and is extremely patient. He immerses himself in reflection, does not manifest his poverty to people, is of easy disposition, and flexible in nature – yet his character is more solid than a rock and more humble than a slave's.'⁴⁴

Al-Saadiq was asked by Sama`ah about the difference between Islam and *Iman*. He replied, '*Iman* is part of Islam but Islam is not part of Iman. Islam is witnessing that there is no god except Allah and affirming that Muhammad is the Messenger of Allah; by it women have been married and inheritances apportioned in the proper manner; most people act in accordance with the outer aspects of it. *Iman* is guidance, and the establishment of Islamic qualities in the heart, and it manifests itself in one's actions. *Iman* ranks higher than Islam. *Iman* shares with Islam in the outward, but Islam has no share with *Iman* in what is within, even though they have common qualities.'⁴⁵

In another *hadith*, Imam al-Saadiq explains the previous *hadith* in the following way: 'The slave is a Muslim before he is a *mu'min* (one who has faith), and is not a *mu'min* until he is a Muslim. Islam comes before *Iman*; thus if a slave commits one of the punishable offences or one of the lesser offences which Allah has forbidden, he has left *Iman* and can no longer be described as having true faith, although the word Islam may still be applied to

---

43   *Nahj*, IV, 735 & 762.
44   ibid.
45   al-Kulayni, II, 25 & 47.

him. If he turns to Allah for forgiveness he returns to the safety of *Iman*. Only rebellious argument and claiming something is forbidden when it is allowed, or claiming something is allowed when it is forbidden, brings him outside the pale of both Islam and *Iman*.'[46]

In describing the qualities of the believer, al-Saadiq has also said, 'A believer should possess eight qualities: he must be honorable in the face of trials, patient when afflicted, thankful when things are going easy for him and content with what Allah has given him of His bounty; he should not oppress his enemies nor burden his friends; he himself feels tired but others feel rested as a result of his exertion. Surely knowledge is the close companion of the believer, kindness is his minister, intellect the general of his armies, gentleness his brother and good behaviour towards others his father.'[47]

Fear of Allah and carefulness in one's behavior (*taqwa*)

Allah, may He be praised, says in His Book:

☼ Be careful of [your duty to] Allah with the care which is due to Him. (3:102)

☼ Surely Allah enjoins the doing of justice and the doing of good [to others]. (16:90)

☼ Surely the most honorable of you with Allah is the one among you most careful [of his duty]. (49:93)

☼ Those among them who do good and guard [against evil] shall have a great reward. (3:172)

☼ And those who are careful of [their duty to] their Lord

---
46   ibid.
47   ibid.

shall be conveyed in companies. (39:73)

☼ And be careful of [your duty to] Allah and know that Allah is with those who guard [against evil]. (2:194)

☼ Surely Allah loves those who are careful [of their duty]. (9:4)

Commenting on Allah's words, 'Surely Allah enjoins the doing of justice and the doing of good,' the Messenger of Allah has said, 'Allah has gathered the meaning of *taqwa* (fearful awareness of Allah in one's every action) in this verse.' He has also said, 'Have *taqwa* of Allah, for in it lies all goodness.' Elsewhere he said, 'Whoever desires to be the most noble of men let him have *taqwa* of Allah.'[48]

'If you carry out the obligatory duties of Islam, then you will be amongst those with the most *taqwa*.'[49]

While advising Abu Dharr, the Messenger said, 'Be very careful to undertake your actions with *taqwa*, for surely there is not loss in actions undertaken therewith. How could there be loss in something which is acceptable in the eyes of Allah? This is based on Allah's verse: "Surely He accepts that which comes from the *muttaqin* (those with *taqwa*)".'[50]

'Superiority in knowledge is more beloved of Allah, may He be exalted, than superiority in worship, and the most superior thing in your religion is carefulness in your behavior.'[51]

Imam `Ali has said, 'There is no honor more worthy than Islam, nothing more noble than *taqwa* and no fortress stronger

---

48	*Mishkaat*, 45-46.
49	ibid.
50	al-Ashtari, II, 62.
51	al-Khisaal, I, 4.

than carefulness in one's behavior.'[52]

It has been related from Imam `Ali that he said, 'Whoever turns in prayer to our *qiblah* [direction of the Ka`bah] in Makkah, eats the animals we have sacrificed, believes in our Prophet, bears witness like us with the words, "There is no god except Allah," and enters our houses, we apply the laws of the Qur'an and Islam to him. No one is superior to another except by his *taqwa*. Truly those with *taqwa* will have the best reward and the most pleasant ending with Allah.'[53]

Imam `Ali was asked to describe the nature of this world. He replied, 'For the allowed things that you enjoy there is a reckoning, and for the forbidden things punishment. If you saw death and its inevitability you would find consolation for loss in this world and its vain delights. Whoever is careful of his duty to Allah with the care due to Him, Allah will grant intimacy with Him without familiarity, riches without wealth, and strength without authority.'[54]

'Those with *taqwa* may be recognized by certain characteristics: they are true in speech and trustworthy, they keep to their agreements, they lack pride or miserliness, they maintain the ties of kinship, are merciful with the weak, keep little company with women, strive to be kind and courteous and strive to acquire knowledge which will bring them closer to Allah. Such people will be well received and will have a most pleasing abode in the end.'[55]

Commenting on the meaning of *taqwa*, Imam `Ali has said, 'Truly *taqwa* of Allah is a medicine for your hearts' illness, and sight for the blindness of your hearts, a cure for your bodies'

52	al-Ashtari, II, 39.
53	*Mishkaat*, 44-47.
54	ibid.
55	ibid.

sickness and a correction of whatever is wrong in your breasts. It is a purification of your character, a making clear of the dimness of your sight; it is a safety from your agitation and fear, and light for the blackness of your gloom.'[56]

Describing the people of *taqwa*, he has said, 'Those of *taqwa* possess qualities of excellence: their speech is correctness, their garment is economy, their gait is humility; they lower their eyes before what Allah has forbidden and they listen to knowledge which is useful to them.'[57]

'I counsel the slaves of Allah to have *taqwa* of Allah, for it is a lasting provision and a sure means of reaching their destination in the hereafter. The most aware and the most respected of men have called others [to Him] by it; He has caused His call to be heard and those who were attentive have gained paradise.

'O slaves of Allah! Truly *taqwa* of Allah protects the friend of Allah from His fire, and has placed such a fear of Him in their hearts that they remain awake at night in worship, and are thirsty for the next world because they have abandoned this world.'[58]

Imam `Ali mentions the verse from the Qur'an, 'Be careful of [your duty to] Allah with the care which is due to Him' [3:102].[59]

'The closest description of the man of *taqwa* is scrupulousness: he combines kindness with knowledge, words with deeds and rarely commits a wrong action, his heart is humble, he is content in himself, he eats little food; he takes the easiest path in his affairs and is zealous in matters of his religion, his desires have been extinguished and his anger stilled. Good is expected of him and he himself is protected from evil. If he is negligent,

---

56 *Nahj, I,* 275; II, 440-452; I, 273.
57 ibid.
58 ibid.
59 ibid.

he is recorded as not being among those who remember Allah; if he is amongst those who remember Allah, he is not counted amongst those who are negligent. He forgives those who cause him harm and gives to him who withholds; he re-establishes relations with those who have broken with him. He is far from their corruption but gentle in his speech to them. He is absent from their bad actions and present for their kind actions. He accepts goodness from them and turns away from evil; he is dignified in the face of calamity and patient when faced with their plotting. He is thankful when things go easily.'[60]

Imam al-Saadiq said, 'The most scrupulous of men are those who stop short of doubtful things.'[61]

Trust in Allah

Allah, may He be praised, says in His Book:

☼ And on Allah should the reliant rely. (14:21)

☼ And whoever trusts in Allah, then surely Allah is Mighty, Wise. (8:49)

☼ And whoever trusts in Allah, He is sufficient for him. (65:3)

☼ Surely Allah loves those who trust. (3:159)

☼ And on Allah should you rely if you are believers. (5:23)

The Messenger of Allah has said, 'If you were to trust in Allah with the trust which is due to Him, He would surely

---

60   ibid.
61   *al-Khisaal*, I, 16.

provide for you as He provides for the birds.'[62]

'If a man relies solely on Allah, Allah will guarantee him all his provision and in such a way as he had not expected; but if a man devotes himself to the world, then Allah will make him rely solely on it.'[63]

It has been related that when the Messenger's family was afflicted by poverty he would say, 'Stand up for the prayer,' adding, 'Our Lord has commanded us to do this, with the words: "And so enjoin upon thy family worship and be constant therein. We do not ask thee for provision: We provide for thee. And the (success of) hereafter is for *taqwa*" [20:132].'[64]

It is related from al-Saadiq that he [the Prophet] would not say of anything that had happened, 'If only something else had happened!' He would not feel regret for anything that had happened, for he had complete trust in the decree of Allah.[65]

'Whoever wishes to be among those of the greatest *taqwa*, then let him place his trust in Allah.'[66]

'Whoever finds happiness in being amongst the strongest, then let him rely on Allah and whoever finds happiness being amongst the noblest of men, then let him fear Allah in his actions; whoever is happy to be the richest of men, then let him be sure of what is in the hand of Allah than that which is in his own hand.'[67]

It is related from Imam al-Baaqir that some riders met the Messenger of Allah on one of his journeys. He asked them who they were. They replied, 'We are believers, O Messenger of

---

62	al-Ashtari, I, 222.
63	ibid.
64	ibid.
65	*Mishkaat*, 17-18.
66	ibid.
67	ibid.

Allah.' He said, 'What is the reality of your belief?' They replied, 'Contentment with the decree of Allah, delegating our affairs to Allah and submitting to what He has ordained.'

He said, 'Those of knowledge and wisdom are close to the sagacity of the prophets: if you are truthful, then you do not build anything that you are not going to live in, and do not amass what you do not need for immediate consumption, and fear in your actions Him to Whom you are returning.'[68]

Imam `Ali has said, 'Faith is based on four pillars: trust in Allah, the handing over of one's affairs to Allah, contentment with the decree of Allah and submitting to what Allah has ordained.'[69]

'A slave will not taste true faith until he realizes that whatever happens to him could not have passed him by, that whatever passes him by could not have happened to him, and that it is Allah Who causes harm or benefit to man.'[70]

Imam al-Saadiq was asked, 'There exists nothing but that it has a terminus, so what is the terminal point of trust?' He replied, 'Certainty.' He was then asked what the terminal point of certainty was, and he replied, 'That one does not fear anything besides Allah.'[71]

Al-Saadiq said, 'Whoever has been given three things will not be denied three things: whoever has been given prayer, will be given the answer to his prayer; whoever has been given thanks, will be given increase; and whoever has been given trust in Allah will be given sufficiency. Have you not read in the Book of Allah, "Whoever trusts in Allah, He is sufficient for him" [65:3]; Allah then says, "If you are grateful I would certainly give you more"

68	ibid.
69	ibid.
70	*al-Haqaa'iq*, 188-189.
71	ibid.

[14:7]; and "Call upon Me, I will answer you" [40:60].'[72]

'Truly riches and nobility are in movement but when they find the place of trust in Allah they come to rest there.'[73]

`Ali ibn Suwayd asked Imam al-Kaazim about Allah's words in the Qur'an: 'And whoever trusts in Allah, He is sufficient for him,' [65:3] and he replied, 'Trust in Allah is of different degrees. There is that of trusting in Allah in all your affairs, so that whatever He does with you, you are content with Him: realize that He will not fail you in respect of the good and abundance in life and realize that control over these things is with Him; trust, therefore, in Allah by placing these matters in His hands; have confidence in Him concerning these and other matters.'[74]

Reflection

Allah commands man to reflect and meditate in many places in the Qur'an, and has praised those who reflect:

☼ Those who reflect on the creation of the heavens and the earth; Our Lord! Thou hast not created this in vain! (3:191)

☼ Do they not then meditate on the Qur'an? And if it were from any other than Allah, they would have found in it many a discrepancy. (4:52)

☼ And He has made subservient to you whatsoever is in the heavens and whatsoever is in the earth, all from Himself, most surely there are signs in this for people who reflect. (45:13)

72	al-Kulayni, II, 65.
73	ibid.
74	ibid.

The Messenger of Allah has said, 'Reflect upon the bounties of Allah, not upon the essence of Allah, for you will never be able to measure the extent of His power.'[75]

'Give to your eyes their just portion of worship.' When asked what he meant, he replied, 'Looking at the Qur'an, reflecting upon it and believing in its wonders.'[76]

Imam ʿAli said, 'Awaken your heart by reflection, and rise from your bed in worship at night, and trust in Allah as your Lord.'[77]

'Reflection leads one to goodliness and action in accordance with it.'[78]

'All goodness is gathered together in three qualities: observance, silence and speech. Observance without contemplation is negligence, silence without reflection is carelessness, and speech without remembrance of Allah is foolish talk.'[79]

'Wonder at man, who observes with a ball of fat [the eye], who talks with a lump of flesh [the tongue], who listens by means of a bone [the inner ear] and breathes through a hole in the flesh [the nose].'[80]

Al-Saadiq said, 'The best worship is to devote oneself to reflection upon Allah and His power.'[81]

Al-Rida said, 'True worship is not [to be found merely] in much prayer and fasting but rather in reflection on Allah's

---

75	*al-Haqaa'iq*, 306.
76	al-Ashtari, 306.
77	al-Kulayni, II, 54-55.
78	ibid.
79	*Mishkaat*, 37.
80	*Nahj* IV, 660.
81	al-Kulayni, II, 16 & 55.

design.'⁸²

Sincerity and Devotion

Allah says in His Book:

☼ Except those who repent and hold fast to Allah and are sincere in their religion to Allah; these are with the believers. (4:146)

☼ Now, surely, sincere obedience is due to Allah [alone]. (39:3)

☼ And they were not enjoined anything except that they should serve Allah, being sincere to Him in obedience upright. (98:5)

☼ He is the Living, there is no god but He, therefore call on Him, being sincere to Him in obedience. (40:65)

☼ Then see how was the end of those warned, except the servants of Allah, the purified ones. (37:73-4)

The Messenger of Allah said, 'O Mankind! There is Allah and there is Satan, truth and falsehood, guidance and going astray, the right path and the wrong path, life in this world and that of the hereafter, the reward of good actions and bad: the good actions belong to Allah and the bad to Satan, may the curse of Allah be upon him.'⁸³

'Whoever wishes to know what is in store for him with Allah surely must understand what is Allah's.'⁸⁴

'Surely for every truth there is a reality. A servant [of Allah]

---

82 ibid.
83 ibid.
84 *Mishkaat*, I I.

cannot attain the reality of sincerity until he dislikes people praising him for something which Allah has done.'[85]

Imam `Ali said, 'Contentment is his who devotes his worship and prayer sincerely to Allah and whose heart is not occupied by what the eye sees, and who does not forget Allah because of what his ears hear, and whose breast [i.e. heart] is not troubled by what is given to others.'[86]

Al-Saadiq was asked the meaning of Allah's words, '[In order] that He may try you – which of you is best in deeds,' [67:2] and he answered, 'This does not mean the greatest number of deeds, but rather the most correct deeds: truly, correctness comes from fear of Allah and a good and sincere intention. Perseverance in a deed until one finishes it is the hardest of deeds. A sincere deed is one for which you want no one's praise but Allah's; indeed, the intention is better than the deed itself, rather, the intention is a deed.' Then he read Allah's words, 'Say: everyone acts according to his manner,' [17:84] and explained it as meaning, 'according to his intention.'[87]

Justice

Allah has said in His words of revelation:

☼ Allah commands you that when you judge between people you judge with justice. (4:58)

☼ Say: my Lord has enjoined justice. (7:29)

☼ Certainly We sent Our apostles with clear arguments, and sent down with them the Book and the Balance that men may conduct themselves with equity. (57:25)

---

85 ibid.
86 al-Kulayni, II, 16.
87 ibid.

☼ And the heaven, He raised it high, and He made the Balance. (55:7)

☼ Surely Allah enjoins the doing of justice and the doing of good and the giving to kinsfolk. (16:90)

☼ Allah bears witness that there is no god but He, and [so do] the angels and those possessed of knowledge, maintaining His creation with justice.(3:18)

☼ And call to witness two men of justice from among you, and give them right testimony for Allah. (65:2)

☼ Two just persons among you shall judge. (5:95)

The Messenger of Allah said, 'An hour's justice is better than seventy years' worship, rising at night, and fasting by day; and a moment of tyranny in governance is worse than sixty years of crime.'[88]

'Whoever accompanies a tyrant in order that he may help him – while he is aware that he is a tyrant – has left the fold of Islam.'[89]

'Whoever gives of his wealth to support the poor and is just with people of his own accord, is a true believer.'[90]

It has been related by al-Sajjad that the Messenger of Allah said in his last speech, 'Contentment is the lot of those who have refined their behavior, purified their character, cleansed their hearts, who possess beauty in their speech and appearance, are of good reputation, who give away the excess of their wealth, who refrain from superfluous speech and who are just with

---

88   al-Ashtari, II, 60.
89   al-'Amili, 'Izz al-Din, *Nur al-Haqiqah,* 132.
90   al-Kulayni, II, 144-147.

people of their own accord.'[91]

Imam ʿAli has related that Allah said in a *hadith qudsi* (a *hadith* directly from Allah via the tongue of His Prophet), 'My anger is greatest towards men who oppress those who are without helpers. If anyone takes away the wealth of others, Allah will take away his wealth.'[92]

Imam ʿAli said, 'Truly upright citizens prosper under a just leader [Imam], and perish under a corrupt one.'[93]

He also said, at the moment when he returned to the Muslims what ʿUthman had taken for himself while he was caliph, 'By Allah, if I had found that he had married women [meaning by virtue of his authority over the wealth of the Muslims] and taken possession of female slaves, I would have returned them, for surely in justice there is amplitude. If a man finds justice constricting, then oppression will be even more constricting for him.'[94]

When Imam ʿAli handed over the governorship of Egypt to Muhammad ibn Abi Bakr, he commanded him to deal justly with the citizens, saying, 'Treat them kindly, be gracious to them, extend to them the benefits of your position and be fair in the way you regard different ranks of men, so that the powerful do not desire you to commit injustice in their favor and the weak do not despair of your justice towards them; truly Allah will ask your servants about the smallest and greatest of your deeds, about the deeds made in public and those hidden from view. Indeed, if He punishes, then you were surely worthy of the punishment, and if He forgives, then He is the most generous.'[95]

91	ibid.
92	al-ʿAmili, *Nur al-Haqiqah,* 132.
93	al-Haakim, *al-Hayat,* II, 296.
94	ibid. II, 198 (from *Nahj,* III, 543).
95	ibid.

Mu`awiyah ibn Sufyan asked Khalid ibn Mu`ammar why he loved `Ali ibn Abi Taalib. He replied, 'I love him for three qualities: for his compassion when he becomes angry, for his truthfulness when he speaks, and for his justice when he is generous.'[96]

Imam `Ali found a coat of mail belonging to him in the hands of a Christian, so he brought him before the judge, Shurayh, in order to bring a legal action against him. The Imam declared that he had neither sold it nor given it away as a gift. The judge then asked the Christian to explain himself. He replied, 'This coat of mail belongs to none other than myself.' Then he [the judge] asked Imam `Ali if he had any other evidence. He replied that he had not and, therefore, the judge decided in favor of the Christian. The Christian walked away for a while, then he returned and said, 'Truly I bear witness that these laws are from the prophets! Imam `Ali takes me before his own judge – and the judge reaches a verdict against him.'[97]

It is related by Imam al-Saadiq that Imam `Ali said, 'Surely if a man deals fairly with people of his own accord, then Allah will increase his share of honor and power.'[98]

Imam al-Saadiq said, 'Three kinds of men will stay closest to Allah on the day of Resurrection until the reckoning has been completed: the man who, when angry, does not allow his power to drive him to oppress those under him; the man who walks between two others and does not take sides with either of them in the slightest degree; and the man who speaks the truth, whether it is for him or against him.'[99]

'Justice is sweeter than water to a thirsty man; there is nothing

---

96	al-Ashatari, II, 75.
97	al-Haakim, II, 216.
98	al-Kulayni, II, 72 & 148.
99	ibid.

more expansive than justice even when it is practiced only to a small degree.'[100]

'Act out of fear and respect Allah and be just, for surely you yourself criticize those who are not.'[101]

Having a good opinion of Allah

It is related that Imam al-Baaqir said, 'We have found in the book of `Ali ibn Abi Taalib that the Messenger of Allah said from the pulpit, "By Him Who is the only God! A believer is not given the best in this world or the next unless he has a good opinion of Allah and places his hope in Him, shows good behavior and refrains from talking behind the backs of the believers. By Allah, Who is the only God, whoever has a good opinion [of Allah], Allah does not punish after he has turned to Him for forgiveness, unless he has a bad opinion of Allah and does not place his hope in Allah, behaves badly and talks ill of the believers. By Allah, there is no god but Him! If a believing servant has a good opinion of Allah, then Allah is as the opinion of the believing servant. This is because Allah is generous, and all good is in His hand; He would feel embarrassed if a believing servant had thought well of Him and placed his hope in Him and He were to go against this good opinion and hope in Him. Therefore, have a good opinion of Allah and maintain your desire for Him".'[102]

It is related that the Prophet said, 'Allah has slaves who spend according to the size of their property and He has slaves who spend in accordance with their good opinion of Him.'[103]

The Messenger of Allah said, 'You must not die without a

100	ibid.
101	ibid.
102	ibid.
103	al-`Inaathi, II, 17.

good opinion of Allah, for truly a good opinion of Allah is the price of entering the Garden.'[104]

The Messenger asked Allah not to take the reckoning of his *ummah*'s deeds in the presence of the angels, prophets, or the rest of the nations, so that their faults may not be revealed to them; rather, he asked that He take them to account in such a way that only Allah and himself may see their mistakes. Allah then replied, 'O My beloved, I am more compassionate with My slaves than you: if you are loath to have their mistakes revealed to others, then I am loath to expose them even to you, and so I call them to reckoning Myself, so that no one may see their shortcomings other than Me.'[105]

From amongst the sayings dealing with having a good opinion of Allah is one related by Ibn Mas'ud about a woman from the Ansaar who came to the Prophet with ten children and said, 'O Prophet of Allah, these, my children, are yours – take them to fight for Allah.' The Prophet took them into his closest company and led them into battle. The woman asked after them until nine of them had died as martyrs. Those that had passed away gave her more happiness than those who were still alive, until there remained the youngest: he deviated from the path of good and tended towards wrong action. When he fell ill his mother cared for him and treated him with tenderness and sympathy. He said to her, 'O mother, do you not see, if I had behaved badly towards you, or if I had overstepped my rights with regard to you and there was a fire burning in front of you, would you throw me into it?' 'No,' she replied. Then he said, 'Then do you not realize that the One Who has created me is even more compassionate than the one who has given birth to me?' Thereupon he died, and the Prophet said, 'Be filled with

---

104   *Mishkaat*, 36.
105   al-Shirazi, 57.

joy that your son has been forgiven because of his good opinion of his Lord.'[106]

Al-Saadiq said, 'A good opinion of Allah is desiring nothing but Allah and fearing nothing but your wrong actions.'[107] And elsewhere he said, 'A slave will be brought before Allah on the Day of Resurrection having done wrong to himself by his own actions, and Allah will say to him, "Did I not order you to obey Me? Did I not forbid you to disobey Me?" Then he will say, "Yes, O Lord, but my desires overcame me; if You punish me, then You will not have done me wrong, considering my crime." Then Allah will order him into the fire. Then he will say, "This was not the opinion I had of You." Allah will reply, "What was your opinion of Me?" He will reply, "I had the best of opinions concerning You." Thereupon, Allah will order him into the Garden, and He will say, "Your good opinion of Me has saved you on this last day".'[108]

Imam al-Rida said, 'Have a good opinion of Allah, for truly Allah says, "I am in My believing slave's opinion of Me: if he thinks well of Me then for him there is goodness, if ill, then for him is evil".'[109]

The Trial and the Test

It is reported from al-Saadiq that the Messenger of Allah said, 'Allah has said, "Any slave I wish to bring into the Garden I try in his bodily health, for truly this is an expiation for his wrong actions; or I constrict his provision for him so that because of his suffering he comes to Me without committing any wrong actions, and then I bring him into the Garden. Any slave I wish

---

106	al-'Inaathi, II, 12.
107	al-Kulayni, II, 72.
108	al-Barqi, *al-Mahasin*, 26.
109	al-Kulayni, II, 72.

to bring to the fire I make him healthy in body, thus fulfilling the claims he makes on Me; or I make him secure in his authority, thus fulfilling his demands on Me, or I make death easy for him so that he comes to Me without any merit – and so I make him enter the fire".'[110]

It is related from al-Kaazim that Allah said, 'I have not made the rich man rich because of his generosity towards Me, nor have I impoverished the poor man because of his lack of concern for Me. Rather I have tested the rich by the poor, and if it were not for the poor, the rich would not deserve the Garden.'[111]

When trial, and in particular the trial by which Allah tests believers, was mentioned in the company of al-Saadiq, Abu `Abdallah said that the Messenger of Allah was asked, 'Which people undergo the hardest trial in this world?' 'The prophets,' he replied, 'then their like, and then the like of them. The believer is tested in accordance with the strength of his belief and his good deeds; if anyone perfects his belief and does good actions, then his testing will be more severe, and whoever is weak in his faith and deficient in his actions will have a lesser trial.'[112]

The Messenger of Allah said, 'Truly, the greatest of trials will be compensated by the greatest rewards. If Allah loves a slave, He tests him with the greatest trials: whoever accepts with contentment will find contentment from Allah, and whoever becomes angry with the trials will find anger.'[113]

It is related from al-Baaqir that the Messenger of Allah has said, 'Allah has no need of him who gives no portion of his self or his wealth.'[114]

110	*Mishkaat*, 291.
111	ibid., 288-9.
112	ibid., 293.
113	*al-Khisaal*, I, 18.
114	*Mishkaat*, 292.

It is related that al-Baaqir told of how some people came to ʿAli ibn al-Husayn while he was with ʿAbdallah ibn al-ʿAbbas and mentioned to him the trials of their followers and how it was afflicting them. Two of them came to Husayn and spoke to him about it. Husayn said, 'By Allah, trials and poverty come to those who love us quicker than a galloping horse, quicker than the flood running to the end of its course, and quicker than a drop of rain falling from the sky to the earth. If it were not like this for you, we would realize that you were not one of us. By us are the orphans helped, by us is the religion of Islam carried out, and by us are your wrong actions forgiven.'[115]

Al-Saadiq said, 'If the believer knew the reward contained in affliction he would desire to be rewarded by afflictions containing his doom.'[116]

It is related from the same source that 'Verily, Allah assigns affliction to the believer in [the form of] the gifts He bestows upon him so that he stands his nights in prayer; but should he not do so, Allah assigns to him bodily illness, affliction in his family and property, or one of the catastrophes of this world in order that He may reward him on account of it.'[117]

It is also related that he [al-Saadiq] said, 'Truly the believer calls to Allah in his need and Allah says, "I have delayed fulfillment of his need because of My desire for his prayers." When the Day of Resurrection comes, Allah will say, "My slave, you called on Me for such and such a need and I delayed in replying to you, so your reward is that which you asked for." Thus the believer desires that his prayers not be answered in this world, because of the reward he perceives in their place in the next [world].'[118]

115	ibid. 292-293.
116	ibid. 288-293.
117	ibid. 288-293.
118	ibid.

'Truly Allah gives of this world to those whom He loves and hates, but He does not give faith except to the people of the Chosen One [*al-Mustafa'*, i.e. Muhammad] before His creatures.'[119]

'Poverty is stored up with Allah as is the testimony [there is no god except Allah] and He only gives these two things to those He loves of His believing slaves.'[120]

Truly, if Allah loves a slave He appoints for him two angels, saying, "Delay his obtaining what he desires and constrict his means of living for him so that he calls to Me in prayer, Surely I love to hear his voice".'[121]

Imam Zayn al-`Abideen used to say, 'In truth, I dislike that a man is spared in this world and is not touched by any afflictions.'[122]

Contentment with Allah's Decree and One's Own Destiny

Allah says in His Book:

☼ And it behoves not a believing man and a believing woman that they should have any choice in their matter when Allah and His Apostle have decided a matter. (33:36)

☼ And when He decrees an affair. He only says to it, Be, and it is. (2:117)

☼ ...but – in order that Allah might bring about a matter which was to be done. (8:42)

☼ And the matter has [already] been decided; and [all]

119	ibid.
120	ibid.
121	ibid.
122	ibid.

matters are returned to Allah. (2:210)

☼ Surely your Lord makes plentiful the means of subsistence for whom He pleases and straitens [them]. (17:30)

☼ The command of Allah is a decree that is made absolute. (33:38)

The Prophet said, 'There are four kinds of men whom Allah will not consider on the Day of Resurrection: the rebellious, those who begrudge benefits received, those who deny the decree, and those who are addicted to wine.'[123]

The Prophet was asked about the signs of the last day, and he replied, 'When people have faith in the stars and deny predestination.'[124]

Imam `Ali relates that the Prophet said, 'A slave does not truly believe until he believes in four things: until he bears witness that there is no god except Allah, the One Who has no associate; that I am the Messenger of Allah sent with truth; until he believes in the resurrection after death; and until he believes in the decree.'[125]

It is related by Imam al-Saadiq that the Prophet of Allah said, 'Truly I have cursed seven kinds of men whom Allah has cursed and whom every accepted prophet has cursed before me [among them are the following three]: the one who adds to the book of Allah; the one who denies the decree; and the one who opposes my *sunnah*.'[126]

123	al-Khisaal,I,18.
124	ibid.,I,62;I,199;II,349.
125	ibid.
126	ibid.

Imam al-Kaazim said, 'The man who is negligent with regard to Allah should not accuse Him of delaying his provision nor condemn Him for His decree.'[127]

Imam `Ali used to say in his prayers, 'O Allah, grant me reliance on You, that I may entrust my affairs to You, be content with Your decree and submit to Your command so that I do not wish that something You have delayed should be brought forward and that something You have caused to happen should be delayed, O Lord of the Worlds.'[128]

It is related that Imam al-Baaqir said, 'Truly Allah has made and carried out His decree; He has judged, and acted justly in His judgment. Thus, there is no one who can avert His decree and no one who can defer His judgment; therefore it is incumbent on Allah's creation to submit to what Allah has decreed. If anyone knows Allah and is content with the decree, then the decree will come to pass for him and Allah will increase his reward; but if anyone is angry with the decree, then the decree will come to pass for him just the same and Allah will take away his reward.'[129]

'Truly, we desire to enjoy our family and close relations; we should pray to Allah for that which the decree of Allah has not yet caused to happen, for when the decree comes into being we should not desire what Allah has not desired [in His decree].'[130]

It is related from Imam al-Saadiq that he said, 'The most beloved man is he, who when something occurs which he dislikes, does not show it in his face, and if something occurs which makes him happy, does not show it in his face.'[131]

'How can anyone be called a believer when he gets angry at

127	*Mishkaat*,301-303.
128	ibid.
129	ibid.
130	ibid.
131	ibid.

his destiny, and despises his situation when Allah is governing his affairs? Surely, I guarantee that whoever allows nothing but contentment to enter his heart will have his prayer answered if he calls on Him.'[132]

'Inspect your hearts, for if Allah purifies them of violent movement as a result of anger at something of His making, then you may ask of Him what you wish.'[133]

'As for the Muslim, Allah does not decree anything for him without there being good in it: if he is deprived of completely everything, then there is good in it for him; and if he owns the lands both to the east and to the west there is also good in this.'[134]

'The conditions for belief are that one is content with the decree and is at peace with himself. Contentment with the decree is the most noble of the conditions, necessary for belief, and the best characteristic of a believer. Allah has said, "Certainly Allah was well pleased with the believers" [48:18]. He also says, "Allah is well pleased with them and they are well pleased with Allah" [5:119].[135]

Truly, contentment with the decree is a high spiritual rank obtained only by the truthful and the elite of the believers; surely, the death of Imam Husayn as a martyr on the day of `Ashura' [10th Muharram] is the highest example of perfect contentment with the decree and destiny of Allah. When his thirst became unbearable and he asked for water, they said to him, 'Yield to the governance of `Abdallah ibn Ziyad, so that we can leave you alone.' He replied that he was bound by the governance of Allah and refused to submit to this hateful and oppressive condition, knowing that soon he would be put to death. He then fought until he was killed, content with Allah's decree and what fate had brought with it, thereby adorning his

---

132   ibid.
133   ibid.
134   ibid.
135   al-`Inaathi,II,157-159.

character. [136]

Among the tremendous events of Islam were those which occurred after the battle of Uhud, during which the Muslims were defeated in the first instance. During the battle a number of the elite of the Muhajirun and the Ansaar were killed as martyrs, and the Messenger of Allah was wounded. When the news reached Madinah al-Munawwarah, the wife of one of the Ansaar came out to ask about her husband and was told he had died as a martyr. She then asked about her father and her brother and was told the same things. Then she asked, 'Is the Messenger of Allah safe and sound?' When they replied that he was, she said, 'His being still alive makes up for all the others.'[137]

These purified and righteous people became content with the decree of Allah and were patient in the face of events in order to win this contentment and high spiritual stations with Him. As Allah says, 'Truly He will give the patient their reward and will give without reckoning' [39:10]. He also said, 'No soul knows what has been kept hidden for him as a cooling for his eyes, a reward for what they did' [32:17].

Belief in the Last Day and the Place of Return

Allah says in the Qur'an:

☼ From it [the earth] We created you, and into it We shall send you back, and from it We will raise you a second time. (20:55)

☼ Surely the might of your Lord is great. Surely He it is Who originates and reproduces. (85:12-13)

☼ Allah originates the creation, then reproduces it, then to Him you shall be brought back. (30:11)

---

136   ibid.
137   ibid.

☼ Most surely He Who made the Qur'an binding on you will bring you back to the destination. (28:85)

☼ Do they not consider how Allah originates the creation, then reproduces it? (29:19)

☼ To Him is your return, of all [of you]; the promise of Allah made in truth. (10:4)

☼ And those who disbelieve say: the Hour shall not come upon us. Say: Yea! By my Lord, the Knower of the unseen, it shall certainly come upon you. (34:3)

☼ And when it was said: surely the promise of Allah is true and as for the Hour, there is no doubt about it, you said: We do not know what the Hour is; we do not think [that it will come to pass] save a passing thought, and we are not at all sure. (45:32)

☼ And the measuring out on that day will be just; then as for him whose measure [of good deeds] is heavy, those are they who shall be successful. (7:8)

☼ And the companions of the right hand; how happy are the companions of the right hand! Amid thornless lote-trees, and banana trees [with fruits], one above another. And extended shade, and water flowing constantly, and abundant fruits, neither intercepted nor forbidden, and exalted thrones. (56:27-34)

☼ O soul that art at rest! Return to your Lord, well pleased [with Him], well-pleasing [Him], so enter among my servants, and enter into My garden. (89:27-30)

☼ And whoever desires the hereafter and strives for it as he ought to strive and he is a believer, [as for] these, their striving shall surely be accepted. (17:19)

☼ And We will set up a just balance on the day of

Resurrection, so no soul shall be dealt with unjustly in the least; and though it be the weight of a grain of mustard seed, [yet] will We bring it, and sufficient are We to take account. (21:47)

☼ What! Did you then think that We had created you in vain and that you shall not be returned to Us? (23:115)

☼ O people! If you are in doubt about the raising, then surely We created you from dust...This is because Allah is the Truth and because He gives life to the dead and because He has power over all things. And because the Hour is coming, there is no doubt about it; and because Allah shall raise up those who are in the graves. (22:5-7)

☼ And certainly We created man from an extract of clay... Then after that you will most surely die. Then surely on the day of Resurrection you shall be raised. (23:12-16)

☼ As We originated the first creation, [so] We shall reproduce it; a promise [binding on Us]; surely We will bring it about. (21:104)

The Messenger said, 'O men of `Abd al-Muttalib, surely a leader does not lie to his people. By the One Who has sent me with the truth, indeed you shall die just as you sleep, and you shall be raised up just as you wake up, and after death there is no abode save the Garden or the Fire.'[138]

Counseling the noble companion Abu Dharr, the Messenger of Allah said, 'O Abu Dharr, take account of your own soul before you are taken to account, for surely this is easier than your reckoning to come; measure your soul before it is measured for you, and make yourself ready for the tremendous day when

---

138   al-Muhajjah al-Bayda',I,249.

all souls will be received. Even the hidden is not hidden from Allah. O Abu Dharr, a man is not counted among the pious until he takes his soul to account more severely than the man who takes his partner to account and knows where his food, drink and clothing are from – that is, he knows whether they be of *halal* (permitted) or *haram* (forbidden) origin. O Abu Dharr, if someone does not care where he earns his wealth, Allah will not care by what means he will have him enter the Fire.'[139]

The Prophet said, 'The most intelligent of you is he who takes his own soul to account and acts in accordance with what is to come after death.'

Imam al-`Askari conveyed the response of Imam `Ali to a man who posed the question: 'O Commander of the Faithful, how does a man take account of his own soul?' The Imam replied, 'When the morning has been followed by the evening, a man turns to his soul and says, "O my self, surely this day has passed by you and will never return to you. Allah will ask you about it and the way you have spent it; so what have you done during it? Have you remembered Allah? Have you praised Him? Have you taken care of the needs of the believers? Have you relieved the Muslims of their hardships? Have you taken care of those absent from you, and of your family and your children? Have you restrained yourself from talking badly of your fellow believer in his absence? Have you helped the Muslims? What have you achieved during this day? Do you remember what has happened during this day?" If he remembers that good has come out of it, then he praises Allah and His greatness for his success; if he remembers a wrong action or a shortcoming, he asks Allah for forgiveness and makes a firm intention to change his ways.'[140]

Imam `Ali said, 'If you were to suffer like the one amongst

---

139   al-Hikam I, 419 (from al-Hurr, *Wasa'il al-Shi'ite*, XI,379).
140   ibid.,I,420-421 (from *Nahj*,79 & 1031).

you who has died, you would be fearful and horrified; you would listen and obey. What they have suffered is veiled from you; however, the veil will be drawn aside. Surely, you would realize if you but opened your eyes, and you would listen if you but paid attention; you would be guided if you let yourselves be guided. In truth I say to you, I have made plain to you the explanation and forbidden you from what is forbidden; only men will give the message of Allah after the messengers from the heavens.'[141]

Imam Muhammad al-Jawad and his forefathers reported Imam `Ali ibn al-Husayn as saying, 'When the condition of Husayn ibn `Ali became serious, those with him looked at him and saw he was different from them: as his condition became more and more serious, the color of their faces changed, their horses shook with terror and their hearts trembled, while the face of Husayn and some of his most intimate companions were bright in color, their limbs were at ease, their souls at rest. They said to each other, "Look, he is not worried by death!" Husayn said to them, "Have patience, sons of the noble: death is nothing but a causeway which will lead you over hardship and affliction to wide gardens and eternal ease. Which one of you then would not wish to leave a prison for a palace? As for your enemies, it is as if they are leaving a palace for a prison".'[142]

Imam al-Sajjad used to say when praying, 'O Allah, grant us fear of your promised punishment and desire for your promised rewards, so that for what we call on You becomes pleasurable for us, and for what we seek protection from You becomes grievous for us.'[143]

141	ibid.
142	ibid.,I,422 (from *al-Bihaar,* vol. 44,297).
143	ibid.,I,422 (from *al-Sahifah al-Sajjadiyah,*311).

Remembrance of death

Allah said in His Book:

> ☼ Say: O you who are Jews, if you think you are the favorites of Allah to the exclusion of other people, then invoke death if you are truthful. (62:6)

> ☼ Say: [as for] the death from which you flee, that will surely overtake you, then you shall be sent back to the Knower of the unseen and the seen.(62:8)

> ☼ Every soul must taste death and We will try you by evil and good by way of probation; and to Us you shall be brought back. (21:35)

> ☼ Say: if the future abode with Allah is especially for you to the exclusion of the people, then invoke death if you are truthful. (2:94)

The Prophet of Allah said, 'Increase your remembrance of that which annihilates the pleasures [of this world]'[144] – *that is, smother these pleasures by remembering death until your dependence on them ceases.*

'If animals knew death as man knows death, you would not find any fat ones amongst them to eat.'[145]

Some people asked the Messenger of Allah if certain people would be gathered on the day of Resurrection with those who died as martyrs in the battle of Uhud. 'Yes,' he replied, 'those who remember death twenty times during the day.'[146]

Its excellence [remembrance of death] is that it causes distance from

---

144 al-Ashtari,I,268-269.
145 ibid.
146 ibid.

the world of illusion, and brings about preparations for the next world; forgetfulness of death incites devotion to the sensual pleasures of this world.

The Messenger of Allah said, 'Death is the precious gem of the believer,'[147] *meaning that this world is like a prison for the believer: his time in it is spent in distress caused by his constant disciplining of the self, enduring the demands of his passions and defending himself from Satan. Thus death for him is a release from this torment – like the release of the gem from its casket – as he reaches the place of lasting bliss.*[148]

'Death is an expiation for every Muslim,'[149] – *by this he meant the true Muslim, the genuine believer, from whose hand and tongue people are safe, and those people in whom may be found good behavior.*

The Messenger also said, 'Increase your remembrance of death, for it effaces wrong actions and makes one do without this world. Remembrance of death is counsel enough for you.'[150]

The Messenger of Allah went out of the mosque once and heard people talking and laughing. He said, 'Remember death! By the One in Whose hand is my soul, if you knew what I knew, you would laugh little and weep much.'[151]

A man was mentioned to the Messenger and was much praised. He said, 'How did your companion remember death?' They replied, 'We hardly heard him remembering death.' He said, 'Your companion is not over there [in Paradise with those who had remembered].'[152]

One of the Ansaar asked the Messenger who were the most

---

147 ibid.
148 ibid.
149 ibid.
150 ibid.
151 ibid.
152 ibid.

intelligent and the most noble of men. He replied, 'Those who remember death the most and are the most prepared for it are the most intelligent: they have obtained the honor of this world and are the nobility of the hereafter.'[153]

The Messenger said, 'People are of two kinds. One kind gives rest, and the other kind rests. As for the one who rests, this is the believer when he dies: he finds rest from this world and its trials. As for the one who gives rest, it is the unbeliever: when he dies he gives rest to trees, the animals and a great many people.'[154]

The Prophet said to `Abd Allah ibn `Umar, 'Be in this world as if you are a wayfarer or a stranger, and prepare yourself [by remembering] the dead.'[155]

'The believer finds ease in death by leaving behind that which he was wary of [i.e. *dunya*], and by the speed of his movement towards the One Whom he desires and has hope of.'[156]

One of the Ansaar said, 'O Messenger of Allah, why is it that I do not like death?' The Prophet asked, 'Do you have wealth?' 'Yes, O Messenger.' 'Give out your wealth [in this world for the next]; for surely, man's heart is with his wealth: if he gives it out [for the sake of the next world] he wants to regain it, and if he leaves it [in this world], he desires to remain here with it.'[157]

Al-Saadiq told how Gabriel came to the Messenger of Allah and said, 'O Muhammad, Allah conveys His greetings of peace and says, "Act as you wish, for surely you will encounter Him; love whom you wish, for surely you will be separated from him; and live as you wish, for surely you will die. O Muhammad, night

---

153	ibid.
154	al-Khisaal,I,39.
155	*Mishkaat*,303-305.
156	ibid.
157	ibid.

prayer is the nobility of the believer, and it gives authority to his speech".'[158]

Imam `Ali said, 'O people, fear Allah Who hears you when you speak and knows what you think. Anticipate death, which will reach you even if you flee, and will catch hold of you even as you stand up. Even if you forget Him, He remembers you.'[159]

'Whoever reckons he will be living tomorrow has not given death its true measure of importance.'[160]

He also said, while following a funeral procession and hearing a man laughing, 'It is as if death has been ordained for people other than ourselves, as if the reality in the coffin is only for others and as if those who die are merely travelling to a place from which few return.'[161]

'I am astonished at the man who forgets death although he sees dead people.'[162]

The Messenger said to `Ali, 'Sudden death is ease for the believer and a grief for the unbeliever.'[163]

Al-Saadiq said, 'The Day of Resurrection is like the bride of those who fear Allah.'[164]

'Allah has not created anything more certain and without doubt than death, and yet at the same time something which [in the imagination of the people] is less certain and full of doubt.'[165]

158	ibid.
159	ibid.
160	ibid.
161	*Nahj*, IV, 684-685.
162	ibid.
163	Al-Tabarsi, *Makarim al-Akhlaq*, 439.
164	*al-Khisaal*, I, 13-14.
165	ibid.

The *Barzakh*, or matters pertaining to the time spent in the grave before the Day of Resurrection

Allah says:

☼ We will chastise them twice, then shall they be turned back to a grievous chastisement. (9:101)

☼ And when the graves are laid open, every soul shall know what it has sent before and held back. (82:4-5)

☼ Does he not know when what is in the grave is raised, and what is in the breast is made apparent? (100:9-10)

The Messenger of Allah said, 'The burial place will say to the dead person as he is put into his grave, "Woe to you, O son of Adam. What deluded you in respect of me? Do you not realize that I am the house of trial and the house of darkness, the house of solitude and the house of worms? What deceived you concerning me when you used to pass me by so many times?" Then, if he were one of the righteous, someone will answer the grave for him, saying, "Have you seen how he was one of those who enjoined righteousness and forbade evil?" The grave will say, "Then I will transform [this place] into a green meadow, his body will become light again and his spirit will rise up towards Allah".'[166]

Al-Bara' ibn `Azib relates how he went out with the Messenger to the funeral procession of one of the Ansaar. The Messenger then sat down on his grave, his head lowered, and said three times, 'O Allah, I seek refuge from the torment of the grave...,' and went on saying, 'If the believer is in anticipation of the hereafter, Allah sends angels to him whose faces are like the sun and who carry with them his embalming oil and his shroud;

---

166   al-Ashtari,I,288-290;II,168.

they then sit down ranged as far as the eye can see. When his spirit leaves his body, each angel between the heavens and earth prays over him; the gates are opened for him and there is not a gate but that it desires his spirit to enter through it. Thus when his spirit is raised up and it is said, "And what about this slave of yours, Lord?" He will reply, "Take him back and show him what bliss I have prepared for him, for surely I have promised this to him: 'From it We created you and into it We shall send you back and from it We will raise you a second time' [20:55]." Then surely he will hear the tread of the shoes of those who turn back, until he says to that man, "Who is your Lord? Who is your Prophet? Who is your Imam?" Then he will say, "My Lord is Allah, my Prophet is Muhammad and my Imam is `Ali," and then will enumerate the Imams one by one.

'They will reproach him severely and this will be the last trial he is exposed to. Thus when he replies in the way he does, a herald will proclaim, "You have told the truth" – and this is the meaning of the words of Allah: "Allah makes firm those who believe by firm words" [14:27]. Then an angel will come to him, an angel whose face is beautiful and who is sweet-smelling and pleasantly attired, saying, "Be joyful at the good news of mercy from your Lord, and eternal gardens of bounty ." He will also say, "Allah gives you good news of wealth and the Garden." "Who are you?" the slave will ask, and the angel will reply, "I am your righteous deeds. By Allah, I have heard only of the speed of your obedience to Allah and your unwillingness to disobey Him; thus Allah has rewarded you with good." Thereupon a herald will call for a couch to be prepared for him in the Garden, and that a door to the Garden will be opened. Then he will say, "O Allah, hasten the rising of the Last Day, so that I may return to my family and my wealth." For the unbelievers it will be the opposite: just as the believer will find wealth and blessings, they will find torment.'[167]

It is related that the Commander of the Faithful said, 'If a believer dies, 70,000 angels accompany him in mourning to his grave; when he enters his grave, Munkar and Nakir come and sit with him, saying, "Who is your Lord? What is your religion? Who is your Prophet?" He will reply, "Allah is my Lord, Islam is my religion and Muhammad is my Prophet." Then they will clear a space for him in the grave as far as his eyes can see and will bring food from the Garden; they will cause the breath of life to enter and bring perfume, as mentioned by Allah in His words: "And as for those who have been brought close to Me, theirs is happiness and bounty" – that is, in his grave – "and the Garden of bliss" [56:89] – meaning the Hereafter.'

Then Imam `Ali said, 'When the unbeliever dies, 70,000 of the guardian angels of the Fire will accompany him to his grave. Then he will implore those bearing him, in a voice heard by all those bearing him except man and jinn, saying, "If only I had a chance to return and be like the believers! Take me back, that I may do righteous deeds in the place I have left." The guards will reply, "Certainly not – these are merely empty words." An angel will then call to them, "Such men, if they were sent back, would repeat what they had been forbidden to do." Then when he enters his grave and the people have left him alone, Munkar and Nakir come to him in their most hideous form and stand by him, saying, "Who is your Lord? What is your religion? Who is your Prophet?" Then his tongue will stammer and he will be unable to reply, and they will strike him with a stroke of Allah's torment and will terrify all things. Then the two angels will again ask, "Who is your Lord, what is your religion and who is your Prophet?" He will then reply, "I do not know ." They will then say to him, "You have found out nothing, you have not been

---

167   ibid.

guided and you have not been successful." Thereupon they will open for him a gate into the Fire, causing boiling water to pour over him. This is in accordance with Allah's words: "But if he were one of the liars, astray, his abode will be boiling water and burning in the fires of hell" [56:92].'[168]

The body will disintegrate after its separation from the soul. Allah says, 'Do not reckon that those killed in the way of Allah are dead, rather they are alive with their Lord, provided for and glad with what Allah has given them of His bounty; they are rejoicing at those coming after who have not yet joined them; they have no fear and they will not grieve'[3:169].[169]

The Prophet called out to the rebellious unbelievers killed at the battle of Badr, 'I have found what my Lord promised me was true; so have you found what your lord promised you was true? By the One in Whose hand is my soul, certainly they hear your words, but are unable to reply.' A similar *hadith* is also reported from Imam `Ali concerning those killed during the battle of the Camel.[170]

Al-Saadiq is reported as saying, 'The soul will surely remain in its place: the soul of the believer in space and light, and the soul of the sinner in constriction and darkness – but the body will turn to dust.'[171] From the same source: 'The soul of the believer in his body is like a gem in a casket: if the gem is taken out, the casket is discarded, and is not used to contain the gem again.'[172]

He also said, 'Whoever denies these three matters is not among our followers: the *Mi`raj* (the night ascension of

---

168	ibid.
169	*al-Haqaa'iq*,II,460.
170	ibid.,II,461.
171	ibid.
172	ibid.

Muhammad to Allah), the reality of what takes place in the grave, and intercession (on the Day of Resurrection).'[173]

The Place of Assembly of the Day of Resurrection

Allah says in His Noble Book:

> ☼ And We shall gather them together on the day of Resurrection on their faces, blind and dumb and deaf. (17:97)

> ☼ And We will set up a just balance on the day of Resurrection. (21:47)

> ☼ And you shall only be paid fully your reward on the Resurrection day. (3:185)

> ☼ Surely your Lord will judge between them on the Resurrection day concerning that in which they disagreed. (10:93)

> ☼ And on the day of Resurrection you shall see those who lied against Allah; their faces shall be blackened. (39:60)

> ☼ There would be naught but a single cry, when lo! they shall be brought before Us. (36:53)

> ☼ The day when they shall hear the cry in truth; that is the day of coming forth. (50.42)

When asked about the length of the Day of Resurrection, the Messenger of Allah replied, 'By the One in Whose hand is my soul, in truth it will be so short for the believer that it will be easier for him than the prescribed prayers he used to pray in the

---

[173]   al-Kaashaani,*al-Muhajjah al-Bayda'*, I,248 *(from alSaduq,al-Ama li,*177).

world.'[174]

On another occasion the Messenger said, 'Some people will be raised in such ugly forms that apes and pigs will appear beautiful in comparison with them.'[175]

'People will be gathered together on the Day of Resurrection in three groups: riding, walking, or on their faces.'[176]

The Prophet was asked why he did not lead a life of ease and comfort. He replied, 'How should I lead a life of ease, knowing the trumpet-blower has the horn in his mouth and is crouching, listening with his ear for the order to blow?'[177]

☼ 'And the trumpet shall be blown, so that all who are in the heavens and all those that are in the earth shall swoon, except such as Allah please; then it shall be blown again, then lo, they shall stand up awaiting' [39:68].

'On the Day of Resurrection people will be raised up barefoot and naked, isolated and exhausted by profuse sweating – even from their earlobes.'[178]

It is related that Sawdah, the wife of the Prophet, said, 'O Messenger of Allah, will we be able to see each other's private parts?' He replied, 'People will be too preoccupied to notice; each one will be concerned by a matter which will allow him no time for other things.'[179]

Imam `Ali has said, 'On the Day of Resurrection, Allah will raise the people from their graves solitary, having nothing about them, and beardless, together on one plane; then they will be

---

174 al-Kaashaani, *Qurrat al-`Uyun*, 480.
175 ibid. 479.
176 ibid.
177 ibid.
178 al-Ashtari, I, 294.
179 ibid.

driven by light and gathered together by darkness, until they stand on the threshold of the place of assembly; they will climb on top of each other, jostling others out of the way, preventing others from moving forward, their breath becoming heavier and heavier, sweat pouring from them, the noise and clamor increasing while their cries rise higher and higher.'[180]

Al-Saadiq has said, 'Take account of yourselves, before you are taken to account. Truly, on the Day of Resurrection, there are fifty places of standing, each place a standing of a thousand years.' Then he recited, 'On the day whose length extends fifty thousand years' [70:4].[181]

The Garden and the Fire

Allah says in His Book of Wisdom:

☼ And hasten to forgiveness from your Lord; and a Garden, the extent of which is as the heavens and the earth; it is prepared for those who guard [against evil]. (3:133)

☼ Surely whoever associates [others] with Allah, then Allah has forbidden him the Garden, and his abode is in the Fire. (5:72)

☼ And the dwellers of the Garden will call out to the inmates of the Fire: Surely we have found what our Lord promised us to be true. (7:44)

☼ Surely Allah has bought of the believers their persons and their property for this, that they shall have the garden. (9:111)

☼ Whoever obeys Allah and His Apostle, He will cause

---

180   *Qurrat al-'Uyun,* 480.
181   ibid.

him to enter gardens beneath which rivers flow. (4:13)

☼ Not alike are the inmates of the Fire and the dwellers of the Garden. (59:20)

☼ Surely those who guard [against evil] are in a secure place, in gardens and springs. (44:51-2)

☼ Then be on your guard against the Fire of which men and stones are the fuel. (2:24)

☼ Those who say: O Lord! Surely we believe, therefore forgive us our faults and save us from the chastisement of the Fire. (3:16)

☼ Our Lord! Thou hast not created this in vain! Glory be to Thee, save us then from the chastisement of the Fire. (3:191)

The Messenger of Allah said, 'Surely every one of you will stand in front of Allah and He will say, "Did I not give you wealth?" The person will reply, "Yes," then he will look to his right and will not see anything except the Fire, then he will look to his left and will not see anything but the Fire. Thus everyone should guard himself from the Fire, even if it is (in giving) half a date and if he does not find this then a kind word. Then He will say, "O son of Adam, what enticed you away from Me? What were you doing when you did what you did?"'[182]

'Surely the first parts of my community to enter the Fire will be the two cavities.' They said, 'O Messenger of Allah, what are the two cavities?' He replied, 'The private parts and the mouth; and that by which most people will enter the Garden is awe of Allah and good character.'[183]

---

182   al-Ashtari,I,297.
183   al-Khisaal,I,78&93.

'Truly there are stations in the garden only reached by the just Imams of those who maintain strong ties with their relations and those who are patient with their families.'[184]

'By the One Who sent me in truth as a proclaimer of good news: Allah will never torment with fire a man who believes in His unity; those with belief in His unity will act as intercessors and be interceded for.'[185]

'The Ruh al-Amm, Jibril [Gabriel], informed me that there is no god except Him. When mankind is standing, the earliest and the latest generations gathered together, *Jahannam* will be brought forward crashing, destructive, roaring and hissing, driven by a thousand reins, each rein held by a hundred thousand angels, rough and harsh in appearance.'[186]

Al-Saadiq has said, 'Fever is a precursor of death; it is Allah's prison on this earth and it is like an exhortation to the believer to avoid the Fire.'[187]

BELIEF IN PROPHETHOOD

Creation's Need of the Prophets and Messengers

Allah says in the Qur'an:

☼ Certainly We sent Our apostles with clear arguments, and sent down to them the Book and the Balance that men may conduct themselves with equity. (57:25)

☼ Surely We have revealed to you as We revealed to Nuh, and the prophets after him, and We revealed to Ibrahim and Isma'il and Ishaq and Ya`qub and the tribes, and `Isa

---

184	ibid.
185	*Qurrat al-`Uyun*, 491-492.
186	ibid.
187	ibid.

and Ayyub and Yunus and Harun and Sulayman and We gave to Dawud the Psalms. And [We sent] apostles We have mentioned to you; and to Musa, Allah addressed His word, speaking [to him]; [We sent] apostles as the givers of good news and as warners, so that people would not have a plea against Allah after the [coming of] apostles; and Allah is Mighty Wise. (4:163-5)

☼ When their apostles came to them from before them and from behind them saying, serve nothing but Allah. (41:14)

☼ And all We relate to you of the accounts of the apostles is to strengthen your heart therewith. (11:120)

☼ Those who deliver the messages of Allah and fear Him, and do not fear anyone but Allah; and Allah is sufficient to take account. (33:39)

☼ And certainly We raised in every nation an apostle saying: Serve Allah and shun the Shaytan. So there were some of them whom Allah guided and there were others against whom error was due; therefore travel in the land, then see what was the end of the rejecters. (16:36)

☼ And We made them Imams who guided [people] by Our command, and We revealed to them the doing of good and the keeping up of prayer and the giving of alms, and Us [alone] did they serve. (21:73)

Imam al-Saadiq relates that the Messenger of Allah said in one of his speeches, 'He desired to distinguish Himself by His Oneness when He veiled Himself in His light, and ascended in His sublimity and hid Himself from His creation, and sent Messengers to them that they be the evident proof of Himself for His creation, and that His Messengers to them be witnesses over them; He raised up amongst them prophets, bringers of good news and warners, to destroy those who were doomed to destruction by the clear evidence, and to give life to those who flourished by the clear evidence. Thus He allows the slaves to reflect about their Lord concerning that of which they were ignorant: they recognize Him by His Lordship after they had denied Him, and they affirm His Oneness by His divinity after they had not co-operated.'[188]

Imam `Ali, talking about the raising up of prophets and messengers said, 'Allah has chosen prophets from amongst Adam's descendants who, through revelation, accept [divine] contracts and are entrusted with delivery of the divine message.

'He has sent His Messengers amongst them and has sent His prophets one after another to fulfill the contract of the *fitrah* [the original, primordial nature of man], and to remind them of the blessing which had been forgotten. Delivery of the message and calling men to Him is a proof [of Him]; the prophets transmit treasures of wisdom and knowledge and they show man the decreed signs.'[189]

The Commander of the Faithful, `Ali, said, 'He has sent His Messengers and has marked them out from other men by His revelation. He has made them a proof of Himself over His creation, so that the proof is not allowed to become the responsibility of those other men and they are given no opportunity for finding excuses [in order not to believe]; He has invited them with words of sincerity to the path of truth.'[190]

Imam al-Saadiq has said, 'The leaders of the prophets and the messengers are five in number: they are those messengers

---

188 al-Saduq, *al-Tawhid*, 45.
189 al-Haakim I,122 (from *Nahj* 33 & 437).
190 ibid.

of divine resolution around whom turns the millstone [of existence] – Nuh, Ibrahim, Musa, `Isa and Muhammad.'[191]

It is recorded in *Misbah al-Shari`ah* that Imam al-Saadiq said, 'Truly Allah has given His prophets access to the stores of His bounty, His generosity and His mercy; He has instructed them from the treasures of His knowledge and has singled them out above the whole creation for Himself. Their behavior and reactions are to be found in no other persons in all creation, such that he has made them a means to Him for the rest of the creation and has made love of Him and obedience to them a way to gain His contentment. Of opposition to and denial of them, He has made a reason for His anger. He has ordained that each nation should follow the way of life of their messenger. He has refused to accept the worship of anyone except those who obey and revere the messengers; and knowledge and love of the messengers is with Allah as is their dignity, honor and veneration. Allah has revered all His prophets: You cannot reduce them in rank or stature so that they resemble beings inferior to them. Moreover, you should not use your intellect to understand their stations and reactions and behavior except by means of explanation and proof taken from Allah's Book, or by adopting the consensus of opinion of those men of spiritual understanding who have used proofs which affirm the messengers' qualities of excellence and their high ranks. How can one reach truth without knowledge of Allah? If you compare their words and behavior with others inferior to them, you have betrayed their company and denied their knowledge, and are ignorant of their distinction with Allah, and so you yourself have fallen from the stations of true belief and knowledge: thus beware!'[192]

Allah has raised the prophets in excellence over the angels;

---

191 *Qurrat al-`Uyun*, 405-406.
192 *al-Muhajjah al-Bayda'*, I, 226.

thus He ordered His angels to make prostration to Adam. In Allah's words, And when We said to the angels: make obeisance to Adam they made obeisance, all but Iblis; he refused. (2:34)

Moreover Allah has raised them in excellence over all creation: Surely, Allah chose Adam and Nuh and the descendants of Ibrahim and the descendants of `Imran over the nations. (3:33)

The Prophet of Allah said, 'O `Ali! Allah has preferred the messengers over even His intimate angels and He has preferred me over all the prophets and messengers. This excellence after me is for you, O `Ali, and for the Imams after you: truly the angels are as our servants and the servants of those who love us.'[193]

It is reported that the number of prophets is 124,000 and the number of those delegated by them is the same, since for every prophet there is an executor of his teachings whom he appoints by Allah's command. All of them have come with the truth from the realm of the Truth. Thus their speech is the speech of Allah and their commands the commands of Allah; obedience to them is obedience to Allah and disobedience to them is disobedience to Allah. Surely they never speak except by divine inspiration.[194]

The Mission of the Seal of the Prophets

Allah says:

> ☼ He it is Who sent His Apostle with guidance and the religion of truth, that He might cause it to prevail over all religions, though the polytheists may be averse. (9:33)

> ☼ O you who believe! Answer [the call of] Allah and His Apostle when He calls you to that which gives you life. (8:24)

---

193   ibid.,I,227.
194   ibid.

☼ Certainly an Apostle has come to you from amongst yourselves; grievous to him is your falling into distress, excessively solicitous respecting you; to the believers [he is] compassionate, merciful. (9:128)

☼ O Prophet! Surely We have sent you as a witness, and as a bearer of good news and as a warner, and as one inviting to Allah by His permission, and as a light-giving lamp. (33:45-46)

☼ And We have not sent you but as a mercy to the worlds. Say it is only revealed to me that your God is one God; will you then submit? (21:107-8)

☼ Muhammad is not the father of any of your men, but he is the Apostle of Allah and the Seal of the prophets; and Allah is Cognisant of all things. (33:40)

☼ Certainly you have in the Apostle of Allah an excellent exemplar for him who hopes in Allah and the Last Day and remembers Allah much. (33:21)

☼ I deliver to you the messages of my Lord, and I offer you good advice and I know from Allah what you do not know. (7:62)

☼ Whoever obeys the Apostle, he indeed obeys Allah. (4:80)

☼ Most surely it is the Word of a most honored messenger... One [to be] obeyed, and faithful in trust. (81:19,21)

The Messenger of Allah warned his people in accordance with Allah's command: 'And warn those of your people close to you' [26:214]: 'O tribe of `Abd al-Muttalib, truly by Allah I do not know a man from among the Arabs who has come to his people with anything better than that with which I have come to you. Indeed, I have come to you with the best of this world and the next, and Allah, may He be exalted, has commanded me to call you to Him.'[195]

Imam `Ali said, 'We witness that there is no god except Allah and Muhammad is His slave and messenger, sent with the truth, a leader and a guide towards Him. He has led us out of error by means of him and He has saved us from ignorance by him; whoever obeys Allah and His Messenger has obtained a tremendous victory and a generous reward, but whoever disobeys Allah and His Messenger has fallen into great loss and will be given a painful punishment.'[196]

'Thus Allah sent Muhammad with the truth, to lead His slaves from worshipping idols to worshipping Him. Allah has instructed him through the Qur'an and has made him firm and strong , so that the slaves may know their Lord when they previously had been ignorant of Him.'[197]

'And I witness that Muhammad is His bondsman and Messenger: He has sent him with the acclaimed *Din*, transmitted knowledge, the written book, the shining light, the dazzling brightness, and the enacted command thereby removing doubt and ambiguity, establishing clear proof with evidences, and giving a warning through signs.'[198]

'Truly Allah has sent Muhammad to bring His slaves away from worshipping His slaves to worshipping Him, away from transaction with His slaves to a transaction with Him, from obedience to His slaves to obedience to Him, and from the

---

195   *al-Ghadir*,II,279.
196   *al-Tawhīd*,33.
197   *Nahj*,III,446;I,22-24;IV,742.
198   ibid.

authority of His slaves to His own authority.'[199]

'Truly Allah sent Muhammad at a time when none of the Arabs knew how to read, nor were any claiming prophecy; he urged them to settle down in one community, and informed them of the means whereby they might save themselves: thereafter their lances became straight and ordered and their battle ranks confident of victory.'[200]

'Allah sent His messenger to fulfill his promised term, and to perfect his prophecy by continuing the divine transaction undertaken before him by the rest of the prophets. He sent a messenger whose reputation was well-established and whose birth was noble, at a time when people of the earth were composed of different nations and temperaments, and had diverse livelihoods; there were those who worshipped Allah in their behavior, while others were openly heretical or called on gods other than Allah. He guided them all from the path of error by means of Muhammad and He rescued them from ignorance by his rank.'[201]

'Allah sent him to call people to the truth and to be as a witness over creation; he transmitted the message of his Lord, unremitting, never negligent. He fought for Allah against his enemies, never weakening nor finding excuses in the face of difficulties. He was the Imam of those who feared Allah and the eye of discernment of those who accepted guidance.'[202]

Imam al-Saadiq has said, 'Allah has entrusted His Messenger with a task not entrusted to anyone else of His creation: He has demanded that he go out to his people alone, without any other group there to help in the struggle; this He has not demanded

---
199　　ibid.
200　　ibid.,I,73 & 18-19.
201　　ibid.
202　　ibid.

of anyone else of His creation, either before or after him.' Then he recited the Qur'anic verse, 'So fight in the way of Allah; this is not imposed on you except in relation to yourself' [4:84].[203]

The Life Story of the Prophet Muhammad

His Names

His most famous name is Muhammad, being mentioned so in the Qur'an:

> ☼ 'Muhammad is the Apostle of Allah, and those with him are firm of heart against the unbelievers, compassionate amongst themselves.' (48:29)

This name is derived from the Arabic word *hamd* (praise), as is the name Ahmad:

> ☼ '... And giving the good news of an Apostle who will come after me, his name being Ahmad.' (61:6)

Al-Shahid (the Witness) is also one of his names:

> ☼ 'How will it be, then, when We bring from every people a witness and bring you as a witness against these?' (4:41)

He is also called a Prophet of mercy:

> ☼ 'And we have not sent you but as a mercy to the worlds.' (21:107)

> ☼ He is called *al-Amin* (the Faithful and Trustworthy) by Allah: 'One to be obeyed and faithful in trust.' (81:21)

> ☼ He is called the last of the Prophets: 'But he is the Apostle of Allah and the Seal of the Prophets.' (33:40)

---

203   al-Kulayni, VIII, 274.

The Birth and Death of the Prophet

Most sources are in agreement that his birth was at sunrise on the 17th of Rabi` al-Awwal, in the Year of the Elephant, on Friday. He passed away on Monday the 18th of Safar, in the eleventh year after *hijrah*, although there are numerous traditions which report his death as being on other days. Muhammad lived for sixty-three years, and had lived in Makkah for exactly forty years when the first revelation came upon him. He remained a further thirteen years in Makkah and then emigrated to the Illuminated City, Madinah, where he remained for ten years.[204]

The Genealogy of the Prophet

Muhammad was the son of `Abd Allah ibn `Abd al-Muttalib ibn Hashim ibn `Abd al-Manaf ibn Qusayy ibn Kilab ibn Murra ibn Ka`b ibn Lu'ayy ibn Fihr ibn Malik ibn al-Nadir (of the tribe of Quraysh) ibn Kananah ibn Khuzaymah ibn Mudrikah ibn Alyas ibn Mudar ibn Nazar ibn Ma`ad ibn `Adnan. He lived with his father for two years and four months (less than this, according to some; it is also reported that he was born after the death of his father). He then lived with his grandfather, `Abd al-Muttalib, for eight years. After the death of his grandfather, his uncle Abu Taalib took him into his care: he treated him generously, protected him and helped him in deed and word for as long as he lived.

Muhammad married Khadijah when he was twenty-five-years old. His uncle Abu Taalib died when Muhammad was forty-six, and three days later Khadijah also passed away. Muhammad named this period the year of grief.[205]

---

204 al-Irbilli, *Kashf al-Ghummah*, I, 16.
205 ibid.

The Prophet's Everyday Behavior

The Prophet Muhammad would constantly implore and humbly pray to Allah that He adorn him with the noblest of conduct, saying in his prayers, 'O Allah, improve my character and my behavior,' and, 'O Allah, keep me away from unseemly behavior.' Allah answered his prayer and revealed the Qur'an to him; He made his character such that 'His character was the Qur'an.'[206]

The Qur'an describes him by saying, 'Truly you are of a tremendous character' [68:4]; and about the importance of the Prophet's behavior, he himself also said, 'I have been sent to perfect nobility of behavior.'

Allah has given directives concerning the Prophet's behavior in the following verses:

☼ Take to forgiveness and enjoin good and turn aside from the ignorant. (7:199)

☼ And be patient and your patience is not but by [the assistance of] Allah. (16:127)

☼ Surely Allah enjoins the doing of justice and the doing of good [to others]. (16:90)

☼ And they should pardon and turn away. Do you not love that Allah should forgive you? (24:22)

☼ Shun much suspicion, for surely suspicion in some cases is a sin, and do not spy nor let some of you backbite others. (49:12)

There are many other verses which refer to his character and behavior.

---

206   al-Muhajjah al-Bayda', IV, 120-126.

The Messenger of Allah has said, 'By the One Who has my soul in His hand, none will enter the Garden except those who have good behavior.' He has also said, 'Truly, Allah has encircled Islam with nobility of character and righteous actions.'[207]

The following aspects of noble behavior might be mentioned: enjoying healthy social relations; spending one's energy in undertaking kindly actions, establishing peace; feeding people; visiting sick Muslims, whether they be righteous or astray; accompanying the funeral procession to the grave; having good relations with one's neighbors, be they Muslim or non-believers; showing respect for the older generation; forgiveness and peacemaking between people; having generosity, nobility and tolerance; greeting people with the word salam (peace); suppressing one's anger; defending Islam; and rendering loathsome [to oneself and others] lying, backbiting, slander, miserliness, oppression, deviousness, trickery, bad relations between people; breaking off family relations, pride, haughtiness, deceit, envy, injustice, tyranny and violence.

According to the consensus of scholars, jurists and historians, the Messenger of Allah was the gentlest of people, the most courageous, the most just, the most forgiving and the most generous; he would not sleep for a single night while there was a dinar or a dirham remaining in his house; if any money remained in his possession, he would not return to his house until he had given it away in charity or in generosity.[208]

He used to mend his own shoes and patch his clothes; he would serve by performing household jobs and would help by cutting up the meat with the womenfolk. He was the most modest of men, never allowing his glance to linger when looking at someone's face. He would accept an invitation from both freeman and slave. He would accept presents, even if it were a draught of milk, and give back similar presents. He would not eat out of charity. When he ate, he would eat what was within easy reach, and never reclining. He never ate his fill of bread for three consecutive days for as long as he lived, and this was out of a desire to discipline himself — not because of

---

207 ibid.
208 ibid.

poverty or miserliness. He would attend feasts, visit the sick, witness burials and walk amongst his enemies without a guard. He would sit with the poor and bereft and share their meals.[209]

BELIEF IN IMAMATE

Necessity of the existence of the Imam after the Prophet

Allah says in the Qur'an:

☼ And there is not a people but a warner has gone among them. (35:24)

☼ [... and there is] a guide for every people. (13:7)

☼ And on the day when we will raise up in every people a witness against them from amongst themselves, and bring you as a witness against these... (16:89)

☼ He it is Who has revealed the Book to you; some of its verses are decisive, they are the basis of the Book, and others are allegorical; then as for those in whose hearts there is perversity, they follow the part of it which is allegorical, seeking to mislead, and seeking to give it [their own] interpretation except Allah, and those firmly rooted in the knowledge. (3:7)

☼ Only Allah is your *Wali* and his Apostle and those who believe, those who keep up prayers and pay the poor-rate while they bow. (5:55)

☼ O Apostle! Deliver what has been revealed to you from your Lord; and if you do not, then you have not delivered

---

209   ibid.

His message, and Allah will protect you from people. (5:67)

☼ This day have I perfected for you your religion and completed My favor on you and chosen for you Islam as a religion. (5:3)

☼ And We made of them Imams to guide Our command when they were patient, and they were certain of Our communications. (32:24)

The Messenger said, 'Among every generation of my nation after me there will be the just ones who will dispel the folly of those bearing rancor [towards us], and who will deny the false claims of liars and the [false] interpretations of the ignorant.'[210]

'Surely, your Imams are those persons who lead you to Allah; therefore look to whom you take as leaders in your religion and in your prayer.'[211]

'Truly your Imams are your delegates to Allah, so pay attention to your *deen* and your prayer.'[212]

'There are twelve from amongst my Household to whom Allah has granted my [degree of] understanding, my knowledge, and my wisdom and He has created them from my character and constitution. Woe to those after me who treat them with arrogance, and who break my ties of blood and family with them; what is the matter with them? Allah will not allow my intercession to reach them.'[213]

'After me there are twelve, the first of them being you O `Ali, and the last of them being the Qa'im – the upright and

---

210 ibid.,I,231.
211 al-Haakim,I,125 (from *al-Bihaar*,vol.88,99).
212 From al-Haakim,I,125.
213 *al-Muhajjah al-Bayda'*,I,244.

unflinching one, at whose hand Allah will open both east and west.'[214]

The Messenger also said, 'Allah has mercy on my caliphs,' and when someone asked him who his caliphs were, he replied, 'Those who love my *sunnah* and teach it to the slaves of Allah.'[215]

Al-Saadiq said, 'Allah has delegated His affair to no one of His creation but the Messenger of Allah and the Imams. For Allah has said, "We have revealed the Book with the truth that you may judge between people by means of that which Allah has taught you" – and this matter is continued with those who inherit [his knowledge] after him.'[216]

'A slave is not a believer until he knows Allah and His Messenger, all of the Imams, the Imam of his time, and returns his greeting.' He then said, 'How can he know the last when he does not know the first?'[217]

Al-Baaqir said, 'If a man dies without having an Imam, then his death is like that of someone living in the *jahiliyyah* [the age of ignorance before Islam]: people will not be forgiven until they have recognized their Imam.'[218]

`Isa ibn al-Sirri is quoted as saying, 'I asked Abu `Abd Allah [al-Saadiq] to explain to me the foundations on which Islam is built, such that if I held fast to them my actions would be purified and anything of which I remained ignorant thereafter would not harm me. Al-Saadiq replied, "Bearing witness that there is no god but Allah, and that Muhammad is the Messenger of Allah; affirming what he brought from Allah; giving a portion of your wealth away as alms, as a purification; and recognizing the *wilayah*

214	ibid.	
215	al-Haakim,II,339.	
216	al-Kulayni,II,8 & I,180.	
217	ibid.	
218	al-Haakim,I,127 (from *al-Bihaar*,vol.23,77).	

(of Allah) and the *wilayah* of the family of Muhammad. Surely the Messenger of Allah has said, 'If a man dies without having an Imam, then his death is like that of someone living in the *jahiliyyah*'.'[219]

☼ Allah says, 'Obey Allah and obey the Apostle and those in authority from among you.' (4:59)

Describing the Imam, he [Imam al-Saadiq] has said, 'It is by means of him that Allah spares people's lives, reconciles people to each other, resolves the affair of people, joins what is broken, clothes the naked, satiates the hungry and affords security to those who fear.'[220]

Imam al-Sajjad said, 'O Allah, bless the righteous persons of his Household whom You have chosen for Your affair, whom You have made custodians of Your knowledge, the guardians of Your religion, Your caliphs on Your earth, and Your proof to Your slaves – those whom You have purified from all corruption and iniquity by Your will, and whom You have made the means of reaching You and the pathway to Your Garden.'[221]

'Thus he is the safe abode of those who seek refuge, the cave of the believers, the staff of those who hold fast and the light of the worlds. O Allah, give thanks to Your *wali*, for that with which You have blessed him, and establish by him Your Book, Your laws, Your *shari`ah* and the *sunnah* of Your Prophet, and by him restore the marks of the religion which the unjust have caused to disappear.'[222]

Imam al-Baaqir has said, 'Even if a man were to stand all

---

219   al-Kulayni,II,21 & I,314.
220   ibid.
221   al-Haakim,II,382 *(from al-Sahifah al-Sajjaadiyah,334-338).*
222   ibid.

night in prayer and fast during the day, give all his wealth away in charity, and go on pilgrimage every year for the rest of his life, while not recognizing the *wilayah* of the *wali* of Allah and not taking him as his *wali*, Allah would not be beholden to reward him and he would not be counted among the people of belief.'[223]

Al-Saadiq said, 'The earth is never left without an Imam who prescribes what is permitted by Allah and forbids what is prohibited by Him. This is referred to in Allah's words, "On the day when We call each people with their Imam" [17:71]. The Messenger of Allah has said, "Whoever dies without an Imam has died the death of the *jahiliyyah*".'[224]

The Siraat is the pathway to knowledge of Allah. There are two Siraats: the Siraat in this world and the Siraat of the next. The Siraat of this world is the Imam whom the people are obliged to obey – whoever recognizes him in this world and follows his guidance will pass over the Siraat which is the bridge across Jahannam in the next world. But whoever does not recognize him in this world will lose his footing on the next, and will perish in the fire of Jahannam.[225]

Necessity of Obedience to the Imam after the Prophet

Allah says in the Qur'an:

☼ O you who believe! Obey Allah and the Apostle and those in authority among you. (4:59)

☼ Surely those who swear allegiance to you do but swear allegiance to Allah: the hand of Allah is above their hands. Therefore whoever breaks [his oath], he breaks it only to the injury of his own soul, and whoever fulfils what he has

---

223 al-Hurr,I,91.
224 al-Haakim,II,382 (from *al-Bihaar*,vol.8,12).
225 *al-Muhajjah al-Bayda'*,I,197 & 250.

covenanted with Allah, He will grant him a mighty reward. (48:10)

☼ Then We have made you follow a course in the affair; therefore follow it, and do not follow the low desires of those who do not know. (45:18)

When Allah revealed to His Prophet the words: 'O you who believe! Obey Allah and the Apostle and those in authority among you.' Jaabir ibn `Abd Allah al-Ansaari is related to have asked, 'O Messenger of Allah, we know who Allah is, and who is His Messenger; but who are "those in authority", obedience to whom Allah has compared to obedience to you?' The Prophet replied, 'They are my caliphs, O Jaabir, and the Imams of the Muslims after me; the first of them is `Ali ibn Abi Taalib, then comes al-Hasan, then al-Husayn.'[226]

When Allah revealed the verse: 'And warn the closest of your kin,' [26:214] the Messenger called together the tribe of `Abd al-Muttalib, they being approximately forty men, amongst whom were his uncles. In a long speech he said, 'Allah has commanded me to call you to Him; so which of you will act as my *wazir* [advisor] in this matter and be my brother, act as my delegate after death and my caliph amongst you?' The people all shrank back except `Ali who was the youngest of them; he stood up and said, 'I, O Prophet of Allah, will be your *wazir* in this matter.' The Messenger of Allah grasped him by the shoulders, saying, 'Truly this man is my brother, inheritor and caliph amongst you – so listen to him and obey him.'[227]

Imam `Ali said, 'Fear Allah and obey your Imam, for surely

---

226 ibid.
227 al-Amili, `Abd al-Husayn Sharaaf al-Din, *al-Muraaja`aat*, 155 (from *Tabari* and Ibn al-Athir).

righteous citizens will prosper with a just Imam just as corrupt citizens will perish with a corrupt Imam.'[228]

'O people, the one who has the most claim in this matter is he who is the strongest amongst them in dealing with it and the most knowledgeable concerning Allah. If anyone stirs up discord, he will be reprimanded; and if he refuses to listen, he will be killed.'[229]

Imam al-Sajjad said, 'O Allah, truly You have assisted Your religion at all times by means of an Imam whom You have established as a source of knowledge for Your slaves and a light in Your lands; and this You have done after joining him in a compact of protection and friendship, and have made him the means to Your contentment. Thereupon You have made obedience to him obligatory, and have warned against disobeying him and have commanded men to follow his orders, and to avoid what he has forbidden lest someone go forward in front of him or fall behind.'[230]

Imam al-Saadiq said, 'People will not be righteous except with an Imam and the earth will not be put in order except by an Imam.'[231]

Al-Husayn ibn `Ali came out to his companions and said, 'O people, truly Allah only created His slaves so that they may come to know Him, so that when they know Him, they may worship Him, and then by worshipping Him they may do so without worshipping any besides Him.' A man then said to him, 'O son of the Messenger of Allah, by your father and mother, what then is knowledge of Allah?' He replied, 'That the people

---

228   al-Haakim,II,385 (from *al-Bihaar*,vol.8,472).
229   ibid.,II,384 (from *Nahj*,IV,557).
230   ibid.,II,378 (from *al-Sahifah*,337).
231   ibid.,II,385 & 393 (from *al-Bihaar*,vol.23,22 & vol.5,312).

of each age know the Imam whom they are obliged to obey.'[232]

Al-Saadiq explained Allah's words, 'Whoever is granted wisdom, is indeed given a great good,' as meaning obedience to Allah and knowledge of the Imams.[233]

'The core of the matter, its essence and key, the door to all things and contentment of the Merciful, lies in obedience to the Imam after having obtained knowledge of him.'[234]

'We are a people obedience to whom Allah has made obligatory; you will find perfection in the Imam, and ignorance of him is inexcusable.'[235]

'We are a people obedience to whom Allah has made obligatory; to us belong the spoils of war and to us is the best part of wealth. It is we who possess certainty of knowledge, and we are those envied by others whom Allah mentions in the Qur'an: "Or do they envy the people for what Allah has given them of His grace?" [4:54]'[236]

When Imam al-Rida was asked if obedience to him was obligatory, he replied it was – the same level of obedience as that given to `Ali ibn Abi Taalib.[237]

Imam al-Saadiq was once asked whether the Imams acted and demanded obedience in a similar fashion. 'Yes,' he replied.[238]

It is related that al-Saadiq said, 'Allah has made obedience to us obligatory; people will only find ease through obedience to us, and they have no excuse for ignorance of us. Whoever

---

232	ibid.
233	al-Kulayni I,185-188.
234	ibid.
235	ibid.
236	ibid.
237	ibid.
238	ibid.

recognizes us is a believer, and whoever denies us is a non-believer; and whoever neither recognizes us nor denies us is gone astray until he returns to guidance – and that is obedience to us, made obligatory by Allah. If they die while they are astray, then Allah will do with them as He pleases.'[239]

A man asked Imam al-Baaqir what was the most preferred action – an action which brought a slave near to Allah, obedience to Allah, obedience to His Messenger or obedience to those in authority. 'Love of us is belief and hate of us is disbelief,' he replied.[240]

The Family of the Prophet

Allah says in His Book of Revelation:

> ☼ Allah only desires to keep away the uncleanness from you, O people of the House! And to purify you with a [thorough] purifying. (33:33)

> ☼ ... Say: Come let us call our sons and your sons and our women and your women and our selves and your selves, then let us be earnest in prayer. (3:61)

> ☼ And hold fast by the covenant of Allah all together and be not disunited. (3:103)

> ☼ And [know] that this is My path, the right one, therefore follow it. (6:153)

> ☼ O you who believe! Obey Allah and obey the Apostle and those in authority among you. (4:59)

> ☼ So ask the followers of the Reminder if you do not know. (16:43)

---

239   ibid.
240   ibid.

☼ And whoever acts in hostility to the Apostle after that guidance has become manifest to him and follows other than the way of the believers, We will turn to that which he has [himself] turned and make him enter hell. (4:115)

☼ You are only a warner and [there is] a guide for every people. (13:7)

☼ These are those upon whom Allah bestows favors from among the prophets and the truthful and the martyrs and the good. (4:69)

☼ Only Allah is your Friend and His Messenger and those who believe, those who keep up prayer and pay the poor-rate while they bow. And whoever takes Allah and His Messenger and those who believe for a guardian, then surely the party of Allah are they that shall be triumphant. (5:55-6)

☼ Surely Allah and His angels bless the Prophet; O you who believe! Call for divine blessings on him and salute him with a [becoming] salutation. (33:56)

These verses and others, over three hundred in number, have been revealed by Allah specifically with regard to the family and progeny of Muhammad. This is the consensus of opinion of most commentators and historians over the centuries.[241]

The Messenger of Allah said, 'O people! I have left amongst you two things, and if you take hold of them, you will never go astray: they are the Book of Allah and my progeny.'[242]

'Surely, I am about to be called and I will answer the call. I am leaving with you two precious things; the Book of Allah and

---

241   al-Muraaja'aat, 65-79.
242   ibid., 51 & 53.

my progeny. The Book of Allah is like a cable stretching from heaven to the earth, and my progeny is the people of my House [Ahl al-Bayt]. Truly the Subtle, the All-Knowing has informed me that these two things will never part company until they come to the watering at the fountain [in the Garden]. Therefore, look to see how you invest my authority in these two things.'[243]

When the Messenger returned from the final pilgrimage, he gave a speech at Ghadir Khumm, in which he said, 'It is as though I have answered the call; truly I have left with you two precious things, one more tremendous than the other: the Book of Allah and my progeny.'[244]

The Messenger of Allah said about his progeny, 'Do not go ahead of them and so perish, do not fall behind them and so perish, and do not try to instruct them, for surely they are more knowledgeable than you.'[245]

'Truly my progeny is like the ark of Noah floating amongst you: whoever embarks thereon is saved, and whoever stays behind will be drowned.'[246]

'The likeness of the people of my Household is as the gate of forgiveness of the tribe of Israel: whoever enters it is forgiven.'[247]

'The stars are protection and security for the people of the earth; and the people of my Household are protection and security for my nation when disputes occur in matters of religion. If a tribe of Arabs disagrees with people of my Household (concerning the laws of Allah), they fall into dispute

---

243	ibid.	
244	ibid.	
245	ibid.,54-61.	
246	ibid.	
247	ibid.	

and become the allies of Satan.'[248]

'Whoever finds delight in living my life and dying my death and dwelling in the Garden of Eden laid out by my Lord, should bear allegiance to `Ali after me, and then bear allegiance to his delegated authority, and should follow the people of my Household, for they are my progeny; they have been created from the same clay as myself, and have been provided with my understanding and my knowledge. Woe to those of my nation who deny their excellence, who are thus breaking off relations with my family: Allah will not extend my intercession to them on the day of Resurrection.'[249]

The Messenger said in one of his speeches, 'O people, truly excellence, nobility, honor and authority belong to the Messenger and his progeny, so do not allow usurpers to lead you astray.'[250]

'Therefore, raise the people of my Household to the same position as the head in relation to the body, and the eye in relation to the head; it is only by means of eyes that the head guides itself.'[251]

'Have love for us, the people of the Household, for whoever meets Allah and loves us will enter the Garden by our intercession. By the One in Whose hand is my soul, a slave's actions are of no use except with knowledge of what is due to us.'[252]

'Even if a man were to plant his feet between the corner of the Black Stone and the place where Abraham stood, praying and fasting but nevertheless harboring a dislike for the family of Muhammad, he would still enter the Fire.'[253]

---

248   ibid.
249   ibid.
250   ibid.
251   ibid.
252   ibid.
253   ibid.

Talking about the family of the Prophet, Imam `Ali said, 'So where are you going and what are you imagining? The indications are there to see and the signs are clear. The lamp has been raised high, so how can it lead you astray? How are you so blind, when amongst you are the progeny of the Prophet? They are the pinnacle of truth, the landmark of this religion and the tongue of truthfulness. Visit them as you would the best of houses where the Qur'an is remembered, drink their knowledge as the thirsty drink from a pool. O people, accept this from the tongue of the last prophet: from amongst us there will die someone who has not yet died, and someone whose body will turn to dust as those from amongst us who have died and are turning to dust; but in fact his body will be neither old or decayed. Thus do I speak about that which you have no knowledge of, for surely the greater part of truth lies in that which you know nothing of; and forgive those who can provide no proof to you against Him – for I am he. Am I not working amongst you with the greater of two precious things [i.e. the Qur'an], and leaving you the lesser of the two [Hasan and Husayn]; and I have planted amongst you the flag of the faith.'[254]

'Look to the family of the Prophet, follow them in their excellence and imitate their actions; they will never lead you away from guidance and never make you return to wickedness. If they remain firm in one place, remain firm yourselves; if they move, move as well, but do not go ahead of them and thus overshadow them.'[255]

---

254   al-Haakim,I,125 *(*from *al-Muraaja`aat*,47).
255   ibid.

The Commander of the Faithful, Imam `Ali ibn Abi Taalib

His names, titles, genealogy, and death

`Ali ibn Abi Taalib ibn `Abd al-Muttalib, whose genealogy corresponds with that of the Prophet, was the last of the sons of Abu Taalib, being born after Taalib, `Aqil and Ja`far. His mother was Faatimah bint Asad ibn Hashim ibn `Abd al-Manaf, and she was as a mother to the Messenger of Allah, who was brought up in her home and was grateful for her kindness. She was one of the first to believe in him together with the rest of those who left Makkah for Madlnah. When she died, the Prophet shrouded her in his own shirt, and made a pillow for her in the grave to protect her from the pressure of the earth; he gave her this special treatment in recognition of her rank with Allah.[256]

Amongst `Ali ibn Abi Taalib's other names were Abu al-Rayhanatayn and al-Murtada. His titles were Commander of the Faithful, Prince of the Believers, Husband of the Devotee of Allah [i.e. Faatimah], the Waali, the Appointed Guardian, the Bold in Attack, the Emir of the Righteous and the Slayer of the Corrupt.[257]

His birth and martyrdom

He was born in the sacred House [the Ka`bah] in Makkah on Friday, the 13th of Rajab in the thirtieth Year of the Elephant. None before or after him had been born in the House of Allah, and this represented a great honor from Allah.[258]

Imam `Ali was the first male to be invited to submit to Islam by the Prophet. He accepted and from that moment onwards never ceased to help in the propagation of the religion, to

---

256 al-Mufid, *al-Irshad*, 10.
257 al-Irbilli, I, 67-75.
258 al-Mufid, 9-12.

help in the fight against idol-worshippers and protect the faith. For 23 years he stood alongside the Messenger of Allah after the latter had received his mission, thirteen of them spent in Makkah before the migration to Madinah with the Prophet, sharing his trials and taking upon himself the greatest of the Prophet's difficulties. After the migration, he spent ten years in Madinah protecting the Prophet from the idol-worshippers, fighting against the non-believers with the Prophet and acting as a personal bodyguard against his enemies until Allah took the Prophet to His garden and raised him to the highest of stations. The Commander of the Faithful was 33 years old at the time of the Prophet's death.[259]

His Imamate lasted thirty years after the time of the Prophet, and during this period he was caliph of the Messenger of Allah for five years and six months. He was tried and tested by the opposition of the hypocrites, by those who broke their pact and deviated from the *din* just as the Messenger had been tested, while being prevented from governing according to prophecy, by fear for the Muslims, restrictions and banishment.[260]

The Commander of the Faithful was martyred before daybreak on Thursday, the 21st of Ramadan, 40 AH, by the sword of Ibn Muljim al-Muradi, may Allah curse him, in the Kufa mosque.

His position and role in the establishment of Islam

It is related by Ibn `Abbas that one day Imam `Ali looked into the faces of the people and said, 'Truly I am the brother of the Messenger of Allah and his *wazir*. You are aware that I was the first of you to believe in Allah and His Messenger, that I am his

---

259 ibid.
260 ibid.

brother and I share his genealogy. Moreover, I am the father of his grandchild, husband of the mother of his progeny and mistress of the women of the world. I am his most beloved among you and the one in whom he has the most trust; I am also the most effective in killing and wounding the enemy.'[261]

Abu Sa`id al-Khudri relates how he heard the Messenger of Allah talking to Faatimah, who had come to him that day crying and saying, 'O Messenger of Allah, the women of the Quraysh have reproached me because of `Ali's poverty.' He said, 'Are you not content, O Faatimah, that I have married you to your husband when he was the first man to embrace Islam and the most knowledgeable of men? Allah has examined the people of the earth and chosen your father, and made him a prophet. He then examined the people again and chose from among them your husband and made him the appointed guardian. Allah then revealed to me that I should marry you to him. Do you not see it as Allah's honor and respect for you that your husband is the kindest of men, the most knowledgeable and the first of them to submit to Islam?' Faatimah then smiled and rejoiced at the good news.[262]

Al-Hakim in his *Mustadrak* relates a hadith, whose authority is recognized by al-Bukhari and Muslim, that the Messenger of Allah rested in Ghadir Khumm on his return from the final pilgrimage and said, 'It is as if I have been called and have answered. Surely I have left amongst you two precious things, one of them greater than the other: the Book of Allah and my progeny. So be careful how you follow me in these two matters, for they will never be separated from each other until they lead me to the fountain.' He continued, 'Allah is my only master and I am the master of every believer.' Then he took hold of `Ali's

---

261 al-Irbilli,I,80.
262 al-Mufid,24.

hand saying, 'Whoever has taken me for his master, then this man is his protector. O Allah, protect him who has taken him as his protector, and be an enemy to him who is an enemy to him.'[263]

Al-Hakim relates on the authority of Zayd ibn al-Arqam that the Messenger of Allah said, 'Whoever wishes to live my life and to die my death and live in the Garden promised to me by my Lord, should take as his protector `Ali ibn Abi Taalib, for certainly he will never lead you away from guidance and will never lead you astray.'[264]

Al-Bukhari, Muslim, Ibn Hanbal, Ibn Majah and others [all famous compilers of hadith] relate on the authority of Imam `Ali ibn Abi Taalib, Ibn `Abbas, Zayd ibn al-Arqam, Ibn `Umar, al-Bara' ibn `Azib, Umm Salama and others, that the Prophet said to `Ali (when leaving him at Madinah at the time of the battle of Tabuk), 'Are you content that you are to me as was Harun to Moses – except that there is no prophet after me?'[265]

Al-Tabarani in *al-Kabir* and al-Bayhaqi in his *Sunnah* relate that the Messenger of Allah said to `Ali, pointing to him with his hand, 'This man was the first to believe in me and will be the first to take my hand on the day of Resurrection; he is the greatest of friends and the most discriminating between truth and falsehood, and he is the prince of believers.'[266]

Al-Tabarani in *al-Kabir* and al-Haakim in *al-Mustadrak* relate that the Messenger of Allah said, 'I am the city of knowledge, and `Ali is the gate; so whoever desires knowledge should come to its gate.'[267]

263	*al-Muraaja`aat,* 53,59,165,200-202.
264	ibid.
265	ibid.
266	ibid.
267	ibid.

Ibn Majah, al-Tirmidhi, al-Nasa'i, Ibn Hanbal and others relate that the Messenger of Allah said, at the time of the final pilgrimage, `Ali is from me and I am from `Ali. No one can discharge my duty instead of me except `Ali.'[268]

Imam al-Hasan ibn `Ali ibn Abi Taalib

His birth, names, titles and death

His mother was Faatimah al-Zahra, the daughter of the Messenger of Allah. He was born in Madinah one night in the middle of Ramadan, in 3 AH, and was known as Abu Muhammad. Seven days after his birth, his mother Faatimah brought him to the Prophet who made the *adhan* (call to prayer) in his ear.[269] The Prophet named him Hasan and sacrificed a goat for him. The Messenger passed away when he was seven years and some months old, eight according to some sources.[270]

Imam Ja`far al-Saadiq related that the character, behavior and dignity of Hasan resembled that of the Messenger of Allah more than any other person.[271]

Al-Zuhri relates on the authority of Anas ibn Malik that no one resembled the Messenger of Allah more than Hasan ibn `Ali.[272]

It is related that Faatimah al-Zahra brought her two sons, Hasan and Husayn, to the Messenger of Allah, giving voice to a grievance which had formed within her: 'O Messenger of Allah, these two are your grandchildren, so grant them some inheritance.' 'As for Hasan,' he replied, 'he has my awe-inspiring

---

268 ibid.
269 al-Irbilli, II, 140.
270 al-Mufid, 187.
271 ibid.
272 ibid.

appearance and my authority; while Husayn possesses my generosity and my courage.'²⁷³

Hasan was the delegate of his father, the Commander of the Faithful, and the guardian of his family, children and companions. Imam `Ali appointed him because of his experience and his truthfulness, writing to him and confirming this in a famous contract.

His titles are many, the most famous being he who fears Allah, the Purified one, the Grandson, and the Protector. The highest of his titles was that given to him by the Messenger, when he described his quality of character as being that of a *sayyid* – meaning a master, lord or prince; the Imams and trusted narrators relate that the Messenger said, 'This son of mine is a *sayyid*.'²⁷⁴

Concerning him and his grandfather, the Messenger, it is related in the *Sahih* of Bukhari and of Muslim, in an unbroken chain going back to al-Bara' ibn al-`Azib, that the latter heard the Messenger of Allah saying, while the child Hasan ibn `Ali was riding on his back, 'O Allah, truly I love him – so make him beloved of You!'²⁷⁵

Al-Tirmidhi relates on the authority of ibn `Abbas, with an unbroken chain of transmission, that one day the Messenger of Allah was carrying Hasan on his back when a woman said, 'You have climbed onto the best of mounts!' 'And he is the best of riders,' said the Prophet.²⁷⁶

Al-Tirmidhi relates in his *Sahih*, on the authority of Anas ibn Malik, that the Messenger was asked which of the family of his household he loved the best. 'Hasan and Husayn,' he said.

---

273   ibid.
274   al-Irbilli,II,145-153.
275   ibid.
276   ibid.

Moreover, he used to say to Faatimah, 'Call my sons to me,' whereupon he would smell them and hold them close to him.[277]

It is also related by al-Tirmidhi on the authority of al-Khudri that the Messenger said, 'Hasan and Husayn are the princes of the youths dwelling in the Garden.'[278]

It is related on the authority of `Abd Allah ibn `Umar that the Messenger said. 'These two are my sweet-smelling herbs of this world.'[279]

It is related by al-Tirmidhi and al-Nasa'i in their *Sahih*, both transmissions through Burayda, that while the Messenger was giving a sermon Hasan and Husayn, both wearing red robes, came along, falling over each other. The Messenger came down the pulpit and lifted them up in his arms, saying, 'Surely Allah's words are true: "Indeed your wealth and children are a trial for you" [64:15]. When I looked at these two boys walking and falling over, I could not wait – I interrupted my speech and lifted them up.'[280]

It is related that `Abbas came to visit the Prophet while he was sick. The Prophet brought him close to him and made him sit on the bed, saying, 'May Allah raise you, O uncle.' `Abbas replied, "`Ali is outside and wants permission to enter.' 'Let him enter,' he said, and `Ali entered together with Hasan and Husayn. Then `Abbas said, 'They are your children, O Messenger of Allah.' 'Yes,' he replied. Then `Abbas said, 'May Allah love you as you love them.'[281]

Ahmad ibn Hanbal has related that the Prophet looked at Hasan and Husayn and said, 'Whoever loves these two and their

---

277	ibid.
278	ibid.
279	ibid.
280	ibid.
281	ibid.

father and mother will be with me in my rank on the Day of Resurrection.'[282]

Evidence of his Imamate

It is related by Imam al-Baaqir that the Commander of the Faithful was giving Hasan instructions, witnessed by Husayn, Muhammad and all his other children, the leaders of his followers and the members of his household. Then the Commander of the Faithful presented him with the Holy Book and a sword, saying, 'My son, the Messenger has instructed me to give you this book and weapon and has commanded to order you, if your time of death is approaching, to present them to your brother Husayn.' Then he went to his son Husayn and said, 'The Messenger has ordered you to give this to your son here,' and he took hold of his son, `Ali ibn al-Husayn, and said, 'O son, Allah has ordered you to give this to your son Muhammad and to give him greetings from the Messenger of Allah and myself.'[283]

His taking of allegiance

Abu Mikhnaf reports that Hasan ibn `Ali spoke on the morning before the Commander of the Faithful died. He praised Allah and glorified Him until he said, 'I am the son of the Bringer of Good News, son of the Warner, son of him who calls to Allah; I am from the family of the Prophet's household, from whom Allah has removed all disgrace and whom Allah has purified completely.' Then ibn `Abbas stood up and said, 'O people gathered here, this is the son of your Prophet and the delegated guardian appointed by your Imam, so take his hand in allegiance.' The people responded and swore allegiance to him

---

282   ibid.
283   al-Kulayni,I,298.

as their caliph on Friday, the 21st of Ramadan, 40 AH. He then appointed his agents and emirs.[284]

Shaykh al-Mufid relates that Hasan made a speech to the people and reminded them of his rights; his father's companions then swore allegiance to him, pledging to fight whoever fought him and to keep the peace with whoever wanted peace. As soon as Mu`awiyah ibn Abu Sufyan learned of the martyrdom of the Commander of the Faithful and of the people swearing allegiance to his son Hasan, he began to sow corruption and to entice the people away from him with huge sums of money; even the commander of Hasan's army, `Ubayd Allah ibn al-`Abbas, hastened to Mu`awiyah's camp after the latter had promised him 100,000 dirhams. The Imam instinctively realized that the people had deserted him, and Mu`awiyah wrote to him offering to make a treaty of peace. Mu`awiyah later had him poisoned by his [Hasan's] wife, Ju`adah bint al-Ash`ath ibn Qays, and died in Madinah in the month of Safar, 50 AH.[285] It is also said that he died on the fifth of Rabi al-Awwal in 49 AH.[286]

Imam al-Husayn ibn `Ali ibn Abi Taalib

His birth, names, titles and death

He was born in Madinah on the 3rd of Sha`ban, 4 AH. His mother was Faatimah al-Zahra, daughter of the Messenger, and he was known as Abu `Abd Allah. His mother Faatimah brought him to his grandfather, the Messenger, who rejoiced at seeing him and called him Husayn. He sacrificed a goat for him.[287] His mother shaved his hair and gave away an equivalent weight in silver as charity, just as she had been commanded by

---

284	al-Mufid,188 & 192.
285	ibid.
286	al-Irbilli,II,210.
287	al-Mufid,198.

the Messenger.[288]

According to the Messenger, Hasan and Husayn are the Lords of the youths of Paradise and the grandsons of the Prophet of mercy. Hasan resembled the Prophet from his head to his chest, and Husayn resembled him from his chest to his legs; they were the two most beloved of all his family and children.[289]

His titles were many, the most famous among them being the Rightly Guided, the Good, the Trustworthy, the Lord, the Pure, and the Blessed; of these the Pure was the most famous, but the most exalted and noble was that given to him by the Messenger when he said of him and his brother, 'Truly they are the Lords of the youths of the Garden.' Likewise, the title of *al-Sibt* (grandson or descendant), which, as is related on good authority, the Messenger used, when he said, 'Husayn is one amongst the descendants [*Sibtun min al-asbaat*].[290]

What was related about him by the Messenger

It is related by Salman al-Farisi that he heard the Messenger saying about Hasan and Husayn, 'O Allah, truly I love them, and I love whoever loves them.' Also, 'Whoever loves Hasan and Husayn, I love; whomever I love Allah loves; and whoever hates them, I hate; whomever I hate, Allah hates, He will cause him to enter the Fire.'[291]

It is related by ibn Mas'ud that one day the Prophet was praying when Hasan and Husayn came and climbed on his back; when he raised his head he held them gently and when he had finished, he sat one on his right thigh and one on his left, saying,

---

288	al-Irbilli,II,216.
289	al-Mufid,198.
290	al-Irbilli,II,198.
291	al-Mufid,198.

'Whoever loves me should love these two.'[292]

It is related by al-Tirmidhi that Ya`li ibn Murrah said he heard the Messenger say, 'Husayn is from me and I am from Husayn. Allah loves whoever loves Husayn. Husayn is a descendant of [my] descendants.'[293]

Proof of his Imamate

Proof of his Imamate has been given by his grandfather, his father, and in the will of his brother, Hasan. Mention has already been made (in the section about the Imamate of his brother Hasan) of the instructions given by the Commander of the Faithful to Hasan, concerning the handing over of the Imamate to Husayn and to his son `Ali ibn al-Husayn after him. Moreover, the Messenger had already announced the Imamate of Husayn, just as he had announced the Imamate of Hasan, with the words, 'These two sons of mine are Imams, be they sitting or standing.'[294]

Imam Husayn did not call people to himself after the death of Hasan because of the prevailing conditions, and because a treaty had been made between himself and Mu`awiyah ibn Abu Sufyan. He kept to the agreement, and so followed in the footsteps of his father and brother in the way he established the Imamate; his actions resembled that of the Prophet at the time when he was banished to live in a valley near Makkah, or when he emigrated from Makkah out of fear of his enemies.[295]

When Mu`awiyah died and the treaty that had prevented Husayn from calling people around him was annulled, he openly

---

292	ibid.
293	al-Irbilli,II,218.
294	al-Mufid,199-200 & 252.
295	ibid.

declared his right to the Imamate, whenever he was able and circumstances permitted, to those who were ignorant of it; then he called for a *jihad* and urged people to battle. Together with his sons and household he set out from Allah's and the Messenger's sacred House towards Iraq, to ask for help from those of his followers who had invited him. He sent on ahead of him his cousin Muslim ibn `Aqil, to call the people to Allah and to have them make allegiance to him for *jihad*. So the people of Kufa gave him allegiance, but it was not long before they broke their pact, abandoning and betraying him. They fought between themselves, killed Muslim and then went out to do battle with Husayn. They surrounded him, preventing him from returning to where he had come from and forced him to a place where he had no means of escape; they then advanced between him and the waters of the Euphrates and killed him. He died a martyr, a warrior of Allah, a man of unflagging perseverance – and a man oppressed and wronged.[296]

He (along with many members of his family and close companions) died on the 10th of Muharram 61 AH at the age of 57, seven years of which he had lived while his grandfather, the Messenger, was alive. He had lived 36 years with his father, the Commander of the Faithful, and 47 years with his brother Hasan. His Imamate lasted for eleven years after that of his brother.[297]

Hadith from the Messenger of Allah and the Commander of the Faithful concerning the killing of Imam Husayn

It is related that Umm al-Fadl bint al-Haarith ibn `Abd al-Muttalib went in to see the Messenger, saying, 'O Messenger, I

---

296   ibid.
297   ibid.

have had a loathsome dream.' The Messenger of Allah asked her what she had seen, and she replied, 'I saw a part of your body being cut off and placed in my room.' 'You have seen a good thing,' he replied. 'Faatimah will give birth to a boy, and he will be placed in your room.' Then Faatimah gave birth to Husayn and brought him into the house of the Prophet, placing him in his room. The narrator then caught a glimpse of the Prophet's eyes running with tears, and said to him,' By your father and mother, O Messenger, what is the matter with you?' 'Jibril [Gabriel] came to me,' he said, 'and informed me that my people would kill this son of mine, and he gave me some earth, red with his blood.'[298]

`Abd Allah ibn Yahya, one of the companions of the Commander of the Faithful, relates, 'We went out with `Ali to Siffin, and when we were facing Ninevah he called out, "Be patient, Abu `Abd Allah, on the banks of the Euphrates." I asked him why he told Abu `Abd Allah to be patient, and he replied, "I went in to see the Messenger and his eyes were filled with tears. I then asked him 'By your father and mother, O Messenger of Allah, why are your eyes filled with tears? Has someone angered you?' But he replied that Gabriel had just left, after having told him that Husayn would be killed on the banks of the Euphrates".'[299]

Imam `Ali ibn al-Husayn

His birth, names, titles and death

He was born in Madinah on Thursday the 5th of Sha`ban 38 AH, while his grandfather was still alive – just two years before his death. He remained with his uncle Hasan for twelve years, and with his father Husayn 23 years. He lived for 34 years after

---

298   ibid.
299   al-Irbilli,II,270.

his father and died in Madinah in 95 AH, at the age of 57.[300]

His father was Imam al-Husayn ibn ʿAli ibn Abi Taalib, and his mother was Shahzanan bint Yazdigird ibn Kusra (i.e. Chosroes, the last of the Persian kings).[301] He was known as Abu'l-Hasan, and he was also called Abu Muhammad or Abu Bakr.[302] He had many titles, the most famous being *Zayn al-ʿAbideen* (the Prince of Worshippers), master of the Worshippers, the Pure One and the Trustworthy.

Proof of his Imamate

It is related, as already mentioned, on the authority of Imam al-Baaqir that when the Commander of the Faithful was giving his last directives to Hasan and Husayn, he took hold of his son Husayn's hand and said, 'My son, the Messenger has commanded you to hand over the book and the sword to your son here.' Then he took hold of his son ʿAli and said, 'My son, the Messenger has ordered you to hand them over to your son Muhammad and to give greetings to him from the Messenger of Allah.'[303]

It is related on the authority of Imam al-Baaqir that when Husayn ibn ʿAli found himself facing the final event of his life he called his eldest daughter, Faatimah, and handed to her a wrapped book and his will, unbound for all to see. ʿAli ibn Husayn was hidden in the crowd and Faatimah handed the book over to him.[304]

In another tradition, Imam al-Saadiq relates that Husayn deposited the book and will with Umm Salamah when he left for Iraq; then when ʿAli ibn al-Husayn returned, she handed

---

300 al-Mufid,253-4.
301 ibid.
302 al-Irbilli,II,286.
303 al-Kulayni,I,298-304.
304 ibid.

them to him.[305]

In the words of Shaykh al-Mufid, *'His Imamate was established because of his many qualities, one being that he was the most excellent of Allah's creation after his father; and the Imamate belongs to the most excellent rather than those surpassed in excellence. He was also the nearest to his father Husayn, and the most rightful claimant to his position after him — by his excellence and genealogy.*

'These qualities of excellence also established his Imamate amongst the members of the Household, invalidating the claim of those who would have the Imamate given to Muhammad ibn al-Hanafiyah.'[306]

Some of his excellent qualities

Sa`id ibn al-Kulthum relates how he was with al-Saadiq, who was talking to him about the Commander of the Faithful. He praised and lauded him as befitted his character, and then said, 'None of his sons and no one from his household resembles him more than `Ali ibn al-Husayn in his modesty and understanding of law.'[307]

On one occasion his son Imam al-Baaqir came to see him, just after he had completed an unparalleled period of worship; he noticed how his color has changed to yellow for lack of sleep, his eyes had become sore from weeping, his forehead bruised, and his nose flattened by prostration, and his legs and feet swollen by his standing in prayer. Al-Baaqir said, 'I could not hold back my tears when I saw him in that state, and I wept in compassion for him. He reflected for a while, then turned to me and said, "O my son, give me some of those manuscripts describing how `Ali ibn Abi Taalib used to worship," I gave them to him and he read

---

305 ibid.
306 al-Mufid,254.
307 al-Irbilli,II,297.

from them a little and then put them down saying, "Who can surpass the worship of `Ali ibn Abi Taalib?"[308]

Al-Baaqir relates that `Ali ibn al-Husayn used to pray during the day and night a thousand cycles of prayer, and the breeze would sway him like a sheaf of wheat.[309]

Al-Saadiq relates how `Ali ibn al-Husayn helped 70 households in Madinah without their knowing it; and when he died they missed his deeds.[310]

Ibn al-A`rabi relates that when Yazid ibn Mu`awiyah sent his army to take control of Madinah, `Ali ibn al-Husayn took 400 women into his protection, assisting them until the army of Musrif ibn `Aqabah (Yazid's commander) had dispersed. The same is also related of him when the Umayyad, ibn Zubayr, left the Hijaz.[311]

One of his sons once fell into a well, causing much anxiety to the people of Madinah, until they managed to pull him out. During all this time the Imam was standing in prayer in his prayer-niche. When they questioned him about this he replied, 'I did not notice anything for I was talking in prayer to a Mighty Lord.[312]

When he was asked why the Prophet became an orphan he replied, 'So that he would not owe anything to anyone in creation.'[313] And when asked who was the noblest of men, he said, 'Whoever does not regard the world as something which ennobles the character.'[314] He also said, 'Beware that you do not

---

308	al-Mufid,256.
309	ibid.
310	al-Irbilli,II,304-320.
311	ibid.
312	ibid.
313	ibid.
314	ibid.

take pleasure in wrong actions, for surely this is worse than the actions themselves.'³¹⁵

He joined his Lord in 93 AH, and was buried in the Baqi` graveyard, next to his uncle Hasan. He was 57 years old at the time of his death.³¹⁶

Imam Muhammad ibn `Ali al-Baaqir

His birth, names, titles and death

Imam Muhammad ibn `Ali al-Baaqir was born in Madinah on the 3rd of Safar, 57 AH. His father was Zayn al-`Abideen `Ali ibn al-Husayn ibn `Ali ibn Abi Taalib, and his mother was Faatimah bint al-Husayn ibn `Ali ibn Abi Taalib; thus he is of both the Hashimi and the `Alawi tribes. His grave is in al-Baqi`, in the city of the Messenger.³¹⁷

He was known as Abu Ja`far, and had three titles: the One Well-Versed in Knowledge, the Thankful, and the Guide. The most famous of these is the Well-Versed (*al-Baaqir*), which he was named because of the depth and breadth of his knowledge.³¹⁸

Proof of his Imamate

Falih ibn Abu Bakr al-Shaybani relates how he was sitting with `Ali ibn al-Husayn and his sons when Jaabir ibn `Abd Allah al-Ansaari came and greeted him. He then took hold of Abu Ja`far al-Baaqir's hand and retired alone with him, saying, 'The Messenger informed me that I would meet a man from his Household, known as Muhammad ibn `Ali and with the title of

---

315	ibid.
316	al-Mufid,254 & 262.
317	ibid.
318	al-Irbilli,II,329.

Abu Ja`far, and that I should give greetings from the Messenger to him.' Jaabir then left, and Abu Ja`far returned to sit with his father, `Ali ibn al-Husayn, and his brothers. When they had prayed the sunset prayer, `Ali ibn al-Husayn asked Abu Ja`far what Jaabir ibn `Abd Allah had said to him, and he replied, 'You will meet a man from the family of my House called Muhammad ibn `Ali with the title of Abu Ja`far; and when you do, convey my greetings to him.' 'How fortunate you are my son,' his father said to him, 'to have been singled out by Allah and chosen by His Prophet from amongst the family of his Household. Do not let your brothers know this, lest they plot against you as the brothers of Yusuf [Joseph] plotted against him.'[319]

Imam al-Baaqir relates that when `Ali ibn al-Husayn was close to death, he brought out a chest he had with him, and told Muhammad to take it. Then it was carried away by four men. When he died, his brothers came and claimed what was in the box saying, 'Give us our share of what is in it." 'By Allah,' he replied, 'there is nothing in it for you! Had there been anything for you, it would not have been handed over to me.' In the box were the sword and the Qur'an of the Messenger.[320]

Al-Baaqir succeeded his father, `Ali ibn al-Husayn; he took over the Imamate after him and surpassed all his other sons in excellence, knowledge, simplicity of life-style and dignity. He was the most illustrious and the most outstanding amongst them, both in his daily affairs and his degree of spirituality. He was the highest of them in dignity, and not one of the sons of Hasan and Husayn demonstrated such knowledge of religion, the traditions, the Qur'an, the life of the Prophet and linguistic skill as was demonstrated by Abu Ja`far. Leading scholars, companions, *taabi`un* (the generation of narrators after the

---

319   al-Kulayni,I,304-305.
320   ibid.

companions) and Muslim jurists all quote him in their chains of narration.[321]

Some of his excellent qualities

Jaabir ibn `Abd Allah reported the Messenger as having told him, 'You will live to meet a son of Husayn, known as Muhammad, who is deeply versed in knowledge. When you meet him, convey my greetings to him.'[322]

Imam al-Saadiq relates that Muhammad ibn al-Munkadir used to say, 'I did not think that such a man as `Ali ibn Husayn could leave a successor because of his excellence, until I saw his son, Muhammad al-Baaqir; I sought to counsel him – and he counseled me.' His [al-Munkadir's] companions asked him, 'What did he counsel you?' He said, 'During the heat of the day I went to the outskirts of the town, where I met al-Baaqir. He was a strong man, yet I found him sitting down leaning against his two servants. So I said to myself, "How can one of the Qurayshi shaykhs be in such a state at this time of the day? How is it that he seeks the comfort of this world? I will surely counsel him." So I drew near and greeted him. He in return greeted me, perspiring profusely. "May Allah restore you," I said to him, "a Qurayshi shaykh at such an hour and in such a state, seeking the comfort of this world! What would you do if death came to you while you were in such a state?" Dismissing his two servants with his hand and sitting up he said, "By Allah, if death came to me now with me in this state, then it would have to come to me when I was in a state of obedience to Allah – and therefore I have no need of you or others; truly I would fear death if it came to me as I was doing something disobedient to Allah." "May

---

321 al-Mufid,262.
322 al-Irbilli,II,336.

Allah have mercy on you," I said, "I wanted to counsel you, and you have counseled me".[323]

On his own account it is reported that he was asked why he reported hadith without a chain of narration. He replied, 'When I narrate a hadith, I do not mention the chain of narrators because it passes from my father to my grandfather to his father, and thence to the Messenger, Gabriel, and Allah.'[324]

He also used to say, 'People are a terrible trial for us; if we invite them to Islam they do not respond to us, and if we abandon them, they will be unable to find guidance by anyone other than us.'[325]

It is related that `Abd Allah ibn `Ata'al-Makki said, 'Never have I seen scholars so reduced in stature as when they are in the company of al-Baaqir! I have seen al-Haakim ibn `Utayba, despite his renown amongst the people, looking like a young child with his teacher when sitting with him. Jaabir al-Ju`fi, when narrating on the authority of al-Baaqir, would say, "The guardian of guardians, the inheritor of the science of the prophets, Muhammad ibn `Ali ibn al-Husayn relates that..."'[326]

Al-Baaqir narrated the history of early times as well as the lives of the prophets and wrote books on military warfare; traditions are attributed to him, and he is used as a source for the rituals of the Hajj, as narrated from the Messenger. Sayings concerning Qur'anic commentary have also been attributed to him.[327]

Three of his children were boys, and one was a girl, their names being Ja`far (al-Saadiq), `Abd Allah, Ibrahim and Umm

---

323 al-Mufid,263-266.
324 ibid.
325 ibid.
326 ibid.
327 ibid.

Salamah. Some say he had more children than this.³²⁸ There is disagreement concerning the year of his death: Shaykh al-Mufid says he died in Madinah in 114 AH at the age of 57, while al-Irbilli says he died in 117 AH.³²⁹ Yet others agree with neither, and say he died when he was over 60 years old. His grave is in al-Baqi` in Madinah, in the same area where his father and his father's uncle, Hasan, lie in the same vault as `Abbas, the uncle of the Prophet.³³⁰

Imam Ja`far ibn Muhammad al-Saadiq

His birth, names, titles and death

He was born in Madinah in 80 or 83 AH. He left this world to join his Lord in Shawwaal 148 AH, and was buried in al-Baqi` with his father, his grandfather and his uncle Hasan.³³¹

His genealogy begins with his father Abu Ja`far Muhammad, the son of `Ali ibn al-Husayn and grandson of `Ali ibn Abi Taalib. His mother was Umm Farwah, the daughter of al-Qaasim ibn Muhammad ibn Abu Bakr al-Siddiq. He was known as Ja`far and Abu `Abd Allah (Abu Isma`il according to some), and amongst his titles, the most famous of them being the Truthful (*al-Saadiq*), were the Patient One, the Favored, and the Pure One. His Imamate lasted for 34 years.³³²

Proof of his Imamate

It is related that Abu al-Sabah al-Kinaani told how Abu Ja`far al-Baaqir looked at Abu `Abd Allah al-Saadiq one day as he was

---

328	al-Irbilli,II,331.
329	al-Mufid,262.
330	al-Irbilli,II,331.
331	al-Mufid,281.
332	al-Irbilli,II,336.

walking along and said, 'Do you see that man? He is one of those about whom Allah says, "We desired to show favor unto those who were oppressed in the earth, and to make them examples and to make them inheritors" [28:5].'[333]

It is related by Jaabir ibn Yazid al-Ja`far that al-Baaqir was asked about the Qaa'im (the successor or executor of affairs); he brought his hand down on Abu `Abd Allah al-Saadiq's shoulders, saying, 'This man, by Allah, is the executor of the affairs of the family of Muhammad.'[334]

Sadir al-Sayrafi is said to have heard Abu Ja`far al-Baaqir saying, 'Happiness for a man is that he possesses a son in whom he recognizes a similar creation, behavior and quality of character; and truly I recognize in my son here a similarity in creation, behavior and quality of character.' He was referring to Abu `Abd Allah.[335]

Some of his excellent qualities

Al-Saadiq was one of the greatest of the family of the Prophet, one of the lords of the family; he possessed vast knowledge, was given to much worship and a total renounciation of the world. *Hadith* have been related on his authority, and a number of renowned Imams learned from him, among them Yahya ibn Sa`id al-Ansaari, Ibn Jurayh, Maalik ibn Anas, Sufyan al-Thawri, Ibn `Uyaynah, Abu Hanifah and others; by taking knowledge from him they were ennobled and increased in excellence.[336]

Ibn Hamdun relates how Abu Ja`far al-Mansur, the `Abbasid Caliph, wrote to Imam Ja`far al-Saadiq asking why he did not

---

333 al-Kulayni,I,306-309.
334 ibid.
335 ibid.
336 al-Irbilli,II,367 & 421,419,414,396,400.

visit them as the rest of the people did. Al-Saadiq replied, 'We have nothing to fear from you and you have nothing concerning the next world that we should desire of you; you enjoy no blessings for which we can come and congratulate you, and even this you do not regard as a misfortune that we might come and console you. Thus, what are we to do if we come to see you?' Then Mansur wrote in reply, 'Keep company with us and give us good advice.' 'Whoever desires the world does not give you good advice and whoever desires the next world does not keep your company,' al-Saadiq replied. 'By Allah,' Mansur said, 'I can now distinguish between the different ranks of people – from those who desire the world to those who desire the Hereafter; in truth, al-Saadiq is of those who desire the Hereafter and not this world.'[337]

Abu Hanifah said to Imam al-Saadiq, 'O Abu `Abd Allah, what gives you patience during the prayer?' He replied, 'Woe to you, O Nu`man! Know that prayer is the sacrifice of every God-fearing man, and that the *hajj* is the struggle of every weak man; for everything there is *zakaat*, and the *zakaat* of the body is the fast; the best of deeds is waiting for Allah's help in a matter; and a man who calls to Allah in word but not in deed is like an archer whose bow has no string. Remember these words, O Nu`man.'[338]

Al-Saadiq was once asked why people became mad for food during times of high prices and their hunger also increased when food was cheap. 'Because they are sons of the earth,' he replied. 'If there is a drought, then they eat through fear of scarcity, and if the harvests are plentiful, then they eat because of the abundance.'[339]

Another time he was asked why Allah had forbidden usury,

---

337   ibid.
338   ibid.
339   ibid.

to which he replied, 'So that people do not stop performing acts of kindness amongst themselves.' Then he added, 'Man has been created with different qualities, yet whatever he has been created with does not include treachery and lying.'[340]

Abu Basir relates how he went to see al-Saadiq, wanting him to give some proof of his Imamate, just as his father al-Baaqir had given proof. 'When I entered, I was in a state of ritual impurity, and he said, "O Abu Muhammad, are you so engrossed by what you were doing that you come to me in a state of ritual impurity?" "I did it deliberately," I replied. "Have you no faith?" he said. "Yes, but I wanted to set my heart at rest." "I understand, O Abu Muhammad. Get up and wash yourself." So I got up, washed and went to join some people seated in my house. Thereupon I told them that he was the Imam.'[341]

In the words of Shaykh al-Mufid, 'People have transmitted knowledge from al-Saadiq, and this knowledge has been taken by camel-riders and spread throughout different countries; no one else amongst the learned of his family has been used as a source of transmission as much as he was, and none of them kept company with the narrators of the traditions as much as he did. Compilers of the traditions have collected the names of all the trusted narrators who relate from him (including the whole range of narrators and their diverse collections), and they number 4,000.'[342]

From amongst his sayings concerning the obligation to gain knowledge of Allah and His religion is the following: 'I have found that man's knowledge resides in four things. The first is that you should know your Lord; the second, that you know how He has created you: the third, that you know what He wishes

---

340 ibid.
341 ibid.
342 al-Mufid, 270-288.

from you; and the fourth, that you know what causes a man to leave his religion.'[343]

From amongst his sayings encouraging men to turn in repentance is the following: 'Delay in repentance is deceiving the self: and continued postponement causes perplexity. Seeking a pretext for not turning to Allah leads to destruction, and anyone who persists in his wrong action believes he is protected from the plot of Allah; no one but losers believe that they are protected from the plot of Allah.'[344]

Imam Musa ibn Ja`far al-Kaazim

His birth, names, titles and death

He was born in Abwa' in 128 AH, and passed away in Baghdad under the imprisonment of al-Sindi bin Shaahik, on the 6th of Rajab, 183 AH, at the age of 55.[345] His father was Imam Ja`far al-Saadiq and his mother was a slave girl known as Hamidah al-Barbariyyah.[346] He was called Abu Ibrahim and Abu Hasan, and was known as the Righteous Slave and He who Suppresses his Anger (*al-Kaazim*).[347] His Imamate lasted for 35 years.

Proof of his Imamate

Musa ibn Ja`far was the most brilliant of al-Saadiq's children in capability and the greatest of them in rank, and was the best known amongst the public. No one of his time was more generous, more noble of character, or more honorable in his social relations. No one of his time was more given to worship;

343	ibid.
344	ibid.
345	ibid.
346	ibid.
347	ibid.

he was the most scrupulous, the most outstanding and the most learned in matters of jurisprudence. All the followers of his father supported his claim to the Imamate and submitted to his command.[348]

Al-Fayd al-Mukhtar relates how he said to Abu `Abd Allah al-Saadiq, 'Take me by the hand and save me from the fire – who is there for us after you?' Just then Abu Ibrahim al-Kaazim (at the time a young boy) came in and al-Saadiq said, 'He will be your companion, so stick close to him.'[349]

The elders among al-Saadiq's companions, his intimate associates and his trusted friends among the righteous and learned in jurisprudence, have narrated clear evidence of the transfer of the Imamate from al-Saadiq to his son al-Kaazim, among them al-Mufaddal ibn `Umar al-Ju`fi, Mu`aadh ibn Kathir, `Abd al-Rahman ibn Hujaaj, Fayd ibn al-Mukhtaar, Ya`qub al-Siraaj, Sulayman ibn Khalid, Safwaan al-Jamaal and others.[350]

This has also been reported by his two brothers Ishaaq and `Ali, the sons of al-Saadiq, both indisputably of scrupulous and excellent character.[351]

Ishaaq ibn Ja`far al-Saadiq relates, 'I was with my father one day when `Ali ibn `Umar ibn `Ali asked him, "May I sacrifice myself in your service – with whom should we and the people seek refuge after you?" He replied, "With him who is wearing the two yellow robes; he will appear to you from the door." It was not long before two hands appeared, clasping the two doors; they then opened and Abu Ibrahim came in.'[352]

348	ibid.
349	al-Kulayni,I,307.
350	al-Mufid,288-289.
351	ibid.
352	al-Kulayni,I,308.

Some of his excellent qualities

Ibn Talhah describes him thus: 'He is an Imam of high rank and importance, given to much worship during the night and constant diligence in service; miracles have been witnessed at his hand. He spends the night in prayer and the day in giving charity and fasting, and because of his extreme kindness and patience with those who have wronged him he is called al-Kaazim. He repays bad action with good and forgives those who mistreat him. He is called the Righteous Slave because of his devotion and worship, and is known in Iraq as "The door of relief for those in need".'[353]

It is related that while he was in the prison of Harun al-Rashid he used to say in his prayers, 'Surely You know that I used to ask You to allow me to devote myself completely to worship of You, O Allah, this You have done, and praise belongs to You.'[354]

He used to pray the supererogatory prayers at night, continuing them until the morning prayer; then he would follow this with prayers until sunrise, and remain in prostration to Allah, praising Him and calling on Him, not raising his head from the ground until midday approached.

He would repeatedly say, 'O Allah, I ask You for ease at death and Your forgiveness at the time of reckoning; Your slave's wrong actions are many, so I pray Your forgiveness be forthcoming.' He would weep for fear of Allah until his beard became wet with tears.[355] A number of scholars have related that al-Kaazim would give away 200-300 dinars at a time, and the phrase 'Musa's Purse' became proverbial.[356]

---

353   *al-Muhajjah al-Bayda'*, IV, 266.
354   al-Mufid, 296-304.
355   ibid.
356   ibid.

He died from poisoning in the prison of Harun al-Rashid, and was buried in the Quraysh graveyard in Baghdad in 183 AH.[357]

Imam `Ali ibn Musa al-Rida

His birth, names, titles and death

He was born in Madinah in 148 AH, and passed away in Tus in the region of Khurasan in the month of Safar, 203 AH, at the age of 55. His Imamate lasted for 20 years.[358] His father was Imam Musa ibn Ja`far al-Kaazim and his mother was a slave-girl known as Takattum, or Umm al-Banin. Imam al-Kaazim named her al-Taahirah when she gave birth to Imam `Ali al-Rida.[359]

He was called Abu al-Hasan the second, his father also being known as Abu al-Hasan. He was known as the Contented One (*al-Rida*), the Patient One, the Trustworthy – the first of these being the most famous.[360]

Proof of his Imamate

After Abu al-Hasan Musa ibn Ja`far, his son Abu al-Hasan `Ali ibn Musa al-Rida became the Imam because he surpassed all his brothers and the members of his family, and because of his manifest knowledge, kindness and scrupulousness; both the common folk and the elite were in agreement on this point, as these qualities were plain to see. Moreover, he was the rightful Imam because of what his father al-Kaazim said to him concerning the Imamate, and the fact that he singled him out for

---

357   ibid.
358   ibid.
359   al-Saduq.`Uyun Akhbaar al-Rida,I,15.
360   *al-Muhajjah al-Bayda'*,IV,281.

this from among his brothers.[361]

In the words of al-Makhzumi, 'Imam Abu al-Hasan Musa ibn Ja`far sent for us, and when we were gathered together he said, "Do you know why I have called you? Witness that my son here is my inheritor, guardian of my affairs and my successor after me".'[362]

Dawud al-Riqqi said to Imam Musa ibn Ja`far, 'May I sacrifice myself in your service! I am growing old, so take me by the hand and save me from the Fire: tell me, who is to be our Master after you?' Pointing to his son Abu al-Hasan al-Rida, he replied, 'This will be your Master after me.'[363]

Al-Husayn al-Sahhaaf relates how he was with Hisham ibn al-Hakam and `Ali ibn Yaqtin in Baghdad when the former said, 'I was with Imam al-Kaazim when his son `Ali came in. "O `Ali ibn Yaqtin," he said to me, "this is `Ali al-Rida, the lord of my sons: I have given him my name and title".'[364]

Husayn ibn Bashir said Abu al-Hasan Musa ibn Ja`far appointed his son, `Ali al-Rida, just as the Messenger appointed `Ali on the day of Ghadir Khumm. Then he said, 'O people of Madinah, this is my successor.'[365]

Some of his excellent qualities

Yazid ibn Salit related, in a long *hadith* from Imam Musa al-Kaazim, 'Surely I will be taken this year. The task will then be undertaken by my son `Ali. He has been given the name of `Ali twice: the first `Ali is `Ali ibn Abi Taalib and the second is `Ali

---

361	al-Mufid,304.
362	al-Kulayni,I,312.
363	al-Mufid,305.
364	al-Kulayni,I,311.
365	`Uyun Akhbaar al-Rida,I,29.

ibn al-Husayn. He has been given the understanding of the first, together with his kindness, knowledge, his readiness to assist others, his love, scrupulousness and religion, while being given the trial of the second, together with his patience in the face of what was imposed on him.'[366]

Ibn Talhah says, "'Ali ibn Musa al-Rida is the third of the 'Alis. His faith flourished, his rank and dignity was elevated, his capability increased, his help and support multiplied and his proof was made manifest to such an extent that the caliph al-Ma'mun had total confidence in him, shared with him his lands and possessions, entrusted him with the business of the caliphate and gave his daughter to him in marriage in public.'[367]

Ibrahim ibn al-'Abbas said, 'I have never seen al-Rida being asked something but that he knew the answer, and I do not see another more knowledgeable than him. Al-Ma'mun would test him by asking about everything, and anything he said in reply would always be taken from the Qur'an. He would complete a reading of the whole Qur'an every three days, and would say, "If I wished to complete it in less than three days, then I would do so; but I never read a verse but that I reflect upon its meaning and in what circumstances it was revealed".'[368]

Ibrahim ibn al-'Abbas also said, 'I have neither seen nor heard anyone more excellent than Abu al-Hasan al-Rida, and I have witnessed things in his presence that I witnessed at the hand of no other. I have never seen him speak harshly to anyone, nor heard him interrupt anyone who was speaking to him. He would never refuse to see to the need of anyone if it were in his power; he would never stretch his legs, or recline in front of anyone sitting with him. I have never seen him rebuking any of

---

366 al-Mufid,306.
367 al-Muhajjah al-Bayda',IV,280-282.
368 ibid.

his servants or slaves, nor spitting or laughing out loud – rather, his laugh was as a smile. When he retired to eat and the food was set down, he would have his servants and slaves sit down with him, even the gatekeeper and the stableman. He would sleep little at night and would fast much. He would never miss fasting for three days every month, saying this was like fasting for a lifetime. He would always be helping people and giving in charity without others knowing about it, especially on dark moonless nights. Do not believe anyone who claims to have seen someone like him in excellence.'[369]

Al-Rida said, 'Imamate is the rank of the prophets, and the inheritance of the spiritual guardians. Imamate is the caliphate of Allah and the Messenger; it is the station of the Commander of the Faithful and the heritage of Hasan and Husayn. The Imamate is like the guiding reins of the *deen*, and the government of the Muslims; it is righteousness in this world and the glory of the believers. Truly, Imamate is the root of a flourishing Islam and its wide-spread branches. Through the Imam are prayer, alms-giving, fasting and pilgrimage perfected, booty and charity become plentiful and the laws and punishments are executed. The Imam makes lawful what Allah has made lawful, and forbids what Allah has forbidden.'[370]

Imam Muhammad ibn `Ali al-Jawaad

His birth, names, titles and death

He was born in the month of Ramadan 195 AH, and died in Baghdad in Dhu al-Qa`dah, 220 AH, at the age of 25. He was buried in the Quraysh graveyard with his grandfather Abu al-Hasan Musa ibn Ja`far. His mother was a Nubian slave-girl

---

369   ibid.
370   `Uyun Akhbaar al-Rida,I,218.

known as Sabikah.³⁷¹

He was known as Abu Ja`far. Abu al-Hasan ibn Muhammad Abi `Abbaad relates how Imam al-Rida would never mention his son Muhammad without mentioning his title and he used to say, 'Abu Ja`far wrote to me and I wrote to Abu Ja`far,' addressing him with great respect although he was still a youth in Madinah.³⁷²

He was given the title of the Elect (*al-Muntajab*) and the Chosen. On his death he left behind `Ali, who became Imam after him, and three other offspring, Musa, Faatimah and Imamah.³⁷³

Al-Ma'mun took a great liking to him when he saw, despite his youth, his excellence of character, his level of knowledge, his wisdom, his courtesy and perfect intellect — qualities not possessed by any of the scholars of his time — and so he married his daughter Umm al-Fadl to him. Al-Ma'mun brought her with him to Madinah where he treated Abu Ja`far with great honor and respect.³⁷⁴

Proof of his Imamate

Ibn Abi `Abbaad reports Abu al-Husayn al-Rida as saying, 'Abu Ja`far is my successor, and the caliph of my family after me.'³⁷⁵

Sayings from al-Rida concerning the Imamate of his son Abu Ja`far have been related by `Ali ibn Ja`far al-Saadiq, Safwaan ibn Yahya, Mu`ammar ibn Khaalid, al-Husayn ibn Bishshaar, Ibn Qiyaamah al-Waasiti, al-Hasan ibn al-Jahm, Abu Yahya al-

---

371   al-Mufid,316.
372   `Uyun Akhbaar al-Rida,II,240.
373   al-Mufid,327 & 319.
374   ibid.
375   `Uyun Akhbaar al-Rida,II,240.

Sin'aani, Yahya ibn Habib al-Ziyat, and many others.[376]

'Ali, the son of Imam Ja'far al-Saadiq, told al-Hasan ibn al-Husayn ibn 'Ali al-Husayn that Allah had given victory to Abu al-Hasan al-Rida, when his brothers and uncles treated him unjustly; whereupon he related a long *hadith*, ending with the words: 'Then I rose and grasped the hand of Abu Ja'far Muhammad ibn 'Ali al-Rida, saying to him, I bear witness that you are my Imam before Allah.' On hearing this, al-Rida began to cry. Then he said, 'Have you not heard my father tell how the Messenger said: "By my father, the offspring of a son of the best of the Nubian slave-girls will be banished and wronged by the murderer of his father and grandfather; he will live in exile, and people will ask of him: Is he dead? Has he perished? Which valley is he travelling through?"' Then I said, 'You have spoken the truth – may I sacrifice myself in your service.'[377]

Abu Yahya al-Sin'aani relates how he was with Abu al-Hasan al-Rida when he had his small son brought in, and he said, 'There has never been born a child of greater blessing for our followers than him.'[378]

Safwaan ibn Yahya said, 'I said to al-Rida, "We used to ask you [what you wanted] before Allah granted you Abu Ja'far, and you would reply, 'May Allah grant me a baby boy.' Allah has granted this to you and our hearts are filled with joy. May Allah preserve you; but when your life comes to an end, who is to take over?" Then al-Rida pointed to Abu Ja'far, who was standing in front of him. 'I then said, "May I sacrifice myself in your service – this boy is only three years old!" "What does that matter to him?" replied al-Rida. "Did not 'Isa (Jesus) demonstrate his

---

376   al-Mufid,317.
377   ibid.
378   al-Kulayni,I,321,494 & 496.

proof when he was less than three years old?"'"³⁷⁹

Some of his excellent qualities

It is related that `Ali ibn Asbaat told this anecdote: 'Abu Ja`far came out towards me, and I looked at his head and legs in order that I might describe his stature to our companions in Egypt. I continued scrutinizing him until he sat down and said, "O `Ali, surely Allah has given proof of Imamate just as He has given proof of prophethood." Then he recited these verses: "And We granted him wisdom while yet a child" [19:12], "And when he had attained his maturity" [12:2], and "[when] he reaches forty years" [46:15]. Thus, wisdom may be given to a child or to a man of forty".'³⁸⁰

`Ali ibn Ibrahim relates on the authority of his father how a group of people from neighboring regions asked leave to see `Ali Abu Ja`far. This he granted, and they asked him a good many questions, all of which he answered, and he was only ten years old at the time.³⁸¹

Da`bal ibn `Ali al-Khaza`i, the famous poet, relates that he came to see al-Rida, who commanded him to do something. He accepted, but omitted to praise Allah. Al-Rida reminded him not to forget to do this. Da`bal relates that he then went to see `Ali Abu Ja`far, who ordered him to do something, and Da`bal answered, 'Praise belongs to Allah.' 'Now you are behaving correctly,' `Ali Abu Ja`far said to him.³⁸²

Ibn Talhah calls Abu Ja`far Muhammad 'the second', for Abu Ja`far Muhammad al-Baqir, his great-grandfather, came

---

379   ibid.
380   ibid.
381   ibid.
382   ibid.

before him. Abu Ja`far al-Jawaad (the Generous) was given this title when he was still a teenager because of the excellence and worthiness of his character. He has two other titles: the Contented and the Chosen One.[383] Al-Tabarsi states that his titles are the God-Fearing, the Elect, and the Chosen.[384] The Iraqis refer to him as the Generous (*al-Jawaad*), and this is the name mentioned on his grave, which lies next to that of his grandfather, Imam Musa.

Imam `Ali ibn Muhammad al-Haadi

His birth, names, titles and death

He was born either in the middle of Dhu al-Hijjah, 212 AH, or in Rajab, 214 AH. He passed away four days before the end of Jamaadi al-Akhirah, 254 AH (or in Rajab of the same year, according to another source), at the age of 41 years and six months.[385] His death occurred in Samarra, to where al-Mutawakkil al-`Abbas had taken him from Madinah, together with Yahya ibn Har'amah ibn A`yin, and he remained there until his death. His Imamate lasted for 33 years. His mother was a slave-girl known as Samaanah.[386]

He was known as 'Abu al-Hasan the third', and his titles were the Advisor, the One who Trusts, the One who Opens or Expands, the Pure One, and the Chosen One. The One Who Trusts (*al-Mutawakkil*) was the most famous of these titles, but he would conceal this and order his companions to avoid using it as it was also the title of the Caliph al-Mutawakkil.[387]

Al-Tabarsi mentions other titles: the Learned One, the

383	*al-Muhajjah al-Bayda'*,IV,295.
384	ibid.
385	al-Kulayni,I,497-498.
386	al-Mufid,327.
387	*al-Muhajjah al-Bayda'*,IV,308-309.

Scholar of the Shari`ah, the Trustworthy, and the Good; he added to these the Guide, and this is the most famous title among the Shi`ites.[388]

Proof of his Imamate

It is related how Isma`il ibn Mahraan said that Abu Ja`far al-Jawaad was among the first to leave Madinah for Baghdad in the first group, and Isma`il said to him as he was leaving, 'I am at your service. I fear for you in this matter, for who will take over after you?' He turned to Isma`il, smiling, and said, 'My exile is not, as you believe, this year.' When he was being brought a second time to Mu`tasim, Isma`il asked him instantly, 'You are leaving now, so who will take over after you?' He wept until his beard was wet, then he turned to Isma`il saying, 'This time there is reason to fear for me. My son `Ali will take over after me.'[389]

Muhammad ibn al-Husayn al-Waasiti relates how he heard Ahmad ibn Abi Khalid, a vassal (*mawla*) of Imam al-Jawaad, saying that he saw the written testimony of Imamate, testifying to it with the words, 'I bear witness that Imam Ja`far Muhammad ibn `Ali delegated the Imamate to his son `Ali personally, and then instructed his brothers; he appointed `Abd Allah ibn al-Masaawir over his inheritance until `Ali ibn Muhammad came of age.'[390]

Imam al-Hasan ibn `Ali al-`Askari

His birth, names, titles and death

He was born in Madinah, in the month of Rabi` al-Thaani 232

---

388   ibid.
389   al-Kulayni,I,323 & 325.
390   ibid.

AH, and died on Friday the 8th of Rabi` al-Awwal, 260 AH, at the age of 28. He was buried at his house in Samarra, where his father had also been buried.[391] His mother was a slave-girl called Hadithah[392] or, according to others, Sawsan.[393]

He was known as Abu Muhammad, and his titles were the Guide (*al-Haadi*), the Lamp (*al-Siraaj*), and al-`Askari (a native of Madinat al-`Asaakir); and he, his father and grandfather were each known by the name of Ibn al-Rida.[394]

Proof of his Imamate

Yahya ibn Yasar al-Qanbari (al-`Anbari, according to others) relates that Abu al-Hasan al-Haadi gave instructions [concerning his succession] to his son al-Hasan four months before he died, 'and he made me witness this together with his servants.'[395]

`Ali ibn `Umar al-Nawfali relates: 'I was with Abu al-Hasan al-Haadi in the courtyard of his house when his son Muhammad (the eldest son, who died before him) passed by, and I said to him, "May I sacrifice myself in your service; will he be our master after you?" "No," he replied," Your master after me will be al-Hasan".'[396]

`Ali ibn Ja`far says, 'I was present with Abu al-Hasan al-Haadi when his son died, and he said to his other son, al-Hasan al-`Askari, "My son, give thanks to Allah, for He has begun an important event for you".'[397]

Abu Bakr al-Fahfaki relates how al-Hasan al-Haadi wrote to

391	al-Mufid,335.
392	ibid.
393	al-Kulayni,I,503.
394	*al-Muhajjah al-Bayda'*,IV,321.
395	al-Kulayni,I,325-326.
396	ibid.
397	al-Mufid,335-342.

him saying, 'Abu Muhammad, my son, is by his character, and by his authority, the worthiest of the family of Muhammad; he is the most reliable; he is the eldest of my children; and he is the successor – the ties of Imamate extend to him, as well as its rulings. Thus, whatever you used to ask me, ask him, for he has whatever you need.'[398]

Dawud ibn al-Qaasimi al-Ja`fari relates how he heard Abu al-Hasan al-Haadi saying, 'My successor will be al-Hasan al-`Askari: you will need no one as a successor besides him.' When Dawud asked him why, he replied, 'Surely you have not perceived the greatness of his character. Moreover, you should not refer to him by his name.' 'How should they refer to him?' Dawud asked. 'Call him "the Proof of the Family of Muhammad," he replied.'[399]

Some of his excellent qualities

Abu al-Hasan al-Haadi's son, Abu Muhammad al-Hasan ibn `Ali al-`Askari became the Imam because he combined qualities of excellence which surpassed all others of his time, and which made him the rightful claimant to the Imamate; he was fit for leadership by virtue of his knowledge and self-denial, his perfection and intelligence, his infallibility, his courage and generosity, the number of good actions he performed, which brought him closer to Allah, and finally by virtue of the fact that his father entrusted the Imamate to him.[400]

Ahmad ibn al-Khaaqaan reports that his father, `Ubayd Allah ibn al-Khaaqaan, said, 'O my son, if the Imamate were taken from our `Abbasid caliphs, no one but he of the tribe of

---

398   ibid.
399   ibid.
400   ibid.

Haashim [i.e. Imam al-`Askari] would have the right to it because of his excellence, his chastity, his self-denial, his acts of worship, the beauty of his character, and his uprightness. If you had seen his father, you would have seen a generous, noble and virtuous man.'[401]

Muhammad ibn Isma`il al-`Alawi tells how Imam Abu Muhammad al-`Askari was once imprisoned in the house of `Ali ibn Awtaamish, who was a bitter enemy of the family of Muhammad and harsh with the family of Abu Taalib. People constantly advised him to punish him in various ways, but not a day had passed before he had submitted to him, not raising his eyes to him out of respect; and when the Imam left his house, no one respected him or talked more highly of him than ibn Awtaamish.[402]

Abu Haashim al-Ja`fari relates thus: 'I complained to Abu Muhammad al-`Askari about the conditions in prison, and he wrote to me saying, "Today you will pray the midday prayer in your house." Thereupon I was freed at midday, and prayed in my own home. I was in straitened circumstances, and wanted to ask him for some dinars by letter, but felt ashamed. Yet when I returned to my house, he sent me 100 dinars and wrote, "Do not feel ashamed or reticent if you are in need: ask for whatever you need, and you will have what you desire, if Allah wills".'[403]

Ahmad ibn Ishaaq relates: 'I went to see `Ali Abu Muhammad al-`Askari and said to him, "It has been related to us on the authority of your father and grandfather that prophets sleep on their back, believers on their right side, hypocrites on their left, and devils on their faces." He replied that this was true, and I continued, "O master, I try to sleep on my right side but I

---

401   ibid.
402   ibid.
403   al-Kulayni,I,508 & 514.

cannot go to sleep." "Ahmad, listen to me." I went closer to him and he said, "Put your hand beneath your robe." I did this, and he drew out his own hand from beneath his robe and placed it beneath mine. Then he rubbed his right hand against my left side and his left hand against my right side three times. Since the Imam did that to me, I can no longer sleep on my left side.'[404]

In the words of Ibn Talhah: 'Surely the supreme virtue and outstanding aspect chosen by Allah for him, the everlasting quality which time cannot erase nor tongues forget, is that the Mahdi is of his progeny, and a part of his flesh and blood.'[405]

Imam Muhammad ibn al-Hasan al-Mahdi

His birth, names and titles

The Imam after Abu Muhammad al-Hasan al-`Askari was his son, who carries the same name and title as the Messenger of Allah. His father delegated power to him secretly and not to any other son, temporal or spiritual power. He was born in the middle of Sha`baan 255 AH.[406]

His mother was a slave-girl known as Nargis. He was five years old when his father died. Allah gave him wisdom and judgment at this age and made him a sign for the worlds. Allah gave him wisdom just as he gave John the Baptist wisdom as a boy, and made him an Imam during his childhood, just as he had made Jesus, the son of Maryam, a prophet in the cradle.[407]

Knowledge of his occultation existed before he was born and precise details of his change of state were known before actual occultation. He was the sword-bearer of the Imams of

---

404	ibid.
405	*al-Muhajjah al-Bayda'*, IV,321.
406	al-Mufid,346.
407	ibid.

Guidance, the Awaited One who establishes truth and the rule of belief. Two occultations took place, one longer than the other; the lesser of the two lasting from his birth to the breaking of the link between him and his followers, which occurred on the death of the deputies (*al-sufaraa*). The major occultation began after the minor one, and will end with his reappearance, sword in hand. The Messenger of Allah said, 'The days and nights will not come to an end until Allah sends to the world a man from my Household. His name will be the same as my name. He will fill the earth with equity and justice as it was filled with oppression and tyranny.'[408]

There now follow some Qur'anic texts and *hadith* of the Messenger and the Imams, which confirm the Imamate of the 'Lord of the Age' (*sahib al-zamaan*) and describe his character, occultation and awaited reappearance.

Imam al-Mahdi

Allah says in His Book:

☼ And we desired to bestow a favor upon those who were deemed weak in the land, and to make them the Imams, and to make them the heirs, and to grant them power in the land. (28:5)

☼ And certainly We wrote in the Book after the reminder that [as for] the land, My righteous servants shall inherit it. (21:105)

The Messenger of Allah said, 'Allah has chosen the next world instead of this world for me and my Household. My Household will undergo trial, banishment and exile, until a people will come

---

408   ibid.

from the east bearing black flags; they will demand wealth and will not be given it, so they will fight and be victorious. Then they will be given what they asked for, but they will not accept it until they hand it over to one of my Household, and he will fill the earth with equity and justice as it was once filled with oppression. Who among you realize this? Whoever amongst you is present [for these events] then he should go to them, even if he has to crawl through snow.'[409]

'The Mahdi is of us, the Family of the Household, and Allah will make him thrive when [the age] is dark [for the Household].'[410]

Sa`id ibn al-Musaayyib related how he was talking with Umm Salama about the Mahdi when she said she had heard the Messenger say, 'The Mahdi is one of the progeny of Faatimah.'[411]

Anas ibn Maalik relates how he heard the Messenger say, 'We are the progeny of `Abd al-Muttalib, and the Lords of Paradise – myself, Hamzah, `Ali, Ja`far, Hasan, Husayn and al-Mahdi.'[412]

'Rejoice in the news of the Mahdi: he is a man of the Quraysh, from my Family, who will appear when men are disputing and earthquakes are widespread. He will fill the earth with equity and justice as it was once filled with oppression and tyranny; the inhabitants of heaven will be content with him, as will be the inhabitants of the earth.'[413]

'The earth will not disappear or be destroyed until someone from my Family whose name is the same as mine rules over it.'[414]

'A man from my Family, whose name is the same as mine,

---

409   Ibn Maaja,II,23,*hadith* no. 4082.
410   ibid.,*hadith* no. 4085.
411   ibid.,*hadith* no. 4086.
412   ibid.,*hadith* no. 4087.
413   al-Hindi,*Kanzal-`Umaal fi Sunan al-Aqwaal wa'l-Af`aal*, vol. 14,205-217.
414   ibid.

will appear; and even if only one day of this world remained, Allah would prolong that day until he appeared.'[415]

'The Mahdi is from my Family and of the progeny of Faatimah.'[416]

'The final hour will not come until the earth has been filled with tyranny and oppression, and a man from my Family will appear who will fill it with equity and justice, just as it was once filled with oppression and tyranny.'[417]

'In Ramadan there will be a tremendous noise; in Shawwaal, a turmoil; in Dhu al-Qa`dah, the tribes will fight against each other; in Dhu al-Hijjah, the pilgrims will burn with thirst; and in Muharram, a voice will call from the heavens, "Surely the elect among mankind will be of such and such a disposition, so listen and obey him".'[418]

`Abd Allah ibn `Abbas relates how the Messenger of Allah said, 'My Caliphs and deputies – those men who are living proof of Allah's guidance for His creation after me – will be twelve in number. The first of them will be my brother and the last my son.' When he was asked, 'O Messenger, who is your brother?' He replied,' `Ali ibn Abi Taalib;' and when he was asked 'Who is your son?' he replied, 'The Mahdi, who will fill the earth with equity and justice as it was once filled with oppression and tyranny.'[419]

`Abd Allah ibn `Abbaas relates how the Messenger of Allah said, 'I, myself, `Ali, Hasan, Husayn, and nine of Husayn's offspring are infallible and pure.'[420]

415	ibid.
416	ibid.
417	ibid.
418	ibid.
419	al-Khuraasaani, *Faraa'id al-Simtayn*, II, 70-75.
420	ibid.

The Messenger said, 'I am the Lord of the Messengers, and `Ali ibn Abi Taalib is the lord of those delegated by Allah. My delegates after me are twelve in number; the first is `Ali ibn Abi Taalib, and the last is al-Qaa'im (the Establisher of Islam).'[421]

'The Mahdi will appear and in front of him will be an angel calling, "Truly this is the Mahdi, so follow him".'[422]

'The Mahdi will appear in the final year of my *ummah* and Allah will shower rain for him. From the earth will appear trees and plants, and he will be given all the wealth of the world; cattle and sheep will multiply, and the *ummah* will become mighty.'[423]

Hudhayfah ibn al-Yamaan related how the Messenger made a speech, saying, 'If there were to remain only one day in the life of the earth, Allah will prolong that day until He sends a man from my progeny whose name will be the same as mine,' Whereupon Salmaan got up and asked the Messenger of Allah from which of his progeny he would come and the Messenger replied, 'From this son of mine' – and he slapped Husayn on the back.[424]

'The Mahdi will have a more striking brow and a more prominent nose than us.'[425]

'The Mahdi will be my progeny, his name will be as my name, his title as my title; he will resemble me in his build and his disposition more than any other person. He will go into a period of occultation and the various nations will fall into confusion and evil ways. Then he will appear as a shining torch and will fill the earth with equity and

---

421	ibid.	
422	ibid.	
423	ibid.	
424	al-Khuraasaani,II,84 (from *Masnad Ahmad ibn Hanbal*,I,196).	
425	al-Khuraasaani,II,88-94.	

justice as it was once filled with oppression and tyranny.'[426]

'Truly `Ali ibn Abi Taalib will be the Imam of my *ummah* and my deputy over it after me, and from his progeny will come my awaited successor; through him Allah will fill the earth with equity and justice as it was once filled with oppression and tyranny. By the One Who has sent me with the truth as a bringer of good news, truly those who are unwavering when talking about him during the time of his occultation are more precious than the philosopher's stone.' Thereupon Jaabir ibn `Abd Allah al-Ansari got up and said, 'O Messenger of Allah, will the deputy from your progeny go into occultation?' 'By my Lord,' he replied, 'Allah will purify through him those who believe, and will destroy those who do not; knowledge of it is concealed from His slaves – so beware, lest you doubt in this matter; indeed, to doubt in one of Allah's concerns is to disbelieve.'[427]

Jaabir al-Ansari relates: 'I went into the company of Faatimah, the daughter of the Messenger, and in her hand was a tablet containing the names of the delegated Imams of her progeny. She enumerated twelve names, the last being al-Qaa'im, three of them bearing the name Muhammad, and four `Ali.'[428]

Imam al-Saadiq has said, 'When Allah permits al-Qaa'im to reappear, he will go onto a raised platform and will call people to him, he will adjure them by Allah, and he will invite them to His truth; he will live amongst them according to the *sunnah* of the Messenger, and will make transactions amongst them according to his own transactions. Then Allah will send Gabriel to him; Gabriel will descend onto the wall surrounding the Ka`bah, saying, "Why are you calling?" The Qaa'im will inform him, and Gabriel will say, 'I will be the first to make allegiance to you: give

---

426 ibid.
427 ibid.
428 al-Mufid,348-364.

me your hand." Then he will stroke his hand. Three hundred and some score men will then appear and swear allegiance to him; he will remain in Makkah until his companions number 10,000 and then he will travel to Madinah.'[429]

The Importance of the Learned (al-`ulama') during the period of the Mahdi's occultations

Allah says in His Book:

☼ Allah bears witness that there is no god but He, and [so do] the angels and those possessed of knowledge. (3:18)

☼ Are those who know and those who do not know alike? (39:9)

☼ And [as for] these examples, We set forth for men, and none understand them but the learned. (29:43)

☼ Only those of his servants who are possessed of knowledge fear Allah. (35:28)

☼ Allah will exalt those for you who believe, and those who are given knowledge, in high degree. (58:11)

The Prophet said, 'The similitude of the learned on earth is like that of the stars in the sky: people take them as a guide in the darkness of the land and sea; if they are blotted out, then those being guided will soon lose their way.'[430]

'The man of knowledge outshines the man of worship in the same degree as the full moon outshines the rest of the stars.'[431]

---

429   ibid.
430   al-Haakim,II,268.
431   al-Kulayni,I,34.

'Looking upon the face of a man of knowledge is worship.'[432]

'Visiting the learned is more beloved of Allah than encircling the House [i.e. the Ka`bah] seventy times.'[433]

'Allah will have mercy on my caliphs.' He was asked, 'O Messenger, who are your caliphs?' 'Those who revive my *sunnah* (life-pattern) and teach it to the servants of Allah.'[434]

'The scholars of jurisprudence *al-fuqahaa`* are the trusted deputies of the Messenger.'[435]

'When acts of *bid`ah* (innovation, not part of the original prophetic life-pattern) appear in my *ummah*, then the learned man will reveal his knowledge; if anyone does not act according to his instructions, then the curse of Allah will be upon him.'[436]

'The elite of the elite are the elite of the learned.'[437]

'The inhabitants of the Fire will be tormented by the breath of the man of knowledge who has abandoned the world for the sake of knowledge.'[438]

Imam `Ali said, 'Whoever honors a man of knowledge has honored Allah.'[439]

'Realize that keeping company with a man of knowledge and obeying him is a way of worship which leads to Allah: obedience to him is a means to good actions and reward; it wipes out bad actions and is a provision for the believers.'[440]

432	al-Haakim,II,271 (from *al-Bihaar*,I,195).
433	ibid.
434	ibid.,II,281.
435	ibid., (from *al-Bihaar*,I,216).
436	al-Kulayni,I,54.
437	al-Haakim,II,324 (from *al-Bihaar*,II,110).
438	ibid.,II,276.
439	ibid.,II,271.
440	ibid.,II,273.

Writing instructions to Ashtar al-Nakha'i when he made him governor of Egypt, he said, 'Study frequently with the learned and discuss with the wise, that you may maintain the prosperity of your domain.'[441]

'The blight of knowledge consists in failing to act according to one's knowledge.'[442]

'Do not turn your knowledge into ignorance or your certainty into doubt: if you have learnt something, then act accordingly; and if you are certain about a matter, then proceed with it.'[443]

'The learned are rulers over the people.'[444]

Al-Saadiq said, 'The men of knowledge are the inheritors of the prophets. This is because the prophets do not bequeath dirhams or dinars, but they leave their *hadith*, whoever takes something from them has taken a tremendous portion of spiritual wealth. Therefore look to where you take your knowledge of the *hadith*: amongst us are the Family of the Prophet's house, who are just and true in every generation; they can disprove the corrupt texts related by the unscrupulous.'[445]

'There are some learned men who believe they should teach only the rich and noble, and do not consider that the poor should be taught: such people are in the third level of the Fire.'[446]

441	ibid.	
442	ibid.	
443	ibid.,II,277.	
444	ibid.,II,281.	
445	al-Kulayni,I,32.	
446	al-Haakim,II,295.	

II: Our Way of Worship

PRAYER (SALAAT)

The Obligatory Prayers at the Appointed Times

Allah says in His Book:

☼ And keep up prayer and pay the poor-rate and bow down with those who bow down... And seek assistance through patience and prayer, and most surely this is most difficult except for the humble ones. (2:43-45)

☼ Attend constantly to prayers and to the middle prayer. (2:238)

☼ Surely prayer is a timed ordinance for the believers. (4:103)

☼ Say to My servants who believe that they should keep up prayer. (14:31)

☼ Surely prayer keeps [one] away from indecency and evil. (29:45)

☼ And keep up prayer and pay the poor-rate and obey Allah and His Apostle. (33:33)

☼ And they attend to their prayers constantly. (6:92)

☼ So woe to the praying ones who are unmindful of their prayers. (107:5)

☼ And [as for] believing men and believing women, they are guardians of each other; they enjoin good and forbid evil and keep up prayer. (9:71)

The most important of the secrets of prayer is intention. The Prophet has said, 'Actions are according to one's intentions, and every man is rewarded according to his intentions.'[447]

'Prayer (like all other acts of worship) is not counted as worship of Allah and is not reckoned as an act of obedience to Him, and therefore rewardable in the next world, unless one desires to come closer to Allah by it and so achieve the reward and salvation from punishment.'[448] These words of the Prophet are in accordance with what Allah says when He urges slaves to 'Call upon Him in fear and hope' [7:56] and elsewhere, 'They call upon us desiring and fearing' [21:90].

Allah promises paradise or threatens with fire in innumerable verses. His slaves will be rewarded according to their capacity, stations and intentions. Thus whoever knows Allah for His beauty, His majesty and His kindness, whoever loves Him, longs for Him and devotes one's worship to Him – Who is worthy of such worship and love – then Allah will love him, save him, single him out and bring him close to Him, spiritually and in the world of the senses.[449] *Allah says in this respect, 'And truly he [Dawud] has an intimacy with Us and a good resting place' [38:25].*

Likewise Imam `Ali said, 'My God, I have not worshipped You because I feared Your fire, nor because I desired Your garden, but because I have found You worthy of worship.'[450]

Some have declared that worship is invalidated if by it one desires reward and salvation from punishment, claiming that this intention is incompatible with true devotion – which is desiring only the face of Allah. Most people may be excused from performing this kind of worship, namely seeking the grace of Allah and proximity to Him, because they only

---

447 al-Muhajjah al-Bayda', IV, 349-371.
448 ibid.
449 ibid.
450 ibid.

understand Him in terms of hope and fear; by remembering the fire they take heed of its torment, and by remembering the garden they stimulate a desire for its reward. If such an intention annulled the validity of worship, then it would be meaningless to instill desire or fear in oneself of the promise of reward and the threat of punishment (mentioned in the Qur'an).[451]

With regard to the above, we should note that al-Saadiq divides worship into three classes. There are three kinds of worship: people who worship Allah out of fear – they are the slaves; people who worship Allah for reward – they are paid slaves; and those who worship Allah out of love for Him – these are freed slaves, and this is the best kind of worship.'[452] His words, 'the best kind of worship' emphasize that the first two kinds of worship are not devoid of excellence, provided that they are performed correctly.[453]

The Messenger, as is related in a famous *hadith*, has said, 'The intention of the believer is better than his action, and the intention of the non-believer is worse that his action.' Explaining this *hadith*, Imam al-Baaqir said, 'The believer's intention is better than his action because he intends good even though he may not achieve it, and the non-believer's intention is worse than his action because he intends and desires evil, although he may not actually achieve it.'[454]

The second of the secrets of worship, sincerity in devotion, has been described as stripping one's intention of any impurities until it is solely for the face of Allah, and making one's prayer an inner dialogue with Allah through His attributes and actions. Sincerity also means the breaking of the self, the removing of desire for this world and devoting oneself to the

---

451   ibid.
452   ibid.
453   ibid.
454   ibid.

next world, until the heart yearns for this alone. The Commander of the Faithful says on the same subject, 'Those who sincerely devote themselves to worship of Allah and prayer to Him, whose hearts are not busy with what the eyes see, who do not forget remembrance of Allah because of what their ears hear, and who are not saddened by what has not been given to others, such people find contentment.'[455]

Allah has reproached some of His slaves for their negligence during prayers, saying, 'Woe to those who pray but who are unmindful of their prayers' [108:4-5], not because they have abandoned the prayers. He also says, 'Establish the prayer for My remembrance' [20:14], and, 'Do not be amongst those who are unmindful' [7:205].[456]

The Prophet says, 'Whoever prays two cycles of prayer, and does not allow his mind to wander to the affairs of this world, will be forgiven for the wrong action he has committed earlier.'[457]

'Truly prayer is being humble, resigned, full of regret and contentment; if a man is not like this, then his prayer is imperfect.'[458]

Some of his wives said, 'The Prophet would converse with us and we with him, but when the time came for prayer it was as if he did not know us, and we did not know him.'[459]

Imam 'Ali's face would change color when he began to make ablutions, out of fear of Allah, and when the time for prayer came, he would begin to tremble. When he was asked what the matter was, he replied. 'The time of trust has come, the trust which Allah offered to the heavens, the earth and mountains,

---

455 ibid.
456 ibid.
457 ibid.
458 ibid.
459 ibid.

from which they turned away and refused to accept.'[460]

The prayer of the person unmindful of what he is saying or doing is not accepted. This is because prayer is an inner discourse, and there is no doubt that speech without presence of mind is not inner discourse with Allah. Speech is an expression of what is in the mind, and it is not correct to express what is in the mind without the heart being present. What, then, is the point of asking Allah (in His own words) to 'Guide us to the straight path' if the heart is unmindful? How can bowing and prostration, which are carried out to glorify Allah, accompany negligence and lack of awareness? Moreover, recitation, remembrance, praise, humility and prayer were given to the slaves of Allah that they may polish their hearts, renew their remembrance and strengthen their faith; but how can this be, if the heart of the slave is closed through heedlessness?[461]

The following spiritual qualities give true life to prayer: awareness of the heart, understanding, glorification, awe of Him, hope and meekness. If you hear the call of the muezzin, remind your heart of the awesome call on the Day of Resurrection and make both your inner and outer self prepared for prayer.

Purify your heart with piety and certainty before purifying your limbs with water. Standing in prayer means standing respectfully, one's body and heart in the hands of Allah, one's head bowed and lowered.

If you turn to say the opening words, 'Allahu akbar', or the prayer, then reflect upon the might of Allah and belittle yourself in the face of His might.

When bowing, be humble, by humbling the heart and the body, and seek the protection of Allah's forgiveness; strive to be filled with the power of your Master and the sublimity of your Lord, and to be empty of self.

Prostration is the highest state of submission: the most noble part of the human body, the face has been lowered to the lowest of matter, the dust.

---

460 ibid.
461 al-`Inaathi,I,313.

When sitting in the final state of the prayer, in which one witnesses that there is one God and Muhammad is His Messenger, then one should be conscious of an overwhelming fear and awe, of meekness, and palpitation of the heart.[462]

Prayer in the Night

Allah says in His Book:

☼ And keep up prayer in the two parts of the day and in the first hours of the night. (11:114)

☼ And enjoin prayer on your followers, and steadily adhere to it. (20:132)

☼ Surely I am Allah, there is no god but I, therefore serve Me and keep up prayer for My remembrance. (20:14)

Jibril came to the Prophet, saying, 'O Muhammad, live as you wish, for truly you will be a dead man; love whom you wish, for you will be separated from them; act as you wish, for you will be rewarded for what you do; and know that a man's nobility comes from standing in prayer at night, and his honor from doing without the help of other men.'[463]

The Messenger said to Abu Dharr, 'O Abu Dharr, Allah says, "My most beloved slaves are those who love each other in a lawful manner, those whose hearts are connected to the mosques, those who ask forgiveness in the early hours of the morning; if I wish to punish the people of the earth, then I remember such people [i.e. the beloved slaves] and divert punishment from them".'[464]

---

462   ibid.
463   al-Khisaal,I,7.
464   al-Ashtari,II,62.

It is related on the authority of Ibn `Abbaas that the Prophet said, 'The most noble of my *ummah* are those who carry the Qur'an in their hearts, and those who stand in prayer at night.'[465]

The Messenger has said, 'Truly Allah has sent revelation to the earth saying, "Tire out those who serve you and serve those who reject you." Surely Allah will place light in the heart of the slave who retires with his Master in the deepest darkness of the night, conversing with Him in prayer; and if he says, "O Lord" then Allah will call out to him saying, "At your service, my slave: whatever you ask of Me, I will surely give you, and if you rely on Me then I will be enough for you." Then He will say to the angels, "My angels, look at My slave – he retires alone with Me in the deepest darkness of the night while the misguided are playing and the negligent are sleeping. Bear witness that I have forgiven him".'[466]

Amongst the detailed instructions given by the Prophet to `Ali were the following: 'Strive so hard to give to the needy that you will say, "I am being extravagant," and take upon yourself the prayer of the night, and take upon yourself the prayer of the night, and take upon yourself the prayer of the night.'[467]

Describing the scrupulousness and piety of his followers, Imam `Ali has said, 'By Allah! They are gentle and patient, and knowledgeable of Allah and His religion; they act only in obedience to Him and according to His command; they are guided by love of Him. They are emaciated through exhaustion and devoted to abstinence in the world; their faces are pale from standing in prayer all night, and bleary-eyed from weeping, their lips dry from remembrance of Allah, their stomachs hollow with hunger. You can recognize their abstinence from their faces, and

---

465   *al-Khisaal*,I,6.
466   *Makaarim al-Akhlaaq*,65 & 80.
467   ibid.

their retirement from the world in their character. Their bad qualities are hidden, their hearts are sad, they are modest and have few needs; they themselves are in distress, and others are at ease by their efforts. Such people are wise, intimate with Allah, and are the elite among the noble.'[468]

It is related that al-Saadiq said, 'The excellence of the believers lies in their praying at night, and their glory in their not causing trouble to others.'[469]

Remembrance of Allah

Allah says in His Book:

> ☼ Therefore remember Me, I will remember you, and be thankful to Me, and do not be ungrateful to Me. (2:152)

> ☼ So when you have performed your devotions, then laud Allah as you lauded your fathers, rather a greater lauding. (2:200)

> ☼ Those who remember Allah while standing, sitting and lying on their sides. (3: 19)

> ☼ And remember your Lord much and glorify Him in the evening and the morning. (3:41)

> ☼ Those only are believers whose hearts become full of fear when Allah is mentioned. (8:2)

> ☼ Except those who believe and do good and remember Allah much. (26:227)

---

468   ibid.
469   *al-Khisaal*,I,6.

The Messenger said to Abu Dharr, 'The most noble of you in the eyes of Allah are those who make the most remembrance of Him and are the most respectful towards and fearful of Him. Remember Allah much, for truly it is a remembrance for you in heaven and a light for you on earth.'[470]

"Whoever sits in the place where he has prayed the dawn prayer, remembering Allah, until daybreak, will have a reward equal to that of performing the pilgrimage to the House of Allah, and he will be forgiven.'[471]

'If you find the meadows of paradise, then linger there.' When asked what the meadows of paradise were, he replied, 'Gatherings of remembrance of Allah.'[472]

'Whenever a group sits down to remember Allah, then a voice calls from heaven, "Stand up! For I have exchanged your wrong actions for good [ones], and I have forgiven you everything." Whenever a number of the inhabitants of the earth sit down to remember Allah, a number of angels sit down with them.'[473]

'Whenever a group of people remember Allah, angels circle around them, covering them with mercy; tranquility descends on them, and they make mention of those making remembrance of Allah amongst themselves.'[474]

'Everything a man says is counted against him, except when he is enjoining good or when he is remembering Allah.'[475]

'My Lord has ordered that my speech be remembrance, my silence reflection, and my looking an exhortation.'[476]

470	*Mishkaat al-Anwaar*, 53 & 57.
471	ibid.
472	ibid.
473	ibid.
474	ibid.
475	ibid.
476	ibid.

Commenting on the words of Allah, 'Thereupon their hearts became hardened until they were as stones or even harder' [2:74], the Messenger said, 'Beware of talking too much without remembrance of Allah, for surely too much talking without remembrance of Allah hardens the heart, and the people furthest away from Allah are those with hardened hearts.'[477]

Imam 'Ali has said, 'Increase your remembrance of Allah, for it is the best of remembrances, and desire what has been promised to those who live their lives fearing Him – for His promise is the truest of promises. Model yourselves according to your Prophet, for his is the best guidance.'[478]

And elsewhere, 'All good is contained in three things: your looking, your silence and your speech. Looking without reflection is negligence, silence without meditation is unmindfulness, and speech without remembrance is idle talk. Happiness will be theirs whose looking is a lesson, whose silence is meditation, whose speech is remembrance, who weep because of their mistakes and by whose hand people are safe from evil.'[479]

Al-Saadiq said, 'Shall I not tell you the most weighty matter which Allah has imposed on His creation? It is much remembrance of Allah. By this I do not mean simply saying *subhaan Allah* [glory be to Allah] or *al-hamdu li'Llah* [praise be to Allah], or *laa ilaaha illa'Llah* [there is no god but Allah] and *Allaahu akbar* [Allah is most great], even though these are words of remembrance; but rather remembering Allah before embarking on an action. If permitted, one goes ahead with the actions; if forbidden, then one leaves it, out of obedience to Allah.'[480]

---

477 ibid.
478 *Nahj al-Balaaghah*, IV, 712.
479 *Mishkaat al-Anwaar*, 53-57.
480 ibid.

Al-Saadiq was asked who were the noblest of creation. He said, 'Those who remember Allah the most, and those who are most knowledgeable through their obedience to Him.'[481]

'People are intolerant of three things: one's turning away from people, a man helping his brother with wealth, and making much remembrance of Allah.'[482]

Supplicatory prayer (du`aa')

Allah says in His Book:

☼ And when My servants ask you concerning Me, then surely I am very near; I answer the prayer of the suppliant when he calls on Me. (2:186)

☼ And your Lord says: Call upon Me, I will answer you. (40:60)

☼ Say: call upon Allah or call upon the Beneficent; whichever you call upon, He has the best names. (17:110)

☼ Call on your Lord humbly and secretly; surely He does not love those who exceed the limits. (7:55)

☼ And they who do not call upon another god with Allah and do not slay the soul, which Allah has forbidden. (25:73)

☼ Surely those whom you call upon besides Allah cannot create a fly, even were they all to come together [for this purpose]. (22:73)

☼ So call not on another god with Allah, lest you be of those who are punished. (26:213)

☼ Say: I only call upon my Lord, and I do not associate

---

481   ibid.
482   ibid.

anyone with Him. (79:20)

The Messenger said, 'As for prayer, it is the essence of worship.'[483]

It is related by al-Baaqir that a man asked the Messenger about the verse, 'Surely those who are too proud for My service shall soon enter hell abased' [40:60]. He said that 'service' here meant supplication, and supplicatory prayer is the best of worship. Concerning Allah's words, 'Most surely Ibrahim was forbearing, tender-hearted, oft-returning to Allah,' [11:75] he said, 'He is forbearing because of his *du`aa.*'

The Prophet was asked what was the best kind of worship, and he replied, 'There is nothing Allah likes better than that He be asked for something He possesses, and the most disliked person in the eyes of Allah is he who is proud in his worship and does not ask for what is in His possession.'[484]

Imam `Ali said, 'The most beloved action on this earth in the eyes of Allah is supplication,'[485] and Imam `Ali was a man of constant supplication.

'Supplication is the key of success and the secret of prosperity. The best kind of supplicatory prayers are those which issue from the breasts of the pure and the hearts of the pious; silent supplication is a means of salvation, and, when made with sincerity, a means of escape from the fire. Whenever anxiety overwhelms a man, then Allah is his place of refuge.'[486]

It is related on the authority of al-Saadiq that he [`Ali] recited the verse, 'Who answers the distressed one when he calls

---

483	*Qurrat al-`Uyun,* 244-246.	
484	ibid.	
485	ibid.	
486	ibid.	

upon Him and removes evil' [27:62], and was asked, 'How is it that we pray and are not answered?' He replied, 'Because you are praying to someone whom you do not know, and are asking for something which you do not understand. Necessity is the essence of religion, but the frequent prayers of those who are blind to the real nature of Allah are an indication of delusion. Whoever does not know the baseness of the self, his heart and his thoughts in relation to the power of Allah is claiming – by his demand – a kind of authority over Allah. He believes, moreover, that his demanding is true prayer; but to claim authority over Allah in this way is to be immodest with Him.'

A man came to Imam `Ali saying, 'I have prayed to Allah and I have not had my prayer answered.' 'You are saying something of Allah which cannot be true,' he replied, 'there are four requirements for supplicatory prayer: sincerity of one's heart, making an intention, knowledge of the means and equity in the matter. When you prayed, did you know of these four requirements?' When the man answered in the negative the Imam told him to learn them.[487]

Imam Zayn al-`Abideen was said to glorify Allah in five ways: 'If you say *Subhaan Allahi wa-bihamdihi* (Glory to Allah with His praise), you are raising Allah above what the polytheists say of Him; if you say *Laa ilaaha illa'Llaahu wahdahu laa sharika lahu* (There is no god but Allah, He has no associate), then you are expressing words of devotion, and no slave says them but that Allah delivers him from the fire, providing that he is neither proud nor tyrannical; whoever says *Laa hawla wa laa quwwatah illaa bi'Llaah* (There is no power and no strength except in Allah), is handing over the affair to Allah; whoever says *Astaghfiru'Llaah wa atubu ilayhi* (I seek forgiveness of Allah and I turn to Him), is neither proud nor tyrannical – the proud are those who persist

---

487   al-Ashtari,I,302.

in their wrong actions, and prefer this world to the next; and whoever says *Al-hamdu li'Llaah* (praise belongs to Allah) has given thanks to Allah for every blessing.'[488]

Al-Saadiq said to one of his companions, 'Maintain the courtesy of prayer: consider to whom you are praying, and how you pray and why you are praying; realize the vastness and might of Allah, and with your heart see that He knows what is in your innermost thoughts, and has knowledge of your heart and what is in it of truth and falsehood. Know, too, the way to your salvation and to your ruin, so that you do not call on Allah for something which contains your ruin while believing that it contains your salvation. Allah says, "And man prays for evil as he ought to pray for good, and man is ever hasty." [17:11]

Reflect about what you are asking for and why you are asking. Prayer involves your paying complete attention to the Truth, immersing your soul in witnessing the Lord, abandoning all choice, and submitting all your affairs, both spiritual and material, to Allah. If you do not fulfill the required conditions of the prayer, then do not expect an answer. Truly He knows what is secret and hidden: sometimes a man asks him for something, but He knows that his real intention is other than that declared in the prayer.

'Know that even though Allah has not obliged us to make supplications, He answers them out of His generosity if we are sincere in our calling on Him. Realize also, then, how it must be for the one who fulfils all the necessary conditions and courtesies of prayer, considering that he guarantees an answer even to someone who prays with mere sincerity.'[489]

He also said, 'So if you fulfill the conditions for prayer as I

---

488   *al-Khisaal*,I,299.
489   *Qurrat al-'Uyun*,244-246.

have mentioned, and devote your heart entirely to His face, then rejoice in one of the following things: either that He grants you what you have asked for in this world, or that He is storing up something greater than this for you, or that He is averting from you an affliction from which you would have perished, had He sent it down upon you.'[490]

The Conditions of Prayer

Whoever prays should fulfill the special conditions and courtesies, in order that Allah may answer his prayer:

He should strive to make his prayers at the 'times of excellence', namely, on the day of `Arafah, which occurs once each year; during the special month of Ramadan; on the Friday of each week; and during the hours before sunrise each night.[491]

He should pray to Allah in a state of purity, facing the direction of the Ka`bah; he should lower his voice until it is only just audible, in a state of extreme humility, respect, longing and fear. Allah says, 'Surely they used to hasten one with the other in deeds to goodness and to call upon Us, hoping and fearing and they were humble before Us' [21:90].

He should also be insistent in his prayers. Al-Saadiq said, 'A believing slave does not insist from Allah, demanding what he needs, but that He grants it to him.'[492]

He should begin the prayer with remembrance of Allah and His glorification, and should not begin with the request itself. Al-Saadiq said, 'If you require something, then glorify the Mighty, the Powerful, and laud and praise Him, in order that He may turn in forgiveness and repel the grievances of the slaves; approach Allah with yearning, and mention what

---

490   ibid.
491   ibid.
492   ibid.

you need. Surely Allah knows what the slave wants before he makes a prayer, but He likes to send him his requirements [after his demanding]; thus if you make a prayer, state what you require. [493]

He should weep when facing Allah, for it is the highest of courtesies. Imam al-Saadiq said, 'When your skin quivers and your eyes fill with tears, be careful, for you have arrived at your goal.' [494]

Prayer made in a group is better than when made alone. Al-Saadiq said: 'If my father were saddened by something he would gather together the womenfolk and children, then he would make a prayer and they would feel reassured.' [495]

His food and clothing should be lawful, and this is the most important of the conditions. The following is related from the Imam: 'Make sure what you acquire is good and by good means, and your prayer will then be answered. If a man lifts a morsel of unlawful food to his mouth, then his prayers will not be answered for forty days.' [496]

He should begin and seal the prayer by blessing the Prophet, as it has been related that blessing on the Prophet and his family are not rejected by Allah. [497]

Humility

Allah says in His Book of Revelation:

☼ Had We sent down this Qur'an on a mountain, you would certainly have seen it falling down, splitting asunder because of the fear of Allah. (59:21)

☼ Successful indeed are the believers, who are humble in

---

493 ibid.
494 ibid.
495 ibid.
496 ibid.
497 ibid.

their prayers. (23:1-2)

☼ ...being lowly before Allah, they do not take a small price for the communications of Allah. (3:199)

☼ Has not the time yet come for those who believe that their hearts should be humble for the remembrance of Allah? (57:16)

☼ They used...to call upon Us, hoping and fearing; and they were humble before Us. (21:90)

☼ And among His signs is this, that you see the earth still [humble]. (41:39)

☼ Their looks cast down, abasement shall overtake them. (68:43)

☼ Their eyes cast down, going forth from their graves as if they were scattered locusts. (54:7)

The Prophet once said, on seeing a man playing with his beard while praying, 'If that man's heart were humbled, then his limbs would certainly be humbled too. Truly those guarded are like the guardian; and thus we find in the prayer, "Oh Allah, make good the guarded and the guardian," meaning the heart and the limbs.'[498]

The Prophet gave instructions to Abu Dharr, saying, 'Surely the first thing that Allah will raise up from this nation of Muslims will be trust and humility, until you will scarcely see a humble, God-fearing man.'[499]

'O Abu Dharr, if you follow a funeral procession, then busy yourself with reflection and humility, and know that in doing so

---

498   al-'Inaathi,I,291-292.
499   al-Ashtari,II,56-59.

you will have truly joined the funeral.'[500]

It has been said that humility is submission to the Truth, and also that humility is the hearts facing the Truth.[501]

It has also been said that the humility of men of spiritual knowledge is the sudden trembling of the heart when it discovers Reality; this is related to the fear and dread mentioned by Allah in the verse, 'Those whose hearts tremble with fear when they remember Allah' [22:35] – and this takes only as long as a palm-frond takes to burn. Muhammad ibn al-Hanafiyyah says, 'Faith is firmly fixed, but certainty occurs during certain moments.[502]

Fear and turning to Allah for Forgiveness

Fear

Allah says:

> ☼ Had We sent this Qur'an on a mountain, you would certainly have seen it falling down, splitting asunder because of fear of Allah. (59:21)

> ☼ [As for] those who fear their Lord in secret, they shall surely have forgiveness and a great reward. (67:12)

> ☼ And do not fear anyone but Allah. (33:39)

> ☼ Only those of His servants who are possessed of knowledge fear Allah; surely Allah is Mighty, Forgiving. (35:28)

> ☼ We have not revealed the Qur'an to you that you may be unsuccessful. Nay, it is a reminder to him who fears. (20:2-3)

> ☼ And he who obeys Allah and His Apostle, and fears

---

500   ibid.
501   al-'Inaathi,I,291-292.
502   ibid.

Allah, and is careful of [his duty to] Him, it is those that are the achievers. (24:52)

☼ And you feared men, and Allah had a greater right that you should fear Him.(33:37)

☼ Allah is well pleased with them, and they are well pleased with Him; that is for him who fears his Lord. (98:8)

The Prophet, giving instructions to Imam ʿAli, said, 'O ʿAli, I advise you to maintain certain qualities in your character. O Allah, help him! The first quality is truthfulness: never allow lies to leave your lips. The second, scrupulousness: do not commit treachery. The third is to fear Allah as if you see Him. The fourth, weep often out of fear of Allah – with every tear He will build a thousand houses for you in paradise.'[503]

'The eyes of every man will be weeping on the Day of Resurrection, except for three kinds of men: the eyes which wept for fear of Allah, the eyes which were lowered before the things Allah has forbidden, and the eyes which stayed awake in the night, following the way of Allah.'[504]

Fear of Allah is the lamp of the heart; by it the believer observes the good and the bad in it, and the reins of knowledge restrain the self from oppression and injustice. The sign of this fear is its constant vigil in secret and in the open, and it issues only from an exceeding gentleness and a complete gnosis. In this respect Allah says, 'Only those of His servants who are possessed of knowledge fear Allah; surely Allah is Mighty, Forgiving' [35:28].[505]

---

503   al-Ashtari,I,40.
504   *al-Khisaal*,I,98.
505   al-ʿInaathi,II,1.

Turning to Him in Repentance

Allah says in His Book of Wisdom:

☼ But He turned to them [mercifully]; surely to them He is Compassionate, Merciful. (9:117)

☼ Except such as repent and believe and do good, these shall enter the garden, and they shall not be dealt with unjustly in any way. (19:60)

☼ Except those who repent and amend and hold fast to Allah and are sincere in their religion to Allah; these are with the believers. (4:146)

☼ But if they repent and keep up prayer and pay the poor-rate, they are your brethren in faith. (9:11)

☼ O You who believe! Repent to Allah with a sincere repentance. (66:8)

☼ Repentance with Allah is only for those who do evil in ignorance... and repentance is not for those who go on doing evil deeds. (4:17-18)

☼ That Allah may reward the truthful for their truth, and punish the hypocrites if He pleases or turn to them [mercifully]. (33:24)

☼ And whoever does not repent, these are they who are the unjust. (49:11)

☼ Surely Allah loves those who turn much to Him [in repentance] and He loves those who purify themselves. (2:222)

Repenting* to Him is freeing the heart of wrong actions and a returning from a distance to a proximity; in other words, stopping wrong actions immediately, and making a resolution to stop them in the future. Moreover, it is striving to understand one's deficiencies in the past.

Turning to Him is obligatory whenever wrong action is committed, and immediately after such an action. One of the conditions is that it be undertaken for the sake of Allah alone, not only for material reasons, social standing or out of fear of the ruler; a second condition is that one be full of regret, namely that the heart be pained and saddened at the wrong action. Regret is the essence of turning to Him in repentance, and the key to genuine repentance.[506]

The Messenger said, 'Regret means turning to Him in repentance, and the one who repents is beloved of Allah; and the one who turns to Him, away from his wrong action, is as one who has not committed any wrong action.'[507]

The fruit and excellence of regret is that one realizes the ugliness of one's wrong actions, the severity of punishment, the weakness of the self in withstanding the punishment, the superiority of the next world and the miserable state of this world, the proximity of death, the delight of gnosis and true spiritual dialogue and the removal of the reasons for repeating one's bad actions. The reasons for continuing a bad action are delusion, love of this world and ambition.[508]

[* It should be noted that the Arabic word, *taaba*, literally means 'to turn'; when applied to man, it comes to mean 'turn repentant', and when applied to God, it means 'turn mercifully'.]

---

506   *Qurrat al-'Uyun,* 285-286.
507   ibid.
508   ibid.

The Messenger has said, 'Allah is more delighted when a slave turns to Him than when a man finds his riding-beast and provisions after they have gone astray during a dark night.'[509]

'There is nothing more beloved to Allah than a youth who turns to Him.'[510]

'Good deeds remove bad deeds just as water removes dirt.'[511]

'Were you to make [so many] mistakes such that they reached the heavens and then you regretted them, Allah would surely turn to you.'[512]

Al-Saadiq said, 'Truly Allah has given those who turn to Him three qualities, and if but one of them had been given, all the inhabitants of the heavens and earth would have gained salvation by it.'

Allah's words, 'Surely Allah loves those who turn much to Him, and He loves those who purify themselves' [2:222], indicate that whomever He loves He will not punish. There is a similar meaning to His words, 'Those who bear the power and those around Him,' to 'That is the mighty achievement' [40:7-9], and His words, 'And those who do not call on other gods together with Allah,' to 'Allah is ever forgiving and merciful' [25:68-70].[513]

Commenting on Allah's words, 'Turn with a sincere turning.' [66:8] al-Saadiq says, 'What is meant here is a turning away from wrong action, never to return again. Allah loves those of His slaves who, having commited wrong actions, turn to Him often in repentance: if a slave turns to Him in sincerity then Allah loves him, and will cover up his faults and protect him.'[514]

---

509   ibid.
510   ibid.
511   ibid.,287-294.
512   ibid.
513   ibid.
514   ibid.

'Delay in turning to Him is self-deception, and continued procrastination is confusion; seeking an excuse not to turn to Allah is ruin. Continued repetition of one's wrong action means one feels secure from the cunning of Allah and no one feels secure from His cunning except people of loss.'[515]

'Turning to Him is obligatory for all people and in all states; no one is exempt from it at all. Allah says, "Turn to Allah, all of you" [24:31], speaking to all men. The light of one's perception also indicates the necessity of turning to Him, since the meaning of turning to Him is to return to the path which leads to worship of Allah, and to distance oneself from the way of Satan; this cannot be grasped except by a man of intellect. The faculty of intellect does not reach maturity until after bodily desires, anger, and the other reprehensible qualities which are Satan's means of deluding men, come to maturity. By this we mean that bodily desires are fully formed in childhood and youth, before the formation of the intellect which comes to perfection around the age of forty. Thus Satan's armies (i.e. sexual desires) are the first to occupy man's body, the first to gain a foothold in his heart and the first to become an intimate friend. Then the intellect, the ally of Allah, appears and begins to try to save the man from the armies of Satan: if it is weak and has not reached perfection, then the realm of the heart will be handed over to Satan; however, if it is strong and has reached maturity, then its first task is to extirpate the forces of Satan by breaking man's desires and reprehensible habits, and by returning to worship. There is no meaning to turning to Him except by returning to the path leading to Allah, and leaving one's desires.'[516]

It is not enough to remedy the excesses of one's desires and disobedience by being resolved to put a stop to them in the future; one must wipe out all

---

515   ibid.
516   ibid.

traces of them from one's past by the light of one's acts of obedience.

The Prophet said, 'Follow up a bad action with a good action and it will cancel it out.'

It is fitting that the good deed which wipes out the bad corresponds to that bad deed; thus, for example, one can make amends for listening to or going to musical entertainment by listening to the Qur'an or by attending meetings where Allah is remembered; one may make up for sitting in a mosque when in a state of ritual impurity by worshipping in it instead. This correspondence (between good and bad action) is, however, not obligatory for the Muslim.[517]

It is necessary that someone who regrets a wrong action should be filled with regret soon after committing this wrong action, and he must also remove traces of his mistakes before they build up in his heart. Should he not do this, then the wiping out of his bad action will not be accepted from him. Allah says, 'Repentance before Allah is only for those who do evil in ignorance, then turn to Allah soon' [4:17]. And this verse is made clear by another, 'Repentance is not for those who go on doing evil deeds, until when death comes to one of them, he says, "Surely now I repent" [4:18].[518]

Al-Saadiq said, 'It may be that a man commits wrong actions, and Allah will bring him to Paradise by his wrong actions.' He was asked how this would be, he replied, 'He commits wrong actions, but all the time he fears Allah and hates himself, so that Allah has mercy on him and allows him into Paradise.'[519]

---

517 ibid.
518 ibid.
519 ibid.

Different Kinds of Wrong Actions

Wrong actions involve either both the slave and his Lord, or only the rights of men over each other.

Imam ʿAli said, 'Wrong actions are of three types: those which are forgiven, those which are not forgiven and those which are committed by someone for whom we hope and fear. As for forgiven sins, Allah punishes the slave for his sins in this world, and Allah is more compassionate and generous than to punish His slave twice. Wrong actions which are not forgiven by Allah are those committed by men upon each other. Truly, when Allah appears unto His creation He will make an oath on Himself saying, "By My power and glory, no crime committed by a transgressor will I overlook." Then He will punish mankind one after the other, until no misdeed is left unpunished; and then He will send them to their reckoning.'

'As for the third kind of wrong action, Allah has hidden it from His creation and has granted the one who committed it repentance. This man then becomes fearful for his wrong action, placing hope in his Lord. We [the Ahl al-Bayt] pray for him and fear for him as he does for himself: we have hope for him and fear punishment for him.'[520]

'Wrong actions may be divided into two: minor and major. Allah says, "If you shun the great sins which you are forbidden to commit, We will do away with your small sins," and also, "Those who keep aloof from great sins and indecencies except the passing idea." The Messenger said, "We cover up for the slave between the five prayers and the weekly Friday prayers, if he has avoided major misdeeds".'[521]

When Imam al-Saadiq was asked about the major wrong

---

520 ibid.
521 ibid.

actions, he replied, 'There are seven major wrong actions for which Allah has made the fire an obligatory punishment: denying the existence of Allah, killing someone, disobedience to one's parents, living off interest while being fully aware of what one is doing, spending an orphan's wealth in an improper way, fleeing the call to war and committing adultery.'[522]

Recitation of the Qur'an

Allah says:

☼ I am commanded that I be of those who submit; and that I should recite the Qur'an. (27:91-92)

☼ And certainly We have made the Qur'an easy for remembrance, but is there anyone who will mind? (54:17)

☼ It is a Qur'an which We have revealed in portions so that you may recite it to the people. (17:106)

☼ Therefore recite what is easy of the Qur'an. (73:20)

☼ Keep up prayer from the declining of the sun until the darkness of the night and the dawn recitation; surely the dawn recitation is witnessed. (17:78)

☼ So when you recite the Qur'an, seek refuge with Allah from the accursed Shaytaan. (16:98)

☼ And when the Qur'an is recited, then listen to it and remain silent, that mercy may be shown to you. (7:204)

☼ Do they not then meditate on the Qur'an? (4:82)

---

522   *Makaarim al-Akhlaaq*, 19-21.

The Messenger said, 'Seek a cure in the Qur'an, for surely Allah says, "And a cure for what is in the breasts" [10:57].'[523]

'I have been given the longer chapters of the Qur'an in place of the Torah, the other hundred chapters in place of the Gospels, and the Faatihah in place of the Psalms. Moreover, I have been especially favored with the Mufassal* [Surah 49 – al-Hujurat – to the end] which are a protection for the rest of the Book.'[524]

'The Qur'an is guidance away from error, a making clear after blindness, a leaving of the false path and a light after darkness.'[525]

'Whoever learns the Qur'an and does not act by it, and who prefers love of the world and its beauty, will deserve the anger of Allah; he will be on a par with those Jews and Christians who threw the Book of Allah behind their backs.'[526]

'Those who make lawful what the Qur'an has forbidden do not believe in the Qur'an.'[527]

'How many a reciter of the Qur'an is being cursed by the Qur'an.'[528]

'Truly those who have learned the Qur'an by heart should be the most humble of men, openly and in secret; they should also be those who pray and fast the most, in open and in secret.'[529]

[* According to others *al-Mufassal* is the portion of the Qur'an from Surah 68 to the end. It is thus named because of its many chapter divisions.]

---

523 al-Kulayni,II,600-601.
524 ibid.
525 al-Kaashaani,246.
526 al-Haakim,II,84.
527 ibid.
528 ibid.
529 ibid.

'Surely it is a book of detailed commentary, exposition and learning.'[530]

'O Ibn Mas`ud, whenever you read the Book of Allah and you come to a verse containing an order or a prohibition, read it again carefully and examine its meaning. Do not be careless in this matter, for a prohibition indicates an end to disobedient acts, and an order indicates good and righteous acts. Truly Allah says, "Then how shall it be when We shall gather them together on a day about which there is no doubt, and every soul shall be fully paid what it has earned, and they shall not be dealt with unjustly?" [3:24].'[531]

'I shall be the first to come upon the powerful and mighty on the Day of Resurrection, together with His Book and my family. Then I will ask them, "What have you done with the Book of Allah and with [the example set by] my family?"'[532]

'The noble people of my community are the repositories of the Qur'an and those who spend their nights in worship.'[533]

'The Qur'an is a guidance from error, a light in grief, safety from destruction, a setting right after going astray, a clear description of temptation, a transmission from this world which indicates the next, and in it is a perfection of your religion.'[534]

Imam `Ali said in one of his speeches, 'Realize that this Qur'an gives advice and never deceives, it guides and never leads astray, it speaks and never lies; no one sits down to read this Qur'an but that he rises from it both decreased and increased – increased in guidance, and decreased in blindness. Know, too, that no one who has read the Qur'an is in need, and there is

---

530   ibid.,II,86.
531   ibid.,II,116.
532   *Qurrat al-`Uyun,*246.
533   *al-Khisaal,*I,7.
534   al-Haakim,II,178 (from *Tafseer al-`Ayaashi,*I,5).

no one who has not read it who is not in need. In it is a cure for the gravest of illnesses, namely denying Allah, hypocrisy, evil conduct and going astray. So call on Allah by it, face Him through your love of it, and do not ask His creation in the name of the Qur'an; the Qur'an is the means by which men face Him. Know that the Qur'an is the intercessor and mediator, the speaker and the believed: whoever makes the Qur'an his mediator on the Day of Resurrection will find intercession through it.'[535]

Imam 'Ali said, in another speech describing the Wise Book of Allah, 'Then He revealed the Book to him as a light whose lamps are inextinguishable, a lantern whose brightness cannot be concealed, a sea whose depths are unknown, a path which does not lead astray whoever is on it, a beam whose light is never dimmed, a discrimination whose proof is never destroyed, a demonstration whose foundation is unshakeable, a cure with which one need have no fear of any illness, a mine of faith and prosperity. In it are the springs of knowledge and its seas, the meadows of justice and its pools; Allah has made it as a stream to quench the thirst of the man of knowledge, a spring for the men of jurisprudence, the destination of the path of the righteous, the cure after which there is no illness. It is knowledge for him who is aware, speech for him who discourses and a ruling for him who acts as a judge.'[536]

Imam 'Ali on giving instructions to his son Muhammad ibn al-Hanafiyyah, said, 'You should read the Qur'an and act according to it: follow its commands and laws and its tolerance or prohibition of certain things. You should stand at night reciting it and read it day and night, for it is a pact between Allah and His Creation, and it is incumbent on every Muslim to examine his commitment to it every day – even if it is only to read fifty

---

535   *Nahj al-Balaaghah*, 376 & 455.
536   ibid.

verses.'[537]

It befits the reader of the Qur'an to take note of the following matters, that he may comprehend the importance and sublime nature of its words, and Allah's generosity and kindness in revealing it from the throne of His Majesty, in such a manner as to be understood by its creation. No one will dispute that man cannot penetrate its astonishing wisdom, just as with their eyes alone they cannot penetrate to the core of the sun, but rather take just enough of its rays to strengthen their sight – using it as an argument and proof in their daily lives.

The reader should magnify the glory of Allah every time he begins to read the Qur'an, and should feel the greatness of Allah in his heart, knowing that what he is reading is not the speech of man; he should know of the great danger in reading His words, for as He says, "None shall touch it save the purified ones." Even the outer cover and the pages themselves are protected from being handled, except by someone who has purified himself. Moreover the inner meanings are veiled from the heart of all but those who have cut themselves off from evil and corruption, and are illumined by a light which comes from praising and honoring Him.

The reader's heart should be awake, and he should get rid of the wanderings of mind and self by glorifying Him. Whoever glorifies Him rejoices in the words he is reading, becomes intimate with them and never forgets them. Reflection follows awareness of the heart: a man's worship is imperfect if he merely listens to the Qur'an without reflecting upon it, and Allah says of such people, 'Do they not then reflect on the Qur'an? Nay, on their hearts there are locks' [56:79].

Imam `Ali speaks in a similar way when he says, 'There is no good in worship without pondering upon its meaning, and no good in reading the Qur'an without reflection: if you are unable to reflect except by repeating the words, then repeat them.'

One should also comprehend from each verse whatever is significant

---

537   *Qurrat al-`Uyun,* 246 & 255.

therein: the Qur'an contains mention of the attributes of Allah and His workings, of His prophets and those who denied them and then perished. It contains mention of His commands and restrictions and a reminder of Paradise and the Fire.

One should realize that the reader himself is meant whenever the Qur'an addresses someone: if he hears an order or a prohibition, then he should consider himself the person being ordered or forbidden to do something; if he hears the stories of earlier generations, then he should know that it is not mere entertainment but rather a teaching by which the reader should learn and act; there is no story in the Qur'an in whose telling there is not some benefit for the Prophet and his ummah, as Allah says, 'To strengthen your heart therewith' [47:24].

The reader's heart should be influenced in different ways according to the different verses, his state fluctuating between sadness, fear, hope and trembling. However perfect his knowledge may be, fear of Allah should dominate his heart. But if constriction of his heart overcomes his appreciation of the Qur'anic verses, then he will not find forgiveness and mercy. These are not to be attained by the gnostic except under certain conditions. Thus Allah says, 'Truly I am the One Who forgives' [20:82], following this with four conditions: 'The one who turns [to Me], who has faith, does good deeds, and who keeps to the path of guidance.'

The reciter of the Qur'an should refine his spiritual state until he actually hears the Qur'an as speech from Allah, not as words coming from himself. There are three degrees of reciters: the lowest is that of the man who recites as if he is reciting humbly and devotedly before Allah. Then there is the man who witnesses in his heart that his Lord is speaking to him kindly, communicating inwardly by His generosity and goodness – such a man is in a state of modesty and reverence, attentiveness and comprehension. The highest station is that of the man who looks at neither himself nor his recitation, rather he confines his concern solely to the speaker [i.e. Allah], and reflects upon Him. This is the station of the intimate, and below it are *various degrees of negligence.*[538]

FASTING *(sawm)*

Allah says:

☼ O you who believe! Fasting is prescribed for you, as it was prescribed for those before you. (2:183)

☼ For a certain number of days; but whoever among you is sick or on a journey, then [he shall fast] a [like] number of days... So whoever does good spontaneously it is better for him, and that your fast is better for you if you did but know. (2:184)

☼ Therefore whoever of you is present in the month, he shall fast therein. (2:185)

☼ Then complete the fast till night, and have not contact with them [your wives] while you keep to the mosques. (2:187)

☼ And the almsgiving men and the almsgiving women, and the fasting men and fasting women, and the men who guard their private parts and the women who guard.... (33:35)

The Messenger has said, 'In the words of Allah, "The fast is for Me and I am its reward."'[539]

Al-Saadiq relates that the Messenger said, 'Fasting is a shield which protects [one] from the ills of this world and is a barrier against the torment of the next. If you fast, then make an intention of restraining the passions of the self, of removing

---

538   ibid.
539   ibid.,268-279.

any desire for the way of Satan, and bring yourself to the station of the contented, neither craving food nor drink, waiting expectantly every moment to be cured from the illness of wrong actions. Moreover, when you fast you should purify your inward self from any impurity, negligence or darkness which cuts you off from sincere devotion to the essence of Allah.'[540]

'Fasting is a shield against the fire. If one of you is fasting, then he should not behave in an obscene or foolish manner, and if someone challenges him or insults him, he should reply, "Truly I am fasting, truly I am fasting."'[541]

'For the person who fasts there are two moments of delight: when he breaks his fast, and when he meets his Lord. By the One Who holds the soul of Muhammad in His hand, the smell from the mouth of the person who fasts is sweeter to Allah than the scent of musk.'[542]

'The fasting person is in continual worship, even if he is sleeping in his bed, and as long as he does not slander another Muslim.'[543]

'Whoever slanders another Muslim annuls his fast and breaks his state of purity, and if he dies [in this state], then he does so deeming lawful [for himself] that which Allah has made unlawful.'[544]

It has been said that even if there were nothing in fasting but a raising of man from the baseness of the animal self to a state resembling the spiritual state of the angels, then this would be excellence and honor enough; in addition to this, however, fasting is also a shield from the fire, protecting from the heat of the passions and anger which cause the fires of hell to burn in the belly of man in this world and which appear again to him in

---

540	ibid.
541	ibid.
542	ibid.
543	ibid.
544	ibid.

the next.⁵⁴⁵

Al-Saadiq said, 'If someone fasts a day for Allah during excessive heat and is afflicted by thirst, Allah will appoint a thousand angels to wash his face and to attend to him until he breaks his fast. Then Allah will say, "How sweet is your scent and your soul! O my angels, bear witness all of you, that I have indeed forgiven him."'⁵⁴⁶

'The sleep of the person who fasts is worship, his silence is glorification, his actions are accepted and his prayers are answered.'⁵⁴⁷

'Surely lying annuls one's fast.' Al-Saadiq was then asked, 'Which one of us does not do that?' He replied, 'It is not what you are thinking, but rather the lies told concerning Allah, His Messenger and the Imams.'⁵⁴⁸

*The above hadith indicates that fasting is made void by lying, backbiting and other matters which are not usually counted by jurists as being among the things which render the fast void.*⁵⁴⁹

Al-Kaazim said, 'Take a sleep after midday, for surely Allah feeds and gives drink to the fasting man while he is sleeping.'⁵⁵⁰

'Fasting has two meanings: the first is a restraint and a leaving – this by its nature is a secret as no action is witnessed by anyone. All acts of worship are witnessed by creation and mankind, but the fast is known only to Allah, for it is action of the inward being undertaken solely for the face of Allah; and its reward is from Allah Himself.⁵⁵¹ The second is that it is a

---

545	ibid.
546	ibid.
547	ibid.
548	ibid.
549	ibid.
550	ibid.
551	ibid.

way of overcoming Satan and the means he uses – namely the desires which he made stronger through food and drink. The Messenger said, "Satan moves through man by means of his blood, so restrict his movement with hunger: desires are rich meadows of opportunity for Satan".[552]

There are three kinds of fast: the fast of the common people, the fast of the elite, and the fast of the ultra-elite. The first kind consists of restraining the stomach and the private parts from fulfilling their desires. The second is preventing one's hearing, sight, tongue, hands, legs, and the rest of the limbs from committing evil.

Al-Saadiq said, 'If you fast, then fast with your hearing, sight, feeling and your skin; and stop all actions undertaken for show or actions which harm people. You should treat the fast with respect. The Messenger once heard a woman insulting her slave-girl while fasting. The Prophet then called for food, bidding her to eat, but she replied, "I am fasting," "How can you be fasting while you insult your slave-girl?" Fasting is not abstention from food and drink alone.'[553]

The fast of the ultra-elite is the fasting of the heart from the world and worldly thoughts, and ridding it completely of everything but Allah. This fast is made void by thinking of anything other than Allah and the next world; reflection upon the world in the way demanded by the religion of Islam is provision for the next world, not for this one.[554]

To summarize, one may say that fasting kills the desires of the self and one's natural passions. In it there is a polishing of the heart and a purification of the limbs; it gives form and strength to

---

552	ibid.
553	ibid.
554	ibid.

both the inner and the outer being. It is a thankfulness for Allah's blessings; by it one learns to treat the poor well, to be humble and God-fearing. Crying out to Allah is a means of refuge in Him, which destroys excessive ambition, lightens the final reckoning and increases one's good actions.[555]

PILGRIMAGE *(hajj)*

Allah has said:

☼ And accomplish the Pilgrimage and the visit [`*umrah*] for Allah. (2:196)

☼ And Pilgrimage to the House is incumbent upon men for the sake of Allah, [upon] everyone who is able to undertake the journey to it. (3:97)

☼ And proclaim among men the Pilgrimage: they will come to you on foot and on every lean camel. (22:27)

☼ Then when you are secure, whoever profits by combining the visit [`*umrah*] with the Pilgrimage [should make] what offering is easy to obtain. (2:196)

☼ The Pilgrimage is [performed in] the well-known months... So whoever determines the performance of the Pilgrimage therein, there shall be no intercourse or fornication or quarrelling amongst one another. (2:197)

☼ They ask you concerning the new moons. Say: They are times appointed for [the benefit of] men, and [for] the Pilgrimage. (2:189)

☼ [This is] an announcement from Allah and His Apostle to the people on the day of the greater Pilgrimage. (9:3)

---

555   ibid.

The Messenger said, 'If anyone should die without having performed the Pilgrimage, then let him die as a Jew if he wishes, or as a Christian if he wishes.'[556]

Al-Saadiq said, 'Know that Allah has only made the *Hajj* obligatory and singled it out from other acts of worship, by mentioning it with His name in His words, "And Pilgrimage of the House is incumbent upon men, [upon] everyone who is able to undertake the journey to it" [3:97] – and has only prescribed a pattern of rites for His Prophet throughout the Hajj in order that it may be a means of imploring His assistance and as an indication of death, the grave, the Resurrection and standing before Him [on the final day].'[557]

He also said, 'If you wish to perform the Hajj, then devote your heart to Allah, stripping it of all preoccupations and obscuring veils and hand over all your affairs to your Creator, trusting in Him at all times whether you are in movement or at rest; submit to the destiny of what He has preordained, and take farewell of the world and its ease, as well as creation, and settle your affairs and debts with other men.'[558]

There are various sayings of the Family of the Prophet concerning Hajj:

Imam `Ali said, 'Hajj to the sanctuary of His House has been made obligatory on you. Allah has made it a sign and token of Islam and a place of safety for those who seek refuge...'[559]

Faatimah al-Zahra said, 'Allah has made faith a means of purification for you from worship of other-than-Him, and the Hajj a means of extolling your religion.'[560]

556	ibid.,276-279.
557	ibid.
558	ibid.
559	al-Haakim,I,245 *(from Nahj,*I,40).
560	ibid. *(from al-Bihaar,*vol. I,110).

Al-Saadiq said to Abaan ibn Taghlab, 'Allah has set up the Ka'bah for the religion of the people, and as a place for men to coexist with each other.'[561]

Al-Saadiq also said, 'Truly Allah has created mankind, and has ordained acts of obedience for them in its religion, and has commanded them to what contains benefit for them in this world. Thus He has made the Hajj a meeting-place for the Muslims of East and West, that they may get to know each other.'[562] And elsewhere he said, "This religion will remain for as long as the Ka'bah remains standing."[563]

Someone asked Imam al-Saadiq about a man who owed him money and whom he had not seen for a long time. He then saw him circumambulating the Ka'bah, and he asked whether he should demand his money. The Imam replied, 'No, neither greet him nor cause him concern until he has left the sacred precinct.'[564]

The secret of the excellence of the Hajj is like the secret in any kind of worship – that is, distancing oneself from desire and withdrawing from the pleasures of the senses, limiting oneself to what is absolutely necessary and devoting oneself entirely to Allah, whether in movement or at rest.[565]

Allah has blessed this ummah by making Hajj a period of pious devotion for them, and he has honored the ancient House by saying that the Hajj is for Him. He has set it up as the goal of His worshippers and has made the area around it a haram – a sanctuary of His House – thereby increasing the importance of His affair. He has made 'Arafaah the assembly-place in the courtyard of His sanctuary, and has emphasized its sanctity by prohibiting hunting and the cutting down of plants. Visitors come to it from every remote path, disheveled, covered in dust, humbled before

---

561 ibid., (from *al-Wasaa'il al-Shi'ite*, 41, 9, 14).
562 ibid.
563 ibid.
564 ibid., I, 264.
565 *Qurrat al-'Uyun*, 273-279.

the Lord of the House, submitting to His Majesty, obedient to His might — they recognize that He transcends the confines of any house, and that He is not contained by any country, thereby increasing their own servitude and slavery, and perfecting their compliance and obligation to Him.[566]

Allah has prescribed tasks for the slaves while on Hajj which are difficult for the nafs [the self and its desires] to accept, and whose meanings the intellect finds difficult to penetrate: the throwing of small stones, for example, and the repeated running between Safaa and Marwah — such actions demonstrate one's complete servitude and slavery to God, and it is evident that the nafs finds no pleasure in running to and fro, or in throwing the stones. One feels a natural aversion to performing them, and the intellect cannot grasp their meanings. The cause of one's action is a mere command, which one obeys because it is obligatory. This is in contrast to giving away one's wealth, which is an act of kindness understood by the intellect, and towards which it is attracted. Likewise, fasting means cutting off desires which are the enemies of Allah, devoting oneself to worship by leaving aside all the other preoccupations, bowing and prostrating oneself in prayer out of humility to Him — this glorification of Allah is also pleasing to the nafs. The Messenger said, 'I am truly at Your service on the Hajj as a slave and servant' and he did not say such words in prayer or other acts of worship.[567]

On leaving his own country the pilgrim should make up for any injustices on his part and should turn sincerely in repentance to Allah; he must set his heart on Him, travelling for remembrance of Him and glorification of His rites, disheveled and dusty, avoiding fine attire.[568]

When he reaches the appointed places at the beginning of the sacred month, he should remember how one leaves this world on death and moves towards the appointed places on the Day of Resurrection, and the terror and anguish which lies between two states.[569] When he puts on the ihraam (the

---

566	ibid.
567	ibid.
568	ibid.
569	ibid.

two-piece, seamless garb of the pilgrim), he should remember the shroud, and that his Lord will see him wrapped up in it: like the ihraam, the shroud is also seamless. He should also realize that saying 'I am at Your service' is a response to Allah's call, and when saying it he should be in a state which alternates between hope and fear.[570]

When he enters Makkah he should realize that he has reached the sanctuary, a place of safety, and he should hope for refuge from Allah's punishment. When he catches sight of the Ka`bah he should fill his heart with respect and awe of the House, to such a degree that it is as if he is witnessing the Lord of the House himself; and he should pray that He grant him provision just as He has granted him a visit to the house.[571]

As for the circumambulation, it is a form of prayer, so he should fill his heart with awe, fear, hope, and love, and realize that in his going round the House he resembles the angels closest to Allah as they circle around His throne. This encircling is a movement of the heart in the presence of the Lord and is not a bodily movement at all.[572]

The running between Safaa and Marwah corresponds to the frequent coming and going of the slave in the courtyard of the King as he manifests the sincerity of his service and his humility, that he be seen by his Lord with the eye of mercy.[573]

As the pilgrim stands on `Arafaah, the thronging peoples, their raised voices and various languages, should remind him of the vast plains of the Day of Resurrection, when the different nations are gathered with their prophets and Imams, each nation following its prophet and hoping for his intercession.[574]

570	ibid.
571	ibid.
572	ibid.
573	ibid.
574	ibid.

PURIFICATION OR POOR-RATE TAX
(zakaat and khums)

Zakaat

Allah says in the Qur'an:

☼ So I will ordain it [i.e. Mercy] for those who guard [against evil] and pay the poor-rate. (7:156)

☼ And keep up prayer and pay the poor-rate and whatever you send before for yourselves, you shall find it with Allah. (2:110)

☼ Surely they who keep up the prayer and pay the poor-rate, they shall have their reward from their Lord. (2:277)

☼ And those who keep up prayers and those who give the poor-rate and the believers in Allah and the Last Day, these it is to whom We will give a mighty reward. (4:162)

☼ If you keep up prayer and pay the poor-rate and believe in My apostles and assist them and offer to Allah a goodly gift, I will most certainly cover your evil deeds. (5:12)

☼ And keep up prayer and pay the poor-rate, and obey Allah and His Apostle.(9:71)

☼ And He has enjoined on me prayer and the poor-rate so long as I live. (19:31)

☼ [Woe to] those who do not give the poor-rate and they are unbelievers in the hereafter. (41:7)

The Messenger said, 'If the poor-rate is not given, the earth will not give up its wealth and blessing.'[575]

---

575   ibid.,257.

Al-Saadiq relates how the Prophet said to his companions one day, 'Wealth which has not been purified [by giving away a part of it as poor-rate] is cursed, just as the body which is not purified – even if it be only once every forty days – is cursed.' He was then asked, 'O Messenger, we are familiar with the purification of wealth, but what is the purification of the body?' He replied, 'That it will be afflicted by disease.' Then the faces of those listening changed color. When the Messenger saw this he said, 'Do you know what I meant by what I said?' They replied, 'No, O Messenger!' He said, 'That a man becomes anxious, is beset by misfortune, that he commits mistakes, that he is afflicted by illness, pricked by thorns, or the like, so that he suffers a throbbing pain in the eye.'[576]

The Messenger said, 'Everything has its means of purification, and that of the body is fasting.'[577]

Imam `Ali has said, 'Take care of faith by giving away in charity, protect your wealth by giving the poor-rate, and avert the waves of misfortune by prayer.'[578]

'Both *zakaat* and prayer have been established as a sacrifice for the people of Islam; whoever gives *zakaat* refines the self, for in it there is an expiation for wrong action, and a barrier and protection from the fire. Let him who gives neither regret nor hanker after what he gave: whoever gives other than for the good of his self, hoping for that which is better than it, is ignorant of the *sunnah*, cheated of his reward and defrauded of his action, and lasting is his sorrow.[579]

'What has been made obligatory is obligatory – carry it out

576	ibid.,267-279.
577	ibid.
578	*Nahj al-Balaaghah*,IV,691.
579	ibid.,II,364-368.

and it will take you to the Garden.'⁵⁸⁰

Al-Saadiq said, '*Zakaat* has been established as a test for the rich and a means of sustenance for the poor. If people were to give *zakaat* [as they should], not one bereft Muslim would remain in need; indeed, he would become free of need by what Allah had apportioned for him. People only become poor, in need, hungry and desperate because of the misdeeds of the rich. It is only right that Allah withhold His mercy from those who deny Allah's right over their wealth. By the One Who created the creation and distributes sustenance, wealth is never lost – at sea or on land – but as a consequence of someone having neglected *zakaat*.'[581]

'The most beloved people of Allah are those whose hands are the most generous, and the most generous people are those who pay *zakaat* from their wealth, and are not niggardly with the believers concerning their wealth and what Allah has made obligatory of it as poor-rate.'[582]

'Nothing more difficult has been imposed on this *ummah* by Allah than *zakaat*. Most perish in this matter: whoever refuses even a penny's worth of *zakaat* is neither a believer nor a Muslim. This is what is meant by Allah when He refers to the unbeliever who says, "Send me back; perhaps I may do good in that which I have left [23:99- 100]".'[583]

'Surely the one who gives *zakaat* is not praised, but rather his *zakaat* is an outward indication that his blood is to be spared and that he be called a Muslim. If he does not give it, then his prayer will not be accepted. You are also obliged to give more from your wealth than your *zakaat*.' He [al-Saadiq] was asked why this

---

580   ibid.
581   *Qurrat al-'Uyun,* 257-259.
582   ibid.
583   ibid.

was so, and he replied, 'Glory be to Allah! Have you not heard Allah's words, "And in their property was a portion due to him who begs and to him who is denied [good]?" [51:19].' He was asked what was this portion due from them. He explained, 'One should assign a specific portion of one's wealth to be given every day, every Friday, or once a month.'[584]

When al-Saadiq was asked to what extent *zakaat* was obligatory on wealth, he replied, 'For the outward letter of the law 25 parts in every 1,000, but as for the inner conscience, then one should not prefer for oneself what one's brother has more need of.'[585]

Referring to the following verses:

☼ And they give food out of love for Him to the poor and the orphan and the captive (76:8);

☼ Those who spend their property by night and by day, secretly and openly (2:274);

☼ If you give alms openly it is well, and if you hide it and give it to the poor, it is better for you (2:271),

Al-Saadiq says, 'What is mentioned here is not *zakaat*; Allah has given you this excess of wealth that you may direct it where He has directed it to be given. He has not given it to you so that you may store it up.'[586]

Allah has made zakaat obligatory on every part of your body, even on every follicle of hair and every glance. The zakaat of the eye is one's observing with deliberation and lowering the gaze before that which

---

584   ibid.
585   ibid.
586   ibid.

excites the desires and passions; the zakaat of the ears is one's listening to knowledge, wisdom, the Qur'an, and instruction and advice concerning religion (in which lies one's salvation), and by avoiding the opposite of this – namely lying, backbiting, and the like. Zakaat of the tongue is giving advice to the Muslims, awakening the negligent, repetition of Subhan Allah ('glory be to Allah') and other words of remembrance. The zakaat of the hand is spending and giving generously from that which Allah has bestowed on you, and using it to write down knowledge and matters of benefit for the Muslims concerning obedience of Allah and control of one's wrong actions. The zakaat of the legs is striving to visit spiritually developed men, gatherings or remembrance of Allah, reforming people, maintaining family ties, struggling in the path of Allah, and undertaking whatever is right for your heart and healthy for your religion.[587]

Khums

Allah mentions the *khums* in the following verse:

> ☼ And you know that whatever thing you gain, a fifth of it is for Allah and for the Apostle and for the near of kin and the orphans and the needy and the wayfarer. (8:41)

When giving instructions to the Commander of the Faithful, the Messenger said, 'O `Ali, `Abd al-Muttalib established five practices in the age of ignorance which Allah caused him to continue in the days of Islam.' He found some treasure and he gave out a fifth of it as charity. Then Allah revealed the verse: 'And know that whatever thing you gain, a fifth of it is for Allah.'[588]

Imam al-Kaazim relates on the authority of his father al-

---

587   ibid.,267-268.
588   al-Hurr,IV,386,385,356,353.

Saadiq that the Messenger said to Abu Dharr, Salmaan al-Farisi and Miqdaad ibn al-Aswad, 'Bear witness for me with the testimony of "There is no god but Allah", that `Ali ibn Abi Taalib is the successor of Muhammad and is the Commander of the Faithful, and that obedience to him is obedience to Allah, His Messenger and the Imams of his progeny; and that love of the family of the Prophet is obligatory on every believing man and woman, together with the prayer at its correct times, paying *zakaat*, and disposing of it to the right persons, and paying the *khums* – a fifth of what each man possesses – to the governor or emir of the Muslims, or to the Imams of his progeny after him. Whoever is unable to pay the fifth but can give a little of his wealth should pay it to the weak amongst the family of the Prophet, the descendants of the Imams. Whoever is unable to do this should give to their followers with whom people do not share food; and in giving out to them he should only desire it for the sake of Allah.'[589]

Imam al-`Askari relates in his Commentary – passed down from his father and grandfathers from the Commander of the Faithful – that the latter said to the Messenger, 'I have heard, O Messenger, that after you there will come a king who is harsh and powerful; he will seize the *khums* and the captives of war and sell them, but they will not be lawful for the buyer because my rightful portion is contained therein. However, I have given away my portion to whomever of my followers possesses a share in this, so that what they need for food and drink may be lawful for them, and that their offspring may benefit by it, and not be children brought up on illegal means.' The Messenger said, 'There is no one who has bettered you in your alms-giving, and even the Messenger has followed your example in this matter. I have made permissible for the followers everything they have

---

589   ibid.

gained and the sale of their portion to one of my followers; neither I nor you have permitted it to other than them.'[590]

Salim ibn Qays relates how he heard the Commander of the Faithful saying, 'It is us whom Allah means by "near of kin," mentioning them immediately after Himself and His Messenger: "Whatever Allah has stored for His Apostle from the people of the towns, it is for Allah and for His Apostle and for the near of kin and the orphans and the needy." Allah has not allowed us to take from charity. Allah has honored His Apostle and ourselves by not feeding us from the alms given by people.'

Al-Saadiq relates how, whenever the spoils were brought before the Messenger, he would take the best part for himself, divide what remained into five parts and would take one-fifth. Then he would divide the other four parts between those who had fought for it, and divide the fifth he had taken himself into a further five parts: Allah's fifth would be for himself, then he would divide the remaining four-fifths between the near of kin, the orphans, the needy and the wayfarer, each receiving his rightful share. The Imam would also take the same share as the Messenger.[591]

Al-Saadiq was asked about the meaning of the verse which mentions *khums* and he replied,' Allah's *khums* is for the Messenger, to be used in the way of Allah; the fifth of the Messenger is for his relations, the fifth of the near of kin for his kinsfolk and allies, and the fifth of the orphans for the orphans of his family. As for the fifth of the needy and the wayfarer – you are aware that we cannot accept charity and it is therefore not lawful for us – it must be given only to the needy and the wayfarer.'[592]

---

590   ibid.
591   ibid.
592   ibid.

Al-Nawfall relates on the authority of Sakuni and al-Saadiq how a man came to the Commander of the Faithful saying, 'I have acquired wealth, but concealed the fact that it has been gained both lawfully and unlawfully. I now want to turn to Allah for forgiveness, but I cannot distinguish what is lawful from what is unlawful.' The Commander of the Faithful replied, 'Give away a fifth of your wealth, for surely Allah is pleased with a fifth of anything, and the remainder is lawful and belongs to you.'[593]

Al-Ridaa wrote to al-Ma'mun saying, '*Khums* is a fifth of one's total wealth, taken at a particular time.'[594]

Sayyid al-Murtadaa relates that when the question of *khums* was raised. Imam `Ali said, 'The spoils of war (*anfaal*) belong to the guardian of the Muslim's affairs, just as they were the Messenger's before.' Al-Murtadaa comments:

Allah says, "They ask you about the anfaal, say: The anfaal are for Allah and the Apostle" [8: 1] – they asked about the anfaal so that they might take them for themselves, and so Allah replied to them in this way. Proof of this is provided in the verse, "So be careful of [your duty to] Allah and set aright matters between yourselves, and obey Allah and His Apostle if you are believers" [8:1] – meaning, obey Allah by not demanding what you have no right to. Moreover, whatever is Allah's and His Messenger's also belongs to the Imam, and the latter also has a portion of the spoils as well.

The spoils are divided into two parts, one part going to the Imam, in accordance with Allah's words in 'The Banishment' [also known as The Gathering, Surah 59]: 'Whatever Allah has restored to His Apostle from the people of the towns, it is for Allah and for the Apostle, and for the near of kin and the orphans and needy and the wayfarer' [59:7]. Here is meant the lands undisturbed by the Muslim cavalry [i.e. acquired from the

---

593 ibid.
594 al-Muhajjah al-Bayda', II,72

conquered peoples without the use of military force]. The other portion is that which is given back to them after having been seized from them in the first place. Allah says: 'I am going to place in the earth a caliph' [2:30] – for the whole earth belonged to Adam and then his elected caliphs. When the tyrants usurped the right given to them by Allah, it fell into the hands of the disbelievers, remaining in the hands of the usurpers until the Messenger Muhammad was sent by Allah. Thereupon it returned to him and his successors. Thus whatever had been seized from them they retook by the sword and this is what Allah has 'restored' to them.[595]

Al-Saadiq said, 'If a nation goes to battle without the permission of the Imam, and they obtain spoils, then all these spoils belong to the Imam; if they do battle with the Imam's permission, then the Imam takes a fifth.'[596]

STRUGGLE IN THE WAY OF ALLAH (jihaad) AND ENJOINING GOOD AND FORBIDDING EVIL (al-amr bi al-ma`ruf wa-al-nahi `an al-munkar)

Struggle in the Way of Allah

Allah says:

☼ And [as for] those who believed and fled and struggled hard in Allah's way, and those who gave shelter and helped, these, truly, are the believers. (8:74)

☼ You shall believe in Allah and His Apostle, and struggle hard in Allah's way. (61:11)

☼ Those who believe in Allah and the Last Day do not ask leave of you [to stay away] from striving hard with their wealth and their lives. (9:44)

---

595 al-Hurr,IV,370 & 369.
596 ibid.

☼ The believers are only those who believe in Allah and His Apostle, then they doubt not and struggle hard with their wealth and their lives in the way of Allah. (49:15)

☼ And whoever strives hard he strives only for his own soul; most surely Allah is Self-Sufficient, above [need of] the worlds. (29:6)

☼ They shall strive hard in Allah's way and shall not fear the censure of any censurer. (5:54)

☼ O Prophet! Strive hard against the unbelievers and the hypocrites and be unyielding to them. (4:73)

☼ Allah has made the strivers with their property and their persons to excel the withholders a [high] degree. (4:95)

☼ And most certainly We will try you until We have known those among you who exert themselves hard, and the patient, and made your case manifest. (47:31)

☼ Say: If your fathers and your sons and your brethren and your mates and your kinsfolk and property which you have acquired, and the slackness of trade which you fear and dwellings which you like, are dearer to you than Allah and His Apostle and striving in His way, then wait till Allah brings about His command. (9:24)

☼ Surely Allah arranges those who fight in His way in ranks as if they were a firm and compact wall. (61:4)

The Messenger was asked what kind of striving in Allah's way was the best. He replied, 'Speaking the truth in front of a tyrannical ruler.'[597]

Some of the companions pointed out to the Messenger that

---

597   *Mishkaat al-Anwaar*, 51.

certain of those who had gone into battle had only left with the intention of gaining booty or captives and the honor of conquest. The Messenger replied, 'Actions are according to one's intention; every man shall have what he intended. If a man left for the sake of Allah and His Messenger, then his departure was for Allah and His Messenger; but if anyone left for the sake of gaining something of this world, or to marry a woman, then his departure was for that which he had left for.'[598]

The Messenger thus clearly states in the above that each man receives from his actions only that which he desires, and obtains only that which he intends – be it of this world or the next. In the words of the Messenger, 'There is a gate in the Garden called "the Gate of those who strive in His way"; they approach garlanded with swords and find it open, and the angels greet them as they stand together in a group. If anyone should abandon striving, then Allah debases him, causing him poverty in his means of sustenance and effacing him in his religion. Surely Allah has honored my nation by the hooves of their horses and the armory of spears embedded in the ground.'[599]

'Whoever delivers the message of a warrior, it is as if he has set free a slave and has accompanied him onto the field of battle.'[600]

'The horses of the warrior will be the warrior's horses in the Garden.'[601]

'All good is in the sword and in the shade of the sword; it is only the sword which shows the true value of men. Swords are the key to the Garden and the Fire.'[602]

---

598   *Qurrat al-'Uyun,* 202.
599   al-Haakim, II, 230.
600   ibid.
601   ibid.
602   ibid.

Abu Dharr asked the Prophet, 'O Messenger, what action is most beloved of Allah?' He replied, 'Faith in Allah and striving in His way.' Abu Dharr then asked, 'What is the best kind of striving?' The Messenger replied, 'Whoever's horse is wounded in battle and its blood is shed – you should do battle for it is the monasticism of my nation.'[603]

Among the lengthy instructions the Messenger gave to Imam `Ali were the words, 'Give freely of your wealth and blood, over and above [what is demanded of you by] your religion.'[604]

The Messenger said, 'Gabriel came to me with a matter which was a cooling for my eyes and a joy to my heart. He said, "O Muhammad, whoever of your *ummah* goes to war and is hit by a sword-point falling from the sky, or the shaft of an arrow, this will be a testimony for him on the Day of Resurrection."'[605]

The Messenger said, 'There are four kinds of striving: enjoining good, forbidding evil, being strong on the battlefield and bearing hatred towards evildoers. Whoever enjoins good is increasing the power of the believers, and whoever forbids evil is putting the hypocrite to spite. Whoever is strong on the battlefield has carried out what is incumbent on him and has protected his religion, and whoever bears hatred towards evildoers has hated for Allah's sake, and Allah will get angry for his sake.'[606]

Imam `Ali said to his companions before a battle, 'Death is a tenacious pursuer – neither the man who is standing still nor the man fleeing escapes from it. Certainly the most honorable death is dying in battle. By the One Who holds me, ibn Abi Taalib, in His hand, a thousand blows of the sword would be lighter than

---

603   al-Ashtari, II, 67 & 91.
604   ibid.
605   al-Shiraazi, *Kalimat Allah*, 184.
606   *Makaarim al-Akhlaaq*, 245.

if I were to die in my bed while in a state of disobedience to Allah.'⁶⁰⁷

Talking about battle, Imam `Ali said, 'Doing battle is one of those gates of the Garden which Allah has specially opened for those He befriends; doing battle is a cloak of piety, the armor of Allah and His protective shield. Whoever abandons it out of dislike will be clothed by Allah in the robe of abasement and the coat of affliction.'⁶⁰⁸

'Faith in Allah and His Messenger and striving in His way are the highest stations of Islam'.⁶⁰⁹

'O Hakam,' Imam al-Baaqir said, 'All of us are sustained by the command of Allah.' Al-Hakam said to him, 'Are you the one who guides (*al-mahdi*)?' 'All of us should guide people to Allah,' he replied. 'Then are you the bearer of the sword and the inheritor of the sword?' asked al-Hakam. He replied, 'All of us are bearers of the sword and the inheritors of the sword.'⁶¹⁰

Al-Baaqir said to Sulayman ibn Khaalid, 'Shall I not inform you of Islam, its roots, branches and crown? Its roots are the prayers, its branches *zakaat*, and its crown is striving in His way.'⁶¹¹

Al-Saadiq said, 'If anyone is killed in the way of Allah, then Allah will ignore his wrong actions.'⁶¹²

Striving in His way is one of the obligatory duties of Islam and one of its pillars. It is a community obligation – that is, if a group of Muslims fulfils this obligation without infringing the deen in any way, then this obligation is lifted from the rest of the community; however, if no

---

607   *Nahj al-Balaaghah*,I,121 & 265.
608   ibid.
609   ibid.
610   al-Haakim,II,233 (from al-Kulayni,I,536).
611   ibid.,II,23-24.
612   ibid.,II,288.

one undertakes it, then the whole community is to blame and is liable to punishment.

Excused from battle are women, children, the elderly, the mad, the sick and anyone who is unable to fulfill the conditions of battle.[613]

Enjoining Good and Forbidding Evil

Allah says in His mighty Book:

☼ [Those who] keep up prayer and pay the poor-rate and enjoin good and forbid evil. (22:41)

☼ Surely prayer keeps [one] away from evil and indecency. (29:45)

☼ You are the best of nations raised up for [the benefit of] men; you enjoin what is right and forbid the wrong and believe in Allah. (3:110)

☼ They believe in Allah and the Last Day, and they enjoin what is right and forbid the wrong. (3:114)

☼ [He] enjoins on them good and forbids them evil, and makes lawful to them the good things. (7:157)

☼ And from among you there should be a party who invite to good and enjoin what is right and forbid the wrong. (3:104)

☼ Surely Allah enjoins the doing of justice and the doing of good [to others] and the giving to the kinsfolk, and He forbids indecency and evil and rebellion. (16:90)

☼ And [as for] the believing men and the believing women, they are guardians of each other; they enjoin good and forbid evil and keep up prayer. (9:71)

---

613 al-Tusi, *al-Nihaayah*, 289.

Al-Saadiq relates how a man from Khath`am came to the Messenger and asked him what the best thing in Islam was. 'Faith in Allah,' he replied. 'What is the next best thing?' asked the man, and the Messenger replied, 'Maintaining good relations with one's family.' 'And after this?' 'Enjoining what is good and forbidding what is evil.' The man then asked 'what acts were most hated by Allah?', and he said, 'Associating others with Allah.' 'And after this?' 'Breaking off family relations, enjoining what is evil and forbidding what is good.'[614]

The Apostle said, 'What will happen to you when your women become corrupt and your youth immoral, and you do not enjoin what is good and forbid evil?' Then he was asked, 'O Messenger, will it come to that?' 'Yes – and worse,' he replied, 'What will become of you when you regard good as evil and evil as good?'[615]

Al-Saadiq said that when the verse 'O you who believe! Save yourselves and your families from a fire'[66:6] was revealed, one of the Muslims sat down and wept, saying, 'I am incapable of saving myself: am I also responsible for my family?' The Messenger said, 'It is enough that you enjoin on them what you enjoin on yourself and that you forbid them what you forbid for yourself.'[616]

According to al-Ridaa, the Messenger used to say, 'When my *ummah* becomes indifferent to enjoining what is good and forbidding what is evil, then they are unleashing the enmity of Allah upon themselves.'[617]

The Apostle is reported to have said, 'There is good in a people so long as they are enjoining what is good, forbidding

---

614 *Mishkaat al-Anwaar*, 49-52.
615 ibid.
616 ibid.
617 ibid.

what is evil and helping one another in goodness: if they do not do these things, blessings will be taken from them and some of them will be set up as overlords over others.'[618]

Imam `Ali said, 'You must enjoin what is good and forbid what is evil – otherwise the worst of men will be placed over you, and the best of you will call out but no one will answer them.'[619]

Imam al-Saadiq was asked about enjoining good and forbidding evil and if it was obligatory for the whole *ummah*. 'No,' he replied. When he was asked why, he said, 'It is obligatory for the one who is strong, who is obeyed by people, and who can discriminate between good and evil – and not on the weak, who do not follow the path of guidance. When asked whence and whither they are going, they reply, "From the truth to falsehood." Proof of this is found in the verse, "And from among you there should be a party who invite to the good and enjoin what is right and forbid the wrong" [3:104] – meaning a particular group, not men in general. Likewise the verse, "And of Musa's people was a party who guided [people] with the truth, and thereby did they do justice," [7:159] in which "Musa's *ummah*" is not mentioned, nor is "all his people" specified; at the time his followers were from different nations. Moreover an *ummah* may be one person or more, as Allah says, 'Surely Ibrahim was an exemplary *ummah*, obedient to Allah' [16:120].[620]

Al-Saadiq also said, 'A believer who is commanded to do good and is forbidden evil will take that advice, and the ignorant person will learn and be instructed; this is not the case for him who wields a lash or a sword.'[621]

618	ibid.
619	ibid.
620	ibid.
621	ibid.

He also said, 'Whoever possesses the following three qualities may enjoin good and forbid evil: he must understand what he is enjoining, he himself must not commit the wrong actions he is forbidding, and he must be just and gentle in his enjoining and forbidding.'[622]

Al-Saadiq reported that the Commander of the Faithful said, 'Whoever leaves off condemning evil with his heart, his hand or his tongue, is a dead person among the living.'[623]

'Enjoining good and forbidding evil are two of the obligatory duties of Islam, and no one is permitted to abandon them or be negligent in their performance.'[624]

Enjoining good and forbidding evil must be performed with the heart, the tongue and the hand as long as one is able, and knows that it will not cause harm to himself or to another of the believers, either now or in the future?[625]

If he knows or firmly believes that it will cause harm to himself or to another believer, either now or in the future, then it is not obligatory upon him – only when he feels safe in all circumstances does it become obligatory.[626]

Enjoining good is undertaken by the hand or the tongue; the former means doing good actions and avoiding evil in such a way as to benefit the people: while the latter means calling people to the good by promising them praise and reward, or restraining them by warning them of the punishment.[627]

622	ibid.
623	ibid.
624	al-Nihaayah, 299.
625	ibid.
626	ibid.
627	ibid.

III: Behavior and Courtesy in Islam

HUMAN VALUES

The Struggle against the Self

The Intellect

Allah says:

> ☼ And He has made subservient for you the night and the day and the sun and the moon, and the stars are made subservient by His commandment; most surely there are signs in this for a people who ponder. (16:12)

> ☼ And [as for] these examples, We set them forth for men, and none understand them but the learned. (29:43)

> ☼ Thus do We make the communications distinct for a people who understand. (30:28)

> ☼ Had we but listened or pondered, we should not have been among the inmates of the burning fire. (67:10)

The Messenger was asked what the intellect (`aql) was and he replied, 'It is performing an action in obedience to Allah; those who obey Allah in their actions are truly the men of intellect.'[628]

The Messenger said, 'If Allah's servants wish to come close to their Creator by performing a good action, then let them do

---

[628] *Mishkaat al-Anwaar*, 248-251.

it by their intellects – this will bring them swiftly forward. We, the prophets, talk to people according to the strength of their intellects.'[629]

'All righteous actions are rewarded, and the best reward results from action issuing from the intellect.'[630]

'Nothing Allah has apportioned to his servants is better than the intellect: the man of intellect asleep is better than the foolish person awake. No messenger or prophet has been sent until his intellect had been perfected and refined above any in his *ummah*, although there may be some who go to greater lengths to try and interpret matters of legal difficulty.'[631]

'Allah has created the intellect from a stored-up light which was hidden within His fore-knowledge, and neither emissary, prophet, nor high-ranking angel has seen it. Then He has made knowledge its self, understanding its spirit, doing without (*zuhd*) its head, modesty (*hayaa'*) its eyes, wisdom its tongue, compassion (*ra'fah*) its purpose and mercy its heart. Then He filled and strengthened it with ten things: certainty, faith, truthfulness, tranquility (*sakeenah*), sincerity, kindness (*rifq*), generosity (`*ateeyyyah*), contentment (*qunu`*), submission (*tasleem*), and patience. Thereupon He spoke to it saying, "Go back," and it went back; "Come forward," and it came forward; then, 'Speak!' and it replied, "Praise belongs to Allah, Who has neither enemy nor rival, to Whom there is no likeness and no comparison and no equal, before Whose might everything is submissive and humbled." Then the Lord said, "By My power and splendor, never have I created anything finer than you, nor anything more submissive to Me than you, and nothing more noble than you; by you My unity is affirmed, by you I am worshipped, and by

---

629   ibid.
630   ibid.
631   ibid.

you I am called upon in prayer; hope is placed in Me through you, I am desired through you, by you I am feared, by you is the reward, and by you the punishment".'[632]

'Never has Allah been worshipped more than by the intellect. A man's intellect is only perfected when it possesses ten qualities [among them]: good is expected of it, and one is safe because no evil comes from it, it makes little of the great amount of goodness issuing from it, and much of the small of good issuing from the intellect of another; it does not tire of the demands of people, and is never weary of seeking knowledge.'[633]

It has been related that the Prophet said to someone, 'O 'Uwaymir, if you increase your use of the intellect you will increase your proximity to your Lord, and in this there is contentment (*ghinah*).' 'How am I to employ the intellect?' asked 'Uwaymir. He replied, 'Avoid what Allah has forbidden and carry out what He has made obligatory, that is how you will be making use of the intellect. Undertake supererogatory good actions – this will increase your intellect in this world and increase your proximity to and respect with your Lord.'[634]

'The crown of the intellect – after faith in Allah – is a harmonious relationship with people.'[635]

Al-Saadiq quotes the Messenger as having said, 'If you are told about the good position of a man, then look to see how good his intellect is, for it is according to how he has used his intellect that he will be rewarded.'[636]

'Ali relates how Gabriel came down to Adam and said, 'O Adam, I have been ordered to have you choose between three

---

632   ibid.
633   *al-Khisaal*,II,433.
634   al-'Amili,*Nur al-Ḥaqiqah*,40-41.
635   *al-Khisaal*,I,15.
636   *Mishkaat al-Anwaar*, 248-251.

things: pick one, and leave the other two.' Adam then asked Gabriel what the three things were, and Gabriel replied, 'Intellect, modesty and religion.' 'I choose intellect,' Adam replied, so Gabriel told modesty and religion to go away and leave him. However, they replied that they had been ordered to stay with intellect wherever it may be. 'So be it,' he said, and re-ascended to heaven.[637]

Imam `Ali said, 'Intellect is a cutting sword; cut away your desires with your intellect.'[638]

'A man is as his intellect.'[639]

'The intellect is the messenger of Truth.'[640]

'The intellect makes good every affair; the fruit of the intellect is correct behavior.'[641]

'The intellect is the vessel of knowledge.'[642]

'Loss of the intellect means losing life. He who has lost his intellect may only be compared with the dead.'[643]

'Man is composed of an intellect and a body; whoever lacks an intellect and is content to remain with the body has not attained perfection – he is like a man without a spirit.'[644]

Speaking to his son Hasan, Imam `Ali said, 'The greatest wealth is the intellect, and the greatest poverty is stupidity.'[645]

Al-Saadiq related how man will not find enjoyment unless he

637	ibid.
638	ibid.
639	al-Haakim,I,42.
640	ibid.
641	ibid.
642	ibid.
643	al-Kulayni,I,27.
644	ibid.
645	ibid.

possesses five things: religion, intellect, courtesy, freedom and good behavior.[646]

The Heart

Allah says:

☼ Most surely there is a reminder in this for him who has a heart. (50:37)

☼ And We put in the hearts of those who followed him [Jesus] kindness and mercy. (57:27)

☼ Then your hearts hardened after that, so that they were like rocks. (2:74)

The Apostle said, 'If a man's heart is sound, then his whole body is sound; if his heart is sick, then his whole body is sick.'[647]

'Everything possesses a source, and the source of piety is the heart of the man of gnosis.'[648]

'Every time a man commits a wrong action, a black spot appears on his heart. If he turns away and desists from wrong action and then seeks forgiveness, then his heart becomes cleansed of it; but if he persists in it, then this is the rust which Allah refers to in His Book, "Nay! Rather, what they used to do has become like rust upon their hearts." [83:14]'[649]

'The following are the hallmarks of misery: dullness of the eye, hardness of the heart, excessive zeal in seeking one's provisions, and persisting in a wrong action.'[650]

---

646   *Mishkaat al-Anwar*, 248-251.
647   *al-Khisaal*, I, 31.
648   *Mishkaat al-Anwaar*, 255-258.
649   ibid.
650   ibid.

'Four things harden the heart: repeated wrong action, excessive discourse with women, disputing with a foolish man – you argue and he argues but it never leads to any good – and keeping company with the dead.' They asked the Messenger who 'the dead' were, and he replied, 'The rich who live in ease and luxury.'[651]

'Four things corrupt the heart and cause hypocrisy to flourish just as a tree flourishes when given water: listening to foolish talk, uttering obscenities, asking favors at the door of the sultan, and longing after booty.'[652]

'There is a lump of flesh in man and if it is healthy and sound, then the rest of the body is healthy; if it is sick, then the rest of the body becomes sick. This lump of flesh is the heart.'[653]

The Commander of the Faithful said, 'Tears dry up when the heart hardens, and the heart only hardens because of the number of one's wrong actions.'[654]

'Surely the heart of man becomes weary as the body becomes weary and bored. Seek out rarities of wisdom for it, for surely the heart's nature is to pursue and retreat; when it is in pursuit, then urge it to extra acts of worship; and when it is retreating, then limit yourself to the obligatory acts.'[655]

Al-Saadiq said, 'Surely the heart is constantly murmuring in the recess of the body, demanding the Truth; if the Truth reaches it, then it finds ease and rest.' Then he recited the verse, 'Therefore [for] whomsoever Allah intends that He would guide him aright, He expands his breast for submission [Islam], and [for] whomsoever He intends that He should cause him to

---

651 ibid.
652 ibid.
653 *al-Khisaal*,I,31.
654 *Mishkaat al-Anwaar*,255-258.
655 ibid.

err, He makes his breast strait and narrow as though he were ascending upwards' [6:125].[656]

'There is nothing more corrupting to the heart than sin – it attacks the heart, persisting until it has overcome and completely overturned it.'[657]

'If you meet, then talk and take counsel with each other, for surely this brings life to the heart.'[658]

'The way to Allah is quicker through the heart than by the body; and movement of the heart is more effective than the movement of actions.'[659]

Commenting on Allah's words: 'Surely the hearing and the sight and the heart, each of these shall be questioned' [17:36], al-Saadiq said, 'The hearing will be questioned about what it has heard, the sight about what it has looked at, and the heart about what it has resolved.'[660]

Knowledge of the Self

Allah says:

☼ Do they not reflect within themselves? (30:8)

☼ We will show them Our signs in the universe and in their own souls, until it will become clear to them that it is the truth. (41:53)

☼ And in the earth there are signs for those who are sure, and in your own souls too; will you not then see? (51:20-21)

656	ibid.
657	ibid.
658	ibid.
659	ibid.
660	ibid.

The Messenger said, 'Whoever knows himself knows his Lord.'[661]

A man came to the Messenger and said, 'O Messenger of Allah, how does one arrive at knowledge of the Real?' 'By knowing oneself,' he replied.[662]

Imam `Ali said, 'Knowledge of the self is the most useful form of knowledge.'[663]

'The self's introspection is a way of caring for its improvement (*salaah*).'[664]

'He who succeeds in knowing himself has gained a mighty victory.'[665]

'The greatest form of knowledge is that a man may know himself.'[666]

'Whoever gets to know himself has arrived at the limits of gnosis and science.'[667]

'The man of knowledge is the man who knows his own capability; ignorant is the man who does not.'[668]

'The man who does not know his own capacity is doomed.'[669]

The renowned scholar Fayd al-Kaashaani said, 'The self is the essence of the spirit worlds (al-jawhar al-malakuti), which is used by the body and subjected to this service by the Lord; it is the core of a man and the reality of his awareness. This spirit essence is also called the breath — as the life

---

661	al-Haakim,I,211.
662	ibid.
663	al-Haakim,I,114.
664	ibid.
665	ibid.
666	ibid.
667	ibid.
668	*Nahj al-Balaaghah,*304,1159.
669	ibid.

of the body depends upon it; the fluctuating heart – as it changes with the movement of perceptions and thoughts; and the intellect – as it gathers knowledge and is associated with the faculty of comprehension. These four terms are also used in other senses according to the context.[670]

The self is described in different ways according to its different states: if it accepts commands and prohibitions with tranquility, and confusion and commotion depart when desires are resisted, then it is called 'the self at rest' (*al-nafs al-mutma'innah*).

Allah says, 'O soul that art at rest ! Return to your Lord, well pleased [with Him], well-pleasing [Him].' If the self or soul has not found tranquility, but tends rather towards desire and anger and is open to their influence, then it is called 'the self-accusing soul' (*al-nafs al-lawwaamah*) because it accuses its owner when he falls short in worship of his Lord. Allah says, 'Nay I swear by the Day of Resurrection; nay, I swear by the self-accusing soul' [75:1].[671]

If the self abandons its fight and submits to the demands of the desires and the tempting call of Satan, it is called, 'the commander to evil' (*al-nafs al-ammaarah bi al-su*'). Allah says through the mouth of Yusuf, 'And I do not declare myself free, most surely [man's] self is wont to command [him to do] evil, except such as my Lord has had mercy on' [12:53].[672]

Al-Kaashaani said, 'It can happen that the heart so totally submits to anger and desire that it is enslaved by them; in this way the heart dies, and its course towards eternal bliss is interrupted. It is also possible, however, that the heart submits to another flank of Allah's army: knowledge, wisdom and reflection. If the opposite happens, and the army of anger and desire conquers the self, then the man will be in great loss, which is the state of most men in this age. Their intellects have been subjected to their desires – in their

---

670	*Qurrat al-'Uyun,* 44-47.	
671	ibid.	
672	ibid.	

*very attempts to see to the needs of the desires – whereas it is the desires that should submit to the intellect whenever the latter requires this.*⁶⁷³

According to al-Kaashaani, man's disposition and character possess four qualities: the rapacious, the bestial, the satanic and the divine.[674]

If anger dominates a man, he will adopt the behavior of the beast of prey, bearing animosity and hate towards people and attacking them both physically and verbally.[675]

If desire dominates him, then he will adopt the behavior of beasts, tending to evil, greed and lust, for example.[676]

If we consider the self from its aspect of lordship – as Allah says, 'The Spirit is one of the commands of my Lord' – then we see that it demands dominion and loves mastery, power and control of all affairs; it loves to gain the monopoly of authority and to escape from the bonds of slavery and humility; it wishes to penetrate all the sciences, and demands self-knowledge, gnosis and comprehension of the realities of all things; it rejoices if people ascribe knowledge to it, and is saddened if it is described as ignorant.

The self, despite sharing their anger and desires, may be distinguished from animals by its satanic quality – it becomes evil, and resorts to trickery and cunning in order to achieve its ends; it also disguises evil actions as good ones. This behavior, and that described above, demonstrate that man combines the qualities of the pig, dog, Satan and the wise man in his character. The pig symbolizes desire, and is despicable for its greed and avidity; furthermore, it resembles human form in color, size and

---

673	ibid.
674	ibid.
675	ibid.
676	ibid.

shape.[677]

The dog symbolizes anger; the dangerous beast or the rapacious dog are not what they are merely by their shape, color or size, but rather by their innate qualities of animosity and rapaciousness. Thus in the belly of man is the rapacity and anger of the beast and the greed and lust of the pig. The pig, by its evil, calls to perversion and corruption, and the beast, by its anger, calls to oppression and vile language; Satan for its part never ceases to incite the desires of the pig and the anger of the wild beast, duping the one by the other, and to present to them in a favorable light those qualities which are an innate part of them.[678]

The wise man – which partly represents the intellect – is responsible for repelling the trickery and cunning of Satan: it reveals the duplicity of Satan by its penetrating perception and dazzling light, and destroys the evil of the pig by setting the dog over it. It crushes desire by using anger and repels the rapaciousness of the dog by setting the pig on it. Then it places all of them under its control. When this happens, then it achieves the correct balance, justice reigns in the kingdom of the body, and everything is regulated according to the Straight Path. If it fails to subject them, then they in turn subject and use it, so that it is constantly resorting to every devious means in order to meet the greed of the pig and satisfy the dog. Thus it is in a constant state of worship of the dog and the pig, and this is the state of the majority of people – their sole concern being their bellies, their sexual appetites and aggressive rivalry.[679]

If the opposite happens and the intellect subjugates them all to the power of the divine qualities, then these divine

---

677   ibid.
678   ibid.
679   ibid.

qualities take root in the heart: knowledge, wisdom, certainty, comprehension of the realities of things, gnosis of their true meanings – by means of the power of knowledge and perception – and freedom from any worship of the desires or anger. By controlling the piggish desires and containing them in correct balance, noble qualities are diffused in the heart: qualities such as purity, contentment, serenity, abstention, scrupulousness, piety, delight, graceful bearing and modesty. By controlling anger and containing it within proper limits the qualities of courage, generosity, nobility, discipline, patience, kindness, tolerance, purity, perseverance, honor and respect appear.[680]

The Faults of the Self

Allah says:

> ☼ Most surely [man's] self is wont to command [him to do] evil. (12:53)

Imam `Ali reported that the Messenger once sent out a fighting force, and when it returned he said, 'Welcome to those who have finished the lesser jihad: now there remains for them the greater jihad.' When asked what the greater jihad was, he replied, 'The jihad of the self. The best jihad consists in striving against the self contained between the two halves of one's body.'[681]

The Messenger said, 'When a man conquers his desires by his knowledge, he possesses useful knowledge; when a man lays his passions beneath his feet, then Satan will flee from his shadow.'[682]

---

680 ibid.
681 *Mishkaat al-Anwaar*, 244-246.
682 ibid.

'Whoever acts in three – or even one – of the following ways will be protected by the Throne of Allah on the day when there will be no protection but His: the man who gives of himself that which he himself asks of people; the man who does not put one foot forward or take another backwards until he knows that Allah's pleasure or displeasure lies in it; and the man who does not find fault in his Muslim brother until he has removed the fault from himself – and he will not be able to remove it until it becomes obvious to him that it is a fault; it is enough that a man be occupied with his own rather than the faults of others.'[683]

Imam `Ali is reported to have said, 'Take care not to follow the desires of the self, for surely its desires are its ruin, and to abstain from them is its cure.'[684]

'A man's knowledge of his own faults is the most useful of knowledges.'[685]

'A man's ignorance of his own faults is the worst of sins.'[686]

'The most dreadful of man's shortcomings is that he is unaware of his own faults.'[687]

'Whoever contents himself with his capabilities will find it is better for him in the long term.'[688]

'Whoever is ignorant of his own power is ignorant of all other powers.'[689]

Imam al-Sajjaad related: 'The right of your self over you is that you use it in obedience to Allah. O son of Adam! You are on the path of goodness as long as your self is counselling

---

683	ibid.
684	ibid.
685	al-Haakim,I,114.
686	ibid.
687	ibid.
688	ibid.,I,115.
689	ibid.

you, taking yourself to account is your concern, fear is your undergarment and sadness your cloak. O son of Adam, surely you will die, be raised up, stand before Allah and be questioned – so be ready to make the reply.'[690]

Al-Saadiq once said to a man, 'Surely you have been appointed as your own doctor; sickness has been explained to you, you recognize the signs of good health and you have been shown the cure – so watch how you take care of yourself.'[691]

He also said, 'Bear your self by yourself: if you do not, no one will bear it for you.'[692]

'Make your heart a companion and devote yourself to him, make your activity a father and care for him, make your self your enemy and fight it, and make what you own as a thing borrowed, and so return it.'[693]

'Restrain yourself from that which harms it before it departs from you, and strive to redeem it just as you strive after your means of subsistence – surely your self is held in pledge against your action.'[694]

'The most useful thing for a man is that he should recognize his own faults before others do.'[695]

Self-Reckoning and Vigilance over the Self

Allah says in His book of Revelation:

☼ And We will set up a just balance on the Day of Resurrection, so no soul shall be dealt with unjustly in the

---

690	*Mishkaat al-Anwaar*, 244-246.
691	ibid.
692	ibid.
693	ibid.
694	ibid.
695	ibid.

least; and though there be the weight of a grain of mustard seed, [yet] will We bring it, and sufficient are We to take account. (21:47)

☼ And the Book shall be placed, then you shall see the guilty fearing what is in it, and they will say: Ah! Woe to us! What a book is this! It does not omit a small thing or a great thing, but numbers them [all]; and what they had done they shall find present [there]; and your Lord does not deal unjustly with anyone. (18:49)

☼ On the day when Allah will raise them up all together, then inform them of what they did; Allah has recorded it while they have forgotten it, and Allah is a witness of all things. (58:6)

☼ On that day men shall come forth in sundry bodies that they may be shown their works. So he who has done an atom's weight of good shall see it, and he who has done an atom's weight of evil shall see it. (99:68)

☼ And guard yourselves against a day on which you shall be returned to Allah; then every soul shall be paid back in full what it has earned, and they shall not be dealt with unjustly. (2:281)

☼ And know that Allah knows what is in your minds, therefore beware of Him. (2:235)

The counsel of the Prophet is regarded as the highest form of accounting for the self. `Ibaadah ibn al-Saamit relates that the Prophet said to a man who had asked for his counsel, 'If you want to undertake something, then reflect upon its consequence; if it is correct, then go ahead with it, and if it is wrong, then abandon it.'

Gabriel was asked about the spiritual state called *ihsaan*. He replied, 'It consists in worshipping Allah as if you can see Him; and even if you cannot see Him, He certainly sees you.'[696]

Allah says, 'Do you not know that Allah sees?' [96:14], and 'Surely Allah ever watches over you.' [4:1].

The Messenger said. 'The intelligent person is he who sees faults in his self, and acts for the hereafter; the stupid person is he whose self pursues its desires and who thinks he is bestowing favors upon Allah.'[697]

Imam al-Zaahid Warraam al-Ashtari said:

People of understanding realize that Allah is watching over them, that they will be questioned at the time of reckoning, and that they will be made to account for everything, however small, for the way they deal with the prohibitions and the way they utilized every moment; thus they know they must always take their selves into account, watch for the truth and be in a state of obedience. Whoever takes his self to account before it is taken to account will have his account lightened for him on the Day of Resurrection, as will the reckoning of whoever prepares his answers before he is questioned. Whoever does not take his self to account and makes little of the hereafter, and follows his passions and seeks pleasures in a shameful and disgusting way, will find no relief from the terror of the Last Day – with the exception of whoever is obedient and patient, and directs his self to do that which is pleasing to his Lord. Allah says: "O you who believe! Be patient, and excel in patience, and remain vigilant, and be careful of [your duty to] Allah, that you may be successful" [3:200].[698]

True obedience is that which is accompanied by taking the self to account – it is incumbent on everyone who believes in Allah and the Last Day that he be aware of the states of his self, both when he is awake and

---

696   al-Ashtari,I,234-248.
697   ibid.
698   ibid.

active and when he is asleep or at rest; moreover, every morning he should empty his heart of all that is other than Him, before he takes up contact with those around him; he should also give advice to seven parts of his body; to his eyes, his ears, his tongue, his stomach, his genitals, his hands and his legs.[699]

'As for the eyes, he should guard them from looking at the private parts of a Muslim, or from looking at him with contempt, and use them instead to look at the wonders of Allah's creation and in reading books of wisdom and knowledge.[700]

'As for the tongue, he should control it and prevent it from talking behind people's backs, lying, backbiting, praising the self, disdaining others or criticizing, cursing or calling evil upon them; he must not speak hypocritically of them but rather allow his tongue to move only in remembrance of Allah and reminding others to do the same; he should use his tongue to teach and guide the servants of Allah to the straight path, and to make amends between disputing parties.[701]

'He should do the same with the other parts of the body. Then he should speak to his self, taking it to account for what has appeared from it and what will appear in the future [saying]: "O self, how great is your ignorance while you claim wisdom and intelligence – you amuse yourself and occupy yourself in foolish talk and [yet] you regard death as a distant thing. You realize, however, that it will come upon you suddenly; so why do you not prepare yourself for it? Have you not reflected upon the words of Allah: Their reckoning has drawn near to men, and in heedlessness are they turning aside [21:1].' [702]

'Why do you not rely on the generosity of Allah in this world? If an enemy intends to do you harm, why do you seek to trick him rather than entrusting him to the kindness and mercy of Allah? If you are overcome

---

699	ibid.
700	ibid.
701	ibid.
702	ibid.

by one of the desires of the world, why do you abandon your soul in seeking after this desire? Do you think that Allah is generous in the next world but not in this? Has He not said: "And there is not an animal in the earth but on Allah is [the responsibility for] its sustenance [11:6]?" And, talking about the next world, He says: "And that man shall have nothing but what he strives for [53:39]."'[703]

'He has entrusted you with the affairs of this world; but you do wrong by your actions and rush after it like an animal. He has entrusted the affair of the hereafter to your efforts, but you neglect it in your pride.' [704]

'Woe to the self — you must not be deceived by the life of this world, nor waste your time: the number of breaths is accounted for, so take advantage of your health before you fall ill, avail yourself of your free time before it is taken up by work; of your wealth before poverty arrives; of your youth before your old age, and your life before your death; prepare yourself for the next world. Do you not realize that whoever devotes himself to the joys of this world — given that only death is to come — will be increased in his grief when he is separated from it?' [705]

'Realize, O self, that there is no substitute for religion and faith; seek help against your self by persevering in your worship at night and by your fasting, by abstaining from company and discourse, and by maintaining family relations and caring for orphans.' [706]

'O self! Cry and weep much and seek help from the Most Merciful; make your complaints to the Most Generous, and do not tire in humbling yourself to Him; it may be that He will have mercy on your weakness; if your distress becomes great, your affliction serious and your patience reaches its limit, then there is no refuge and no security but in your Lord — so flee to Him in humility.' [707]

703	ibid.
704	ibid.
705	ibid.
706	ibid.
707	ibid.

Keeping Watch (al-muraaqabah)

Allah says:

- ☼ Surely Allah ever watches over you. (4:1)
- ☼ Does he not know that Allah sees? (96:14)
- ☼ And Allah is watchful over all things. (33:52)

In a *hadith* whose inspiration comes directly from Allah [*hadith qudsi*], the Messenger says, 'Those who intended wrong actions, but remembered My might and kept Me in sight, will reside in gardens of paradise.'[708]

The Messenger has said, 'The spiritual state of *ihsaan* is to worship Allah as if you see Him: and if you do not see Him then surely He sees you.'[709]

Imam `Ali said, 'Allah has mercy on the man whose desires have been removed from him and whose passions have been extracted from his self; for surely it is a most difficult matter to free the self – it is always inclining to obedience of its desires. Know, too, that the man of faith will not rise or retire at night but that he distrusts his own self, and he will never cease to rebuke and demand more of it.'[710]

Al-Saadiq said, 'The self of a man of faith should not be abased.' When asked what can abase a man's self, he replied, 'He does not engage in something from which he would do better to excuse himself.'[711]

Imam Warraam al-Ashtari relates how when Zulaykhah, the wife of the Pharoah, entered upon Yusuf she went and covered

---

708	*Qurrat al-`Uyun*, 304.
709	ibid.
710	*Nahj al-Balaaghah*, IV, 688.
711	*Mishkaat al-Anwaar*, 244-246.

up the face of her idol before trying to seduce him. Yusuf then said, 'What is the matter with you? Do you feel shame that lifeless objects are watching over you, while you feel no shame that the King, the Mighty One is watching over you?'[712]

A servant of Allah should always watch over his own self when he undertakes any action, supervising it closely, for if the self is neglected, then it will commit acts of oppression and corruption. He should also watch for Allah, whether he be in motion or at rest, by always remembering that He perceives one's innermost thoughts, that He is surveying his servant's action, and is a witness of what every self accomplishes.[713]

There is also the watchfulness of the Companions of the Right [ashaab al-yamin], that is, those who enter paradise: they have certainty of Allah's surveillance of their actions and thoughts, and are not perplexed by Allah's watchfulness, neither in His aspect of kindness nor in His aspect of awe-inspiring might. Their hearts remain in balance, ever heedful of Him. Their modesty before Allah dominates them; they do not take a step until they are sure of where it is leading, and they avoid doing anything which would disgrace them on the Day of Resurrection.[714]

To conclude the subject of accounting for and supervising the self, it should be mentioned that the servant of Allah knows that the intellect is like a merchant where the next world is concerned, and his partner is the self: just as the merchant imposes conditions on his partner, and then keeps watch over him, takes him to account and (if he cheats him or causes him loss to the business) he reprimands and punishes him, exacting a fine from him; so the intellect needs the same treatment in its partnership with the self.[715]

As for imposing conditions, the intellect should exact a contract and agreement from the self — every day and night — that it will not commit any wrong actions and will do nothing to anger Allah, nor will it be negligent in

---

712   *Qurrat al-'Uyun,* 303.
713   ibid., 303-305.
714   ibid.
715   ibid.

the obligatory acts of worship.

As far as the second matter is concerned – watching over the self – the intellect should keep a vigilant eye on it whenever it undertakes any action; the intellect must also be watchful of Allah, whether the self be in motion or at rest.

The third condition is that it should take the self to account at the end of the day, reckoning up its every action just as the trader reckons up with his partners at the end of the year.

Rebuke and punishment are due when the intellect finds the self has cheated it in its dealings, has committed wrong actions and has disregarded the rights granted to the intellect over the self by Allah; it should not then neglect the self, but rather punish it by imposing difficult acts of worship and making it keep to intense spiritual exercises. If the intellect were to neglect it, then it would be easily tempted to return to disobedience of Allah; indeed it would get used to this and it would be difficult to wean it away from disobedience.[716]

Controlling the Passions

The Messenger said, 'Whoever guards against the evil of his stomach, his sex and his tongue has found protection.'[717]

It was a desire of the stomach which caused Adam and Eve to be expelled from the Garden to the abode of abasement and misery: they had been forbidden to eat from the tree, but their desire overcame them and they ate, and so became aware of their nakedness.

On reflection we realize that it is from the stomach that the passions emanate, and that the stomach is a source of disease and corruption; since from it emerge the sexual desires and lust; thereafter appears the wish for wealth and position which are both means of obtaining food and satisfying

---

716   ibid.
717   ibid.,60-64.

lust. Then follows the desire for increase in wealth, position and various degrees of pride, envy and thoughtlessness; then appears the disease of showing off, base pride, rivalry in material possessions and haughtiness – all these then leading to malice, enmity and hatred, which lead a man to acts of injustice, evil and corruption.

The Messenger said, 'Never has a man filled a vessel worse than his own stomach.'[718]

He also said, 'Do not kill off your hearts by excessive eating and drinking: surely the heart, like cultivated land, will die if it is flooded with water.'[719]

'Those of you who have the best standing with Allah are those who remain longest in a state of hunger and reflection; the most hated of you are those who are always sleeping, eating and drinking.'[720]

Al-Saadiq said, 'There is nothing more harmful to the heart of a believer than overeating. It causes two things: hardness of heart and excitement of desire. Hunger is nourishment for the believer, food for the spirit and heart, and health for the body.'[721]

Surely sexual desire is the strongest and most obstinate of man's desires which the intellect has to deal with. People find this sexual craving ugly and are afraid of giving in to its demands, but the abstention of most people – whether through fear or concern for their own dignity – has no reward; whereas excellence and great reward lies in abstaining (through fear of Allah) whenever one has the opportunity to fulfill it and the means are made available, especially when the desire becomes strong. Such men have the spiritual station of 'the Truthful ones', on which matter the Messenger has said, 'Whoever feels passion but abstains,

---

718   ibid.
719   ibid.
720   ibid.
721   ibid.

hides his feelings and dies, has died as a martyr."[722]

The Prophet also said, There are seven kinds of people who will be protected by Allah on the day when there will be no protection except His: among them will be the man whom a rich and beautiful woman sought to entice, and who said, "I fear Allah, the Lord of the Worlds".[723]

If the invisible essence – the spirit – becomes weak and is overcome by the desires and passions then it exposes itself to the hatred of Allah and to clear loss.[724]

If the heart falls under the sway of piggish passions and abandons knowledge, wisdom and reflection, then this will lead to despicable qualities such as impudence, viciousness, dissipation, meanness, hypocrisy, immorality, brazenness, mockery, greed, avidity, flattery, envy and malicious pleasure. Obedience to Satan arises from submission to anger and passion, and the following qualities appear: cunning, trickery, deviousness, slyness, deception, cheating and treachery?[725]

Obedience to the dog-like quality of anger leads to rashness, depravity, pride, conceit, a raging temper, arrogance, vanity, derision, slander, scorn, disdain for creation, evil intent and tyrannical desire.[726]

Behavior becomes fixed in the self as certain actions are repeated and actions issue from the heart by means of the limbs – each limb being capable of good actions which in turn lead to laudable behavior; if wrong actions appear which in turn produce bad behavior, then the movements of the heart and limbs must be checked until good is produced, and they are prevented from doing evil. Man's most fatal enemies are the desires of the stomach, sex and tongue.[727]

722	ibid.
723	ibid.
724	ibid.
725	ibid.
726	ibid.
727	ibid.

Luqman the Wise said to his son, 'If the stomach is filled, then reflection falls asleep, wisdom falls silent and the limbs take rest from worship.'[728]

The advantages of hunger are many: clarity and vigor of the heart, delight in obedience, physical weakness which stops one from committing wrong or being negligent, a stilling of sexual desire, which becomes excessive when the stomach is full, and a driving away of sleep, which by its nature makes one languid, allows one's life to slip away and prevents one from rising in prayer at night. The Messenger said, 'The stomach is the house of disease.'[729]

The aim, however, is to achieve a balance, to find the middle way — when the Messenger found out that some of the Muslims were fasting every day and staying up in prayer the whole night, he forbade them to do this.[730]

Thus it is better that a man neither feel heavy after eating nor suffer pangs of hunger; rather, that he forget his stomach and not let it influence him. The object of eating is to keep alive and to maintain our strength for worship: excessive eating prevents one from worship and pangs of hunger engross the heart and weaken the worshipper. Allah has said, 'Eat and drink and be not extravagant,' [7:31] which summarizes everything mentioned above.[731]

As for sexual desire, it has been given to man to ensure the survival of the species. In order to understand the pleasure of sex it is to be compared with the other delights of the next world; surely if sexual pleasure were to last it would be the strongest of the bodily pleasures. In it there is a sickness, however, which may destroy one's religion and life in this world if it is not controlled and used in a balanced way.[732]

Inordinate sexual desire dominates the intellect and diverts man's

---

728	ibid.
729	ibid.
730	ibid.
731	ibid.
732	ibid.

attention to pleasure-seeking. In this way he is denied access to the path of the next world, or otherwise his observance of religion is reduced to such an extent that sexual indecency dominates; such a desire in a man who allows his fantasy to dominate his intellect leads to animal passions – the intellect is surrendered to the service of desire, whereas the intellect was created to be obeyed by, and not a means of, desire.[733]

Withdrawal from Society and Solitude

The Messenger said, 'Allah gave a revelation to the world saying: Tire out the one who serves you and serve the one who turns away from you; surely the slave who remains alone with his Lord in the depths of a dark night conversing in prayer will have a light placed in his heart by Allah. If he says: O Lord! Allah in His majesty will say: At your service, my slave, ask of Me and I will grant it to you, rely on Me and I will be enough for you. Then He will say to His angels: My angels, look at My slave who has retired in the depths of a dark night while the idle are playing and the negligent are sleeping. Bear witness that I have forgiven him.[734]

'Be scrupulous and exert yourselves; do without the world which does without you. Truly the world is treacherous, temporal and ephemeral; how many a man has been deceived by the world and thus perished; how many a man has trusted in it and has been misled, how many a man has relied on it and has then been tricked and deserted by it. Realize that before you is an awesome road and a long journey, passing over the narrow bridge spanning the Fire. A traveler must have provision: whoever has none on the journey will be ruined – and the best provision is piety.'[735]

---

733   ibid.
734   *Mishkaat al-Anwaar*,255-258.
735   ibid.

On the authority of al-Ridaa, `Ali ibn al-Husayn passed by a man who was asking Allah to give him patience. He said, 'Do not say that, rather, ask Allah for good health and gratitude for good health: surely gratitude for good health is better than patience in the face of misfortune. For the Prophet used to say in prayer: O Allah, I ask of You good health and gratitude for good health in this world and the next.'[736]

Al-Saadiq said, 'Good fortune is his (the undistinguished believer) who understands people and accompanies them in body, but his heart is not with their actions; he knows them in the outward but they do not know him in the inward.'[737]

'Withdrawal from society is worship; a man's sitting in his house brings the least blame upon him.'[738]

'A slave does not devote himself to Allah but that He has him enter the Garden.'[739]

'People of intellect choose withdrawal from society because sincere brothers and intimate friends are few; but they know that the company of the righteous and pious is better than to be solitary and withdrawn; whoever chooses to abandon the elect by his own choice must inevitably be afflicted by the worst of people.'[740]

One of the Sufi shaykhs said, 'Whoever chooses solitude rather than company should refrain from all remembrance except that of Allah, all desire except doing His command, and all demands of the self except what He has ordained.'[741]

Another shaykh said, 'Fast from this world and make your

---

736   ibid.
737   al-Khisaal,I,28.
738   Mishkaat al-Anwaar,255-258.
739   ibid.
740   al-`Inaathi,I,41-63.
741   ibid.

breaking of the fast the next; flee from people as you would flee from a lion.'[742]

One of Allah's servants was asked, 'How do you remain patient in solitude?' He replied, 'I am not alone – I sit in the presence of Allah. If I wish to converse with Him I read His Book and if I wish to converse with Him I pray.'[743]

Scholars have summarized the courtesies of withdrawal from society as follows: the first is that a person should intend to protect oneself from evil by withdrawing oneself from society; then he should seek safety from the evil of the wicked; next he should try to rid himself of his shortcomings by carrying out what is incumbent upon him; then he should concentrate all his energy on worship of Allah; then he should devote himself to knowledge, the act of remembrance , and finally reflection during his withdrawal so that he may reap the fruits of his confinement and avoid excessive contact with others which would waste his time.[744]

Purification and Cleanliness

Allah says:

> ☼ He ... sent down upon you water from the cloud that He might thereby purify you. (8:11)

> ☼ Allah only desires to keep away uncleanness from you, O people of the House! And to purify you a [thorough] purifying. (33:33)

> ☼ And purify My House for those who make the circuit and stand to pray and bow and prostrate themselves. (22:26)

> ☼ And your garments do purify. (74:4)

---

742   ibid.
743   ibid.
744   ibid.

☼ In it are men who love that they should be purified; and Allah loves those who purify themselves. (9: 108)

☼ None shall touch it save the purified ones. (56:79)

☼ So let him who pleases mind it, in honored books, exalted, purified. (80:12-14)

☼ This is more profitable and purer for you; and Allah knows while you do not know. (2:232)

The Prophet said, 'Purity is half of faith; purity is the key to prayer; the *Deen* [religion] has been founded on cleanliness; the worst servant [of Allah] is he who is filthy; let whoever obtains clothing make sure it is clean.'[745]

'Surely your mouths are pathways for the Qur'an, so keep them fresh with the tooth-stick (*miswaak*).'[746]

'Prayer after using the tooth-stick is seventy-five times better than prayer without it.'[747]

'The tooth-stick used to clean the mouth is a means of pleasing the Lord.'[748]

'Just as the tooth-stick removes impurities of food and drink from the mouth, so the defilement caused by wrong actions is removed by humility, submissiveness, rising for prayer in the night and seeking forgiveness before dawn.'[749]

'Just as a person's teeth are kept bright with the tooth-stick, so Allah has created the heart pure and clear and has made remembrance, reflection, awe and respect of Him a means of

---

745   *Qurrat al-'Uyun,* 211-216.
746   ibid.
747   ibid.
748   ibid.
749   ibid.

nourishing it; if the purity of one's heart is defiled by negligence and distress it is made clean by turning to Him and is purified by entrusting oneself to Him – in this way it returns to its original state. Thus Allah says, "Surely Allah loves those who turn much [to Him], and He loves those who purify themselves" [2:222].'[750]

The Messenger said, 'Whoever performs the ablution and mentions the name of Allah has purified the whole of his body, and the sins committed between one ablution and the next are expiated; whoever does not mention His name only purifies that part of the body reached by the water.'[751]

'The elect among the believers may be compared to water: let your purity with Allah in your acts of worship be like purity of water which Allah sends down from the sky, and which He has named "purifying" (*tahuran*). Cleanse your heart by piety and certainty of belief just as you purify your limbs with water.'[752]

Al-Saadiq said, 'If a person mentions Allah's name as he is making the minor ablution, it is as if he has made the major ablution.'

He also said, 'If you want purification and ablution then approach water: in doing so you will approach Allah's mercy, for Allah has made water the key to coming close to and conversing with Him. Just as His mercy purifies wrong actions, so physical defilement is purified by water. Allah said, "And We send down pure water from the cloud" [25:74] and "We have made of water everything living" [21:30]. Just as His mercy has brought every blessing to life in the world, so He has brought life to the hearts through acts of worship.'[753]

Al-Ridaa said, 'The command to perform the ablution exists

---

750   ibid.
751   ibid.
752   ibid.
753   ibid.

so that Allah's servant may be purified as he stands in front of the Wielder of Power in discourse with Him, obediently accomplishing what he has been ordered to do, and cleansed of impurity and defilement; in addition to this the ablution drives away laziness and sleep.'[754]

Thus we may conclude from the aforesaid that there are four degrees of purification: the physical cleaning of the body from defilement; the purification of the limbs from criminal or incorrect action and sin; the purification of the heart from discourteous or odious behavior; and the purification of the core of one's self from everything other than Allah – and this is the purification of the prophets and the truthful believers.[755]

The man of intellect should remember as he goes to relieve himself that there is an ease in ridding himself of the accumulated filth from his body. Imam al-Saadiq has said that it is called relief because one is relieved of the weight of the impurity.[756]

One should also regard the impurities of the self in the same spirit of loathing this filth. One should thus free oneself of illicit or dubious actions and overstepping the divine law; one should lock the self in the prison of fear-of-Him, patience and disregard of desires; one should open the door of humility, regret and modesty to the self and prepare to gain the final protection with Allah in the abode of eternity; and one should taste the satisfaction of pleasing Him – for surely there is no thing equal to this kind of trust in Him.[757]

---

754 ibid.
755 ibid.
756 ibid.
757   ibid.

Noble Behavior

Good Character

Allah says, addressing His Prophet:

> ☼ And most surely you are of a tremendous nature. (68:4)

The Messenger said, 'I have been sent to perfect the nobility of your character.'[758]

Al-Saadiq relates that the Messenger said, 'Allah has chosen Islam as the only *deen*, so keep good company with it.'[759]

It is related on his authority that the Messenger of Allah said, 'Most of my people who gain entry to the Garden will gain entry by having *taqwaa* (fearful awareness of Allah) and good character.'[760]

He also relates that the Messenger said, 'Good character melts sins as the sun melts ice, and bad character spoils an action just as vinegar spoils honey.'[761]

The Prophet said, 'Allah did not perfect the form of a slave or his character without feeling loath to feed his flesh to the fire.' He also said, 'O sons of `Abd al-Muttalib! You will never satisfy people by your wealth alone, so meet them with joy and a cheerful face.'[762]

The Messenger said, 'Good character is half of religion.'[763]

Al-Saadiq relates that a man came to the Prophet saying, 'O Messenger of Allah, which people have the most perfect faith?'

758	*Mishkaat al-Anwaar*, 221-224.
759	ibid.
760	ibid.
761	ibid.
762	ibid.
763	ibid.

'Those of them who have the best character,' he replied.[764]

The Prophet was asked what was the best thing a Muslim could be given, and he replied, 'Good character.'[765]

Imam `Ali said, 'The best character is perfection in manners.'[766]

He also said, 'Cheerfulness is the basis of love, tolerance the burial of faults, conciliation the concealing of shortcomings; and there is no better relative than good character.'[767]

'A Muslim's perfect knowledge of religion is his abstention from talking about that which does not concern him, his lack of hypocrisy, his patience and his good character.'[768]

According to the prophetic traditions and the example from his Household there are four key elements to good character; wisdom, courage, decency and justice. Only the Messenger achieved a perfect balance between these four, and Allah praises him saying, 'And most surely you are of a tremendous nature.' Others vary in their degree of proximity to him, but they must all take him as their model – as the Prophet himself has said: 'I have been sent to perfect the nobility of your character.'[769]

The Qur'an demonstrates this behavior in a description of the believers: 'The believers are only those who believe in Allah and His Apostle – then they doubt not and struggle hard with their wealth and their lives in the way of Allah; they are the truthful ones' [49:15].[770]

Faith in Allah and His Messenger which is free of doubt is achieved by the strength of one's certainty; it is the fruit of the intellect and the perfection of wisdom. The struggle with one's wealth is based on a generosity which

---

764	ibid.
765	*al-Khisaal*,I,30.
766	*Mishkaat al-Anwaar*,223-224.
767	ibid.
768	ibid.
769	*al-Haakim*,I,42.
770	ibid.

stems from disciplining the power of desires, and the struggle with the self is based on a courage which stems from using the power of anger within the confines of the intellect.⁷⁷¹

Allah described a particular group of people as being 'Firm of heart with the unbelievers, compassionate among themselves' [48:29], thus indicating that there is a time for firmness and a time for compassion and that perfection does not depend on firmness or compassion alone.⁷⁷²

Forbearance (hilm)

Allah says:

> ☼ But He will call you to account for what your hearts have earned, and Allah is Forgiving, Forbearing. (2:225)

> ☼ And know that Allah is Forgiving, Forbearing. (2:235)

> ☼ And certainly Allah has pardoned them; surely Allah is Forgiving, Forbearing. (3:155)

> ☼ And those who restrain their anger and pardon men; and Allah loves the virtuous. (3:134)

The Prophet said, 'The most intelligent of people are those who are strictest in matters of courtesy and friendship; and the most prudent of them are those who most restrain their anger.' He also said, 'Whoever lives in courtesy and friendship dies the death of a martyr.'⁷⁷³

A man once asked the Apostle to tell him about nobility of character. He said, 'It means that you should forgive him who has wronged you, re-establish ties with him who has broken

---

771 ibid.
772 ibid.
773 *Mishkaat al-Anwaar*, 216-218.

them off, give to him who has denied you something, and speak the truth even if it is against your own interests.'[774]

'Allah never raises a man by his ignorance, nor abases a man because of his forbearance.'[775]

'A believer will, by his forbearance and gentleness, attain the rank of the scholar who is struggling to solve problems of jurisprudence.'[776]

'There are no two things which combine better than forbearance and knowledge.'[777]

When Allah revealed the verse: 'Take to forgiveness, enjoin good and turn aside from the ignorant' [7:199], Gabriel said, 'O Muhammad, it means that you should be forbearing with the man who has insulted you, forgive the man who has wronged you and give to the man who has denied you something.'[778]

Imam `Ali said, 'Four things are most difficult to achieve: to forgive when angry, to be forbearing in the face of oppression, to be generous in times of scarcity and to be abstinent when alone.'[779]

'The first reward for a man's forbearance is that the people will support him against an ignorant person.'[780]

'If you are not forbearing, then pretend to be so; for the man who imitates a people will soon become one of them.'[781]

The Imam said to Husayn, 'O son, what is forbearance?' He

---

774 ibid.
775 ibid.
776 al-Tabarsi,*Makaarim al-Akhlaaq*,430.
777 *al-Khisaal*,I,4.
778 al-`Inaathi,II,63-76.
779 ibid.
780 al-Ashtari,II,237.
781 ibid.

replied, 'Hiding one's anger and controlling the self.'[782]

When a man from Syria assailed Imam Husayn with insults, the latter made no reply; when he had finished, Husayn said to him, 'I believe you are a stranger – you have talked foolishly. If you had asked wealth of us we would have given it you, if you had required something we would have granted it, if you were to seek guidance from us we would direct you, and if you were to ask us to carry you we would do so.'[783]

Al-Baaqir said, 'Allah loves the modest and forbearing.'[784]

Al-Ridaa said to a man from Qum, 'Fear Allah in your conduct, hold your tongue, be patient and forbearing – a man does not become a worshipper until he is forbearing.' He also said, 'One is not a man of intellect until he is forbearing.'[785]

`Ali ibn al-Husayn has said, 'I like the man whose forbearance prevails in times of anger.'[786]

Al-Baaqir said, 'Nothing is dearer to Allah than that a slave swallow his anger and return it to his heart – and this is achieved by patience or forbearance.'[787]

'Allah will increase the honor – in this world and the next – of the slave who stifles his anger.'[788]

He [al-Baaqir] also said, 'If a person stifles his anger when being in a position to give vent to it, Allah will fill his heart with tranquility and peace until the Day of Resurrection.'

782	*Mishkaat al-Anwaar*, 216-218.	
783	ibid.	
784	ibid.	
785	ibid.	
786	ibid.	
787	ibid.	
788	ibid.	

He also said, 'To swallow one's anger by being patient is the best of deeds.'[789]

According to Hamaad al-Lahhaam, a man came to al-Saadiq saying, 'A certain son of your uncle has been talking about you, mentioning all kinds of scandal and insult.' Thereupon al-Saadiq asked his slave-girl to bring him water so as to make the ablution. When he had made his ablution he returned, and al-Lahhaam said to himself that he would make prayers against the man; but al-Saadiq prayed as follows: 'O my Lord, it is my right – You have granted it to me and You are more generous and magnanimous than I; thus I ask You that you may accord me this right and do not punish him because of me.' Then he was seized with compassion and continued to pray, while al-Lahhaam looked on him in astonishment.[790]

Because of its great merit and rarity, Allah has never honored one of his Prophets more than when He describes him as forbearing. Talking of Ibrahim, He says, 'Most surely Ibrahim was very tender-hearted, forbearing' [9:114].

It has been said, 'Forbearance is not that you are forbearing after being wronged only to take revenge when you are able, but rather it is that you are forbearing after being wronged and that you forgive even when you are capable of revenge.'[791]

After the revolt of the people of Madinah against al-Mansur al-`Abbaasi, the latter consulted Imam al-Saadiq who said to him, 'Sulayman ibn Daawud was given much and he was grateful; Ayyub was tested and was patient; Yusuf was able to take revenge but forgave; and Muhammad (may peace be upon him) was tormented and he tolerated it. Allah has made you one of the offspring of those who forgive and overlook.' Al-Mansur then

---

789   al-Tabarsi,*Makaarim al-Akhlaaq*,430.
790   ibid.
791   al-`Inaathi,II,67-86.

stifled his anger and calmed down.[792]

Forgiveness (`afw)

Allah says:

> ☼ And those who restrain [their] anger and pardon men; and Allah loves the virtuous. (2:134)

> ☼ Take to forgiveness and enjoin good and turn aside from the ignorant. (7:199)

> ☼ Repel [evil] with what is best, when lo! He between whom and you was enmity would be as if he were a warm friend. (41:34)

> ☼ And if you pardon and forbear and forgive, then surely Allah is Forgiving, Merciful. (64:14)

When a man asked the Prophet to explain nobility of character to him, he replied, 'It means that you should forgive him who has wronged you, re-establish ties with him who has broken them off, give to him who has denied you something, and tell the truth even if it is against your own interests.'[793]

According to al-Saadiq, the Messenger said, 'Be forgiving, for surely forgiveness only increases a slave in nobility; be forgiving to each other, and Allah will increase you in honor.'[794]

According to the same source, the Messenger said, 'Accept the excuse of anyone who justifies himself, whether he be in the right or in the wrong; if anyone does not accept his excuse, then

---

792   ibid.
793   *Mishkaat al-Anwaar*,228-229.
794   ibid.

my intercession will not reach him.'[795]

Al-Baaqir relates that the Jewess who poisoned the sheep's flesh eaten by the Prophet was brought before the Prophet, who asked her, 'Why did you do what you did?' She replied, 'I told myself that if he is a prophet then it will not harm him, but if he is merely a tyrant, then the people will be free of him.' And according to al-Baaqir, the Messenger then forgave her.[796]

Imam `Ali said, 'If you overcome your enemy, then make your forgiveness of them gratitude for your position of strength over them.'[797]

Imam `Ali relates how he called to his servant, who did not reply. He called him three times and still he did not reply, so he then got up and saw him lying down, and he said to him, 'Can you not hear me?' 'Yes, I can,' replied the servant. 'Then why did you not answer?' 'I knew you would not punish me, so I felt lazy.' 'Go your way,' said Imam `Ali, 'you are a freed man for the sake of Allah.'[798]

Al-Sajjaad relates, 'If a man to your right insults you, then moves to your left and seeks your forgiveness, then forgive him.'[799]

Al-Baaqir said, 'There are three things in which Allah will only increase a man in honor: forgiveness of him who has wronged you, giving to him who has denied you something, and restoring relations with someone who has broken off relations with you.'[800]

He also said, 'To regret that you have forgiven is better and

---

795	ibid.
796	ibid.
797	*Nahj al-Balaaghah*, IV, 660.
798	al-Ashtari, I, 100.
799	al-Tabarsi, 228-229.
800	ibid.

easier than to regret after inflicting punishment.'[801]

Al-Saadiq said, 'Three qualities belong to the virtues of this world and the next: forgiveness of him who has wronged you, the re-establishment of relations with someone who has broken them off, and forbearance with someone who has behaved foolishly with you.'[802]

He also said, 'The courtesy of the People of the House (*Ahl al-Bayt*) consists of forgiving those who oppress us.'[803]

Modesty (hayaa')

The Messenger said, 'There are two kinds of modesty: the modesty of intellect, and the modesty of foolishness. The modesty of intellect is knowledge, but that of foolishness is ignorance.'[804]

Al-Saadiq relates that the Messenger said, 'Allah has mercy on the slave who feels true modesty in the face of his Lord, who protects his mind and what it perceives, and his stomach and its desires, who remembers the grave and decay of the corpse and remembers the place of return in the next world.'[805]

The Messenger said, 'Feel true modesty before Allah.' When asked how, he replied,' If you are able, then not one of you should retire for the night without seeing his death before him; whoever wants the next world should leave the beauty of this world.'[806]

'Faith is naked and its clothes are modesty, its adornment

801	ibid.
802	ibid.
803	al-Khisaal,I,10.
804	Mishkaat al-Anwaar,233-235.
805	ibid.
806	ibid.

is trustworthiness, its manhood is righteous action, its support scrupulousness. Everything has a foundation, and the foundation of Islam is love of the People of the House.'[807]

'Modesty is not present in anything but that it adorns it, and evil is not present in anything but that it makes it ugly. Every religion has its character, and the character of Islam is modesty.' He also said, 'Modesty is from faith, and lack of modesty is disbelief.'[808]

When a man asked the Messenger for advice, he replied, 'Be as modest before Allah as you would before a man of your people who is spiritually advanced.'[809]

Abu Sa'id al-Khudri relates that the Messenger was more modest than a young virgin.[810]

The Apostle said, 'What the people understood from the first words of prophecy was that if you feel no shame, then do as you wish.' Abu al-Tayyib said, 'These words of the Prophet do not mean that everything is licit, but rather they are a warning and a promise. In other words, do what you wish, for you will be rewarded accordingly.'[811]

Imam 'Ali said, 'People will not see the faults of a man who is clothed by modesty.'[812]

Al-Saadiq said, 'Modesty has ten parts – nine of them are in women and one is in men. When the young girl begins to menstruate, a part of her modesty disappears; when she marries, another part disappears; when she is deflowered, another; and when she gives birth, another – so that five parts remain. If she

---

807 ibid.
808 ibid.
809 ibid.
810 ibid.
811 ibid.
812 *Nahj al-Balaaghah*, IV, 706

is corrupt, then all her modesty disappears; and if she is chaste, then five parts remain with her.'[813]

Al-Saadiq also said, 'Faith and modesty are related to each other – if one of them leaves, its companion follows.'[814]

'Modesty is part of faith, and faith is part of the Garden; hypocrisy is oppression, and oppression of the Fire.'[815]

'Good cannot be hoped for from a man who does not possess three things: the man who does not fear Allah in secret, who does not repent when he grows old, and who feels no shame in wrong action.'[816]

Salmaan al-Faarisi said, 'If Allah wills that a slave should perish, he takes modesty from him; and if modesty is taken from him, then you find him fearful and feared; and if he is fearful and feared, then trust is taken from him; and if trust is taken from him, then you find him like a devil accursed, so curse him.'[817]

Virtue (ihsaan)

Allah says:

☼ If you do good, you do it for your own souls, and if you do evil, it shall be for them. (17:7)

☼ Those among them who are virtuous and guard [against evil] shall have a great reward. (3:172)

☼ ... Then they are careful [of their duty] and practice greater virtue, and Allah loves those who are virtuous. (5:93)

---

813   *Mishkaat al-Anwaar*,230-235.
814   ibid.
815   ibid.
816   ibid.
817   ibid.

☼ For those who do good in this world is goodness, and certainly the abode of the Hereafter is better. (16:30)

☼ Surely Allah enjoins the doing of justice and the practice of virtue and the giving to kinsfolk. (16:90)

☼ And those who restrain [their] anger and pardon men; and Allah loves the virtuous. (3:134)

☼ Surely the mercy of Allah is nigh to the virtuous. (7:56)

☼ Is the reward of goodness aught but goodness? (55:60)

Imam `Ali said, 'Your doing good to a virtuous man moves him to make up for it; and doing good to a vile person merely inspires him to argue about the matter.'[818]

He also said,' Do good to the one who has behaved badly towards you and reward the person who does good to you.'[819]

'Do good as you would like good to be done to you.'[820]

Humility (tawaadu`)

Allah has commanded the best of his creation, the Prophet, to be humble:

☼ And lower your wing [be kind] to whoever follows you of the believers. (26:215)

Allah describes the humble among His slaves by saying:

☼ And the servants of the Beneficent are they who walk

---

818 *Makaarim al-Akhlaaq,* 245.
819 ibid.
820 ibid.

on the earth in humility, and when the ignorant address them, they say: Peace. (25:63)

The traditions also relate that humility produces submissiveness, piety and modesty.

The Messenger said, 'Good fortune is theirs who are humble – but not through poverty, who spend of their wealth which they have gained lawfully, who have mercy on the abased and poor and who keep company with the scholars of law and the wise.'[821]

'No one humbles himself before Allah but that He raises him.'[822]

'My Lord gave me the choice of being one of two things: either to be a slave and a messenger, or a king and a prophet, and I did not know which of the two to choose. At my side was the angel Gabriel, and when I raised my head he said, "Be humble to your Lord," so I replied, "As a slave and a messenger".'[823]

'If you see the humble from among my *ummah*, then humble yourself to them; and when you see the haughty, then treat them with haughtiness – this will be humiliation and an abasement for them.'[824]

The Messenger said to some of his companions, 'Why is it that I do not see sweetness in your worship?' When they asked him what sweetness of worship was, he replied, 'Humility.'[825]

'When the slave humbles himself then Allah raises him to

821	al-Ashtari,I,200.	
822	al-Kaashaani,86.	
823	al-Ashtari,I,200-202.	
824	ibid.	
825	ibid.	

the seventh heaven.'[826]

'Humility only increases a slave in his elevation [with Allah], so be humble, that Allah may have mercy on you.'[827]

'There are three things by which Allah only increases a man in goodness: by humility Allah will only increase a man in elevation, by submission of the self He will only increase a man I honor, and by chastity He will only increase a man in wealth.'[828]

'The most troubled of people are the kings, the most hated the proud, and the most abased are those who treat others with contempt.'[829]

Imam `Ali said, 'There is nothing so esteemed as humility, and no loneliness more lonely than conceit. How strange is the pride of the haughty man, when yesterday he was a sperm and tomorrow he will be a corpse.'[830]

Al-Baaqir said, 'There are three kinds of calamity: when a man expects excessive returns for his work, forgets his wrong actions, and is delighted by his own opinion.'[831]

Imam al-Saadiq said, 'The roots of disbelief are three in number: greed, pride and envy.'[832]

Al-Saadiq said, 'It is a sign of humility that you greet those whom you meet.'[833]

When al-Hasan ibn Jaham asked al-Ridaa for a definition of humility, he replied, 'That you give to people of yourself what you would like them to give you.' 'I am at your service,' ibn Jaham

---

826	ibid.
827	ibid.
828	*Mishkaat al-Anwaar*, 224-229.
829	ibid.
830	ibid.
831	ibid.
832	ibid.
833	*al-Khisaal*, I, 11.

said, 'I would like to know where I stand with you.' He [al-Ridaa] replied, 'Look to how I stand with you.'[834]

The Lord of our ancestors, the Messenger of Allah, is a model of humility: he would visit the sick, follow funeral processions, accept the invitation of kings, ride a donkey, feed his camel, sweep the house, repair his own shoes, patch his clothes, milk the sheep and goats, eat with the servant and grind the corn with him, carry his things to the market and to his family, talk to the poor and sit with the weak, wear torn clothes and sit on the ground.[835]

The Messenger used to talk with humility and with his eyes lowered to the ground; [he used to] give time and attention to his companions and walk behind them, greet people from afar, be gentle rather than rough and scornful, make much of any blessings however small; and if he became angry he would turn away and withhold from company.[836]

Anyone of intellect must realize that abasement lies in pride, haughtiness and vanity, and that good and correctness lie in humility and submissiveness (khushu`). Allah says, 'Then get forth from this [state], for it does not befit you to behave proudly therein' [7:13].[837]

Generosity (sakhaa')

Al-Baaqir relates that the Messenger said, 'The Garden is the abode of the generous.'[838]

Al-Baaqir also relates that the Prophet said, 'Generosity is one of the trees of the Garden which reaches down to the earth – whoever takes a branch from it will be led to the Garden by

---

834   *Mishkaat al-Anwaar*,227.
835   al-`Inaathi,I,287 & 305.
836   ibid.
837   ibid.
838   *Mishkaat al-Anwaar*,229-230.

that branch.'[839]

Al-Jaabir relates that the Messenger said, 'Gabriel has related that Allah has said, "I am content with this religion for myself – only generosity and good character are fitting for it, so ennoble it with these two as far as you are able.'[840]

The Prophet said, 'Allah has fashioned his spiritual intimates with a disposition only for generosity and tolerance.'[841]

Al-Jaabir relates that when the Messenger was asked what kind of faith was the best, he replied, 'Patience and tolerance.'[842]

The Prophet said, 'There are two qualities in creation that Allah loves, and two He hates: the two He loves are good character and generosity, and the two He hates are ill-manners and miserliness.'[843]

It is related from various sources that a man asked the Prophet to show him an action which would bring him to the Garden, and he replied, 'Feeding people, giving greetings and agreeable speech will always be accompanied by [Allah's] forgiveness.'[844]

'Turn away from the sin of a generous man, for Allah will take him by the hand every time he stumbles and help him whenever he is in need.'[845]

Ibn Mas`ud relates that the Messenger said, 'Provision comes quicker to the one who feeds others than the knife to the hump of a camel; and Allah boasts to the angels about the one who feeds others.'[846]

839	ibid.
840	al-Ashtari,I,170-171.
841	ibid.
842	ibid.
843	ibid.
844	ibid.
845	ibid.
846	ibid.

The Messenger said, 'The generous man is close to Allah, close to the people, close to the Garden and far from the Fire. The miser is far from Allah, and far from people, far from the Garden and near to the Fire.'[847]

The Messenger said, 'O `Ali, be generous, for Allah loves the generous – if a man comes to you in need, then see to his need. If he has no kin, you are his kin.'[848]

A man asked Imam `Ali, as he was making the circumambulation of the Ka`bah, to tell him about generosity. 'There are two aspects to your question,' he said. 'If you are talking about creation, then the generous are those who give out as Allah has ordered them; if you are talking about the Creator, then He is the Generous One whether He gives or withholds. This is because if He gives, then He is giving you something which does not belong to you; and if He withholds, He is withholding something which is not yours.'[849]

In reply to something which his son Hasan had asked him, Imam `Ali said, 'O son, what is magnanimity?' Hasan replied, 'Spending freely in ease and hardship.'[850]

Imam `Ali said, 'Miserliness is a disgrace and cowardliness is a defect. Be liberal but not wasteful, prudent but not miserly, and do not be ashamed of giving a small amount; for to withhold is to give even less. I am amazed at the miser, who so quickly brings upon himself the very poverty from which he is fleeing, and who fails to gain the riches he desires. He lives as a poor man in this world, and he will be taken to account as a rich man in the next. Miserliness represents the sum of man's shortcomings and

---

847 ibid.
848 *Mishkaat al-Anwaar*,229-230.
849 ibid.
850 ibid.

leads one to all kinds of evil.'[851]

'Ali ibn al-Husayn said, 'The masters of this world are the generous and the masters of the next are the pious.'[852]

Imam al-Baaqir said, 'A young man who yields to sin but is generous is more beloved of Allah than an old man given to worship but who is miserly.'[853]

Al-Saadiq said, 'The generous and noble man is he who gives of his wealth for a rightful cause.'[854]

He also said, 'The generous man is the slave whose self is only too glad to relinquish something he has desired but which is forbidden, and the slave whose self is content to spend what he has obtained lawfully in obedience to Allah.'[855]

'There is no slave who behaves well and is open-handed without being surely in the protection of Allah, and among those whom He guides until they enter the Garden.'[856]

Al-Saadiq was asked for a definition of generosity. He replied,' Spend your wealth according to what Allah has made incumbent upon you, and see that it reaches the right people.'[857]

Imam al-Kaazim said, 'How ugly is the man who is asked for something and who says no.'[858]

Preference for Others (ithaar)

The Messenger said, 'Any man who experiences a desire but

851	ibid.
852	ibid.
853	ibid.
854	ibid.
855	ibid.
856	ibid.
857	ibid.
858	ibid.

keeps hold of himself will be forgiven.'[859]

'A'ishah reported that the Messenger did not eat his fill for three days in succession for as long as he lived – if he had wanted to, he would have eaten his fill, but he controlled himself.[860]

Allah praises those who prefer others to themselves when he says, 'And they prefer [them] before themselves though poverty may afflict them.' [59:9].

Generosity means spending one's wealth freely on someone else whether he is in need or not, and it is rather difficult to spend freely when one is in need for oneself. Likewise, magnanimity may consist in being liberal with others while one is in need. Miserliness can reach a point where one deprives oneself when in need; how many a miser holds fast to his money and becomes ill but will not treat himself, or desires something and is only deprived of it by fear of its price? If he found it to be free, he would surely fulfill his desire. Thus the one man is niggardly with himself even in need, the other prefers others to himself when he, too, is in need – look at the difference between these two men. Noble behavior is a gift, which Allah gives to whom He pleases. There is nothing greater in magnanimity than preferring others to oneself, for one is being generous with something which one has need of oneself.[861]

Magnanimity is a facet of noble character which emanates from Allah, and to prefer others over oneself is the highest kind of magnanimity; it was one of the qualities of the Messenger, so much so that Allah called him 'tremendous': 'And most surely you are of a tremendous nature' [68:4].

It is said that 'Abd Allah ibn Ja'far went out towards one of his friends one day, halting at a date-grove belonging to a certain tribe, where a young black slave was working. The youth brought

---

859 al-Ashtari,I,172-173.
860 ibid.
861 ibid.

out his lunch just as a dog was entering the garden; it came closer to the youth, who threw a loaf of bread to it. The dog ate it and the youth threw a second, and then a third, which were both eaten as `Abd Allah looked on. He then said, 'What do you have for lunch each day?' 'As you have seen,' replied the youth. 'Why have you preferred the dog over yourself?' asked `Abd Allah. 'This is not the dog's territory,' the young man replied, 'it has just arrived hungry from some distant place, and I disliked driving him away.' `Abd Allah asked how he would manage that day, and he replied, 'I will manage somehow.' `Abd Allah ibn Ja`far then said [to himself], 'Do I really know anything about generosity? Surely this man is more magnanimous than I.' He then bought the youth, the garden and all it contained, freed the youth from slavery and gave it all back to him.[862]

Fear and Hope (khawf wa rajaa')

Allah says:

☼ And for him who fears to stand before his Lord are two Gardens. (55:46)

☼ And as for him who fears to stand in the presence of his Lord and forbids the soul from low desires, then surely the Garden – that is the abode. (79:40-41)

☼ Then whoever follows My guidance, no fear shall come upon them, nor shall they grieve. (2:38)

☼ The angels descend upon them, saying: Fear not, nor be grieved. (41:30)

☼ And how should I fear what you have set up [with Him], while you do not fear to set up with Allah that for which He has not sent down for you any authority? (6:82)

---
862 ibid.

☼ They fear their Lord above them and do what they are commanded. (16:50)

☼ But do not fear them, and fear Me if you are believers. (3:175)

☼ Say: Surely I fear, if I disobey my Lord, the chastisement of a grievous day. (6:15)

☼ ... So remind by the Qur'an him who fears My threat. (50:45)

☼ They fear a day in which the hearts and eyes shall turn about. (24:37)

Habeeb ibn al-Harth came to the Prophet and said, 'O Messenger of Allah, I am a man who commits many wrong actions.' Then turn to Allah, O Habeeb,' he replied. 'O Messenger of Allah, I turn to Him, but then I relapse.' Then every time you commit a wrong action, turn to Him.' 'What if my wrong actions are many?' 'Allah's forgiveness is greater than your wrong actions, O Habeeb.' The Messenger also said, 'When the two recording angels transmit to Allah what they have recorded, and He sees that there is a good action on the first page and a good action on the last, then He says to all the angels, 'Bear witness that I have forgiven My slave what is recorded between the first and the last pages.'[863]

Imam `Ali said, 'Fear of Allah restrains the self and prevents it from acts of disobedience.'[864]

'The best of actions is to achieve a balance between fear and hope.'[865]

863	*Mishkaat al-Anwaar*,120.
864	al-Haakim,I,406.
865	ibid.

'Do not be of those who hope for the next world without acting [for it].'[866]

'Those who have the best opinion of Allah are those who fear Him most.'[867]

'If you are able, then increase your fear of Allah while at the same time having a good opinion of Him.'[868]

Imam al-Saadiq said, 'Fear is the guardian of hearts, and hope is the intercessor of the self. Whoever has knowledge of Allah has fear of and hope in Allah – they are the two wings of faith by which the slave flies to the pleasure of Allah.'[869]

'I am amazed at those who are afraid of four things – how is it that they do not seek refuge in four [statements in the Qur'an]? I am amazed at those who fear – why do they not seek refuge in Allah's words, 'Allah is sufficient for us and the most excellent of Guardians' [3:172]? For I have heard Allah saying after this, 'So they returned with favor from Allah and [His] grace; no evil touched them' [3:173]. I am also amazed at those who are distressed – how is it that they do not seek refuge in Allah's words, 'There is no god but Thou, glory be to Thee; surely I am of those who make themselves to suffer loss' [21:87]? For I have heard Allah say after this, 'So We responded to him and delivered him from grief, and thus do we deliver the believers' [21:88]. I am amazed at those who are the victims of deceit – why do they not take refuge in Allah's words, 'So I entrust my affair to Allah, surely Allah sees the servants' [40:44]. For I have heard Allah saying after that, 'So Allah protected him from the evil [consequences] of what they had planned' [40:45]. I am amazed by those who desire this world and its beauty – why do they not

---

866	ibid.
867	ibid.
868	ibid.
869	ibid.,I,407.

take refuge in His words, 'It is as Allah has pleased, there is no power save in Allah' [18:39]. For I have heard Allah say after this, 'If you (a humble and grateful man) consider me to be inferior to you in wealth and children, then maybe my Lord will give me what is better than your garden' [18:40].[870]

It is clear from the meaning of numerous traditions that it is obligatory upon the believer that he be always either in a state of fear or hope; this means that he fears the punishment of Allah and hopes for His bounty and mercy at the same time. This is indicated in Allah's words: 'And fear Me if you are believers' [3:174].

This fear is necessary for the believer in order that he may shield himself from Allah's punishment and protect himself from sin. This meaning is intended when Allah addresses the Messenger, 'Say: Surely I fear, if I disobey my Lord, the chastisement of a grievous day' [6:15].

The Muslim must also hope for the kindness and generosity of Allah, a hope which calls him to obedience and worship – and should not be duped by pride or lack of fear for His punishment. Allah says, 'Nor let the arch-deceiver deceive you in respect of Allah' [31:33], and He speaks to the idol-worshipper saying, 'While the arch-deceiver deceived you about Allah' [57:14].

There are five kinds of fear: there is the fear (khawf) of those who disobey, the fear (khashyah) of creation, the fear (wajal) of the humble, the fear (rahbah) of the worshipper and the fear (haybah) of the spiritually aware.

Fear (khawf) appears because of wrong actions: Allah says, 'And for him who fears to stand before his Lord are two gardens' [55:46].

Fear (khashyah) appears in man as he perceives his shortcomings. Allah says, 'Those of his servants only who are possessed of knowledge fear Allah' [35:28].

Fear (wajal) appears when one abandons worship: Allah says, 'Those

---

870   Mishkaat al-Anwaar,119.

only are believers whose hearts become full of fear when Allah is mentioned' *[8:2].*

Fear *(rahbah)* appears also because one perceives one's shortcomings. Allah says, *'They used to call to Us, hoping and fearing' [21:90].*

Fear *(haybah)* arises with the witnessing of the truth when the secrets are revealed to the men of knowledge. Allah says, *'And Allah makes you cautious of [retribution from] Himself [3:28].*[871]

Patience (sabr)

Allah says in His Book:

☼ Peace be on you, because you were constant, how excellent, then, is the sequel of the [Heavenly] abode. (13:24)

☼ But if you are patient, it will certainly be best for those who are patient. (16:126)

☼ And those who are constant, seeking the pleasure of their Lord, and keep up the prayer. (13:22)

☼ Surely I have rewarded them this day because they were patient, and they indeed are the triumphant. (23:111)

☼ And if you are patient and guard against evil, truly that is an affair of great resolve. (3:186)

☼ Seek assistance through patience and prayer; surely Allah is with the patient. (2:153)

☼ Our Lord: pour out upon us patience and cause us to die in submission. (7:126)

---

871   *al-Khisaal*,I,281-282.

The Messenger said, 'There are four kinds of patience: patience in longing, in anxiety, in doing without, and in expectation. Whoever longs for the Garden no longer thinks of desires, whoever is anxious about the Fire turns away from what is prohibited, whoever does without in this world considers trials and tribulations easy, and whoever expects death hastens to perform good deeds.'[872]

The Messenger said, 'Patience is half of faith and certainty is faith in totality. If patience were a man, he would be a generous man.'[873]

Al-Saadiq relates that the Messenger said, 'There will come a time when people will not be able to obtain dominion except by killing and showing themselves to be proud and haughty, nor will they be able to obtain wealth except by anger and miserliness, nor love except by abandoning religion and following their desire. If a person living in that age is patient in the face of hatred while he is capable of obtaining love, patient in poverty while able to obtain riches, patient in abasement, while he is capable of glory, Allah will grant him the reward of 50 righteous and trusted men.'[874]

Al-Baaqir relates that the Messenger said. 'The affair of the believer is amazing: Allah does not decree something for him but that there is good in it; if tested, he is patient, and if given something, he is thankful.'[875]

`Ali said, 'There are three kinds of patience: patience in misfortune, patience in obedience, and patience in abstaining from acts of disobedience. Whoever is patient in misfortune and bears it with composure, Allah will grant 300 grades of merit –

---

872   *Qurrat al-`Uyun,* 139.
873   ibid.
874   *Mishkaat al-Anwaar,* 19.
875   ibid., 22.

the expanse between the confines of the earth and the Throne. Whoever is steadfast in acts of obedience, Allah will grant 600 grades – the expanse between each being equal to the distance between the earth and the Throne. Whoever refrains from acts of disobedience will be granted 900 grades – the distance between each grade being equal to that between the earth and the Throne.'[876]

`Ali said, 'Faith is built on four pillars: certainty, patience, striving in the way of Allah, and justice.'[877]

Imam `Ali has said, 'Bear patiently a task whose reward is indispensable to you, and desist from an action whose punishment you are not capable of bearing; withstand the judgment of someone who has nothing but that on which to rely and take refuge in. If trials are met with contentment and patience they are a constant blessing, and if blessings are devoid of gratitude they are an ever-present trial.'[878]

He also said, 'There are two kinds of patience: patience in misfortune is a fine and beautiful thing, but better than this is patience when Allah deprives you of something. Remembrance is of two kinds also: remembrance of Allah in misfortune, and better than this is the remembrance of Allah when He deprives you of something and impedes you.'[879]

Imam al-Baaqir said, 'When my father `Ali ibn al-Husayn was close to death he drew me to his breast saying, 'O son, I give you the same advice as my father gave me, just as his father had given him the same advice: bear the truth patiently, even if it is bitter.'[880]

---

[876]   al-Ashtari,I,40.
[877]   *Qurrat al-`Uyun*,140.
[878]   al-Ashtari,I,40-41.
[879]   *Mishkaat al-Anwaar*,19-26.
[880]   ibid.

Al-Saadiq said, 'People have been commanded to adopt two qualities, but they have ceased to respect them and so their lives are futile: those two qualities are patience and restraint.'[881]

He also said, while advising Hafs ibn Ghayaath, 'O Hafs, whoever is patient is patient but a little, and whoever despairs despairs but a little. You should be patient in all your affairs – Allah has sent Muhammad and commanded him to patience and kindness saying, "And bear patiently what they say and avoid them with a becoming avoidance" [73:10] and "Repel [evil] with what is best, when lo! He between whom and you was enmity would be as if he were a warm friend, and none are made to receive it but those who are patient, and none are made to receive it but those who have a mighty, good fortune" [41:34-35].'[882]

Al-Saadiq said, 'When the believer enters his grave, prayer is on his right, *zakaat* on his left, righteous actions are spread over him and patience bends down at his side, and if he enters the place of questioning, patience says to prayer, *zakaat* and righteous actions, "Take heed of your companion: if you fail him, then I am beneath him".'[883]

Al-Saadiq said, 'Patience has the same relation to faith as the head to the body: if the head is removed the body dies, and if patience is removed faith dies.'[884]

Doing Without (zuhd)

Allah has referred to doing without in Surah al-Hadid, when He said:

☼ So that you may not grieve for what has escaped you,

881	ibid.
882	ibid.
883	ibid.
884	ibid.

nor be exultant at what He has given you (57:23).

The Messenger said, 'Doing without in this world does not mean wearing coarse clothes and eating coarse food, but rather curbing one's expectations.'[885]

A man said to the Messenger of Allah, 'Tell me of some actions I could do which would make me beloved of Allah in heaven and beloved of the people on earth.' He replied, 'Desire what is with Allah, and Allah will love you, and do without what is with the people, and they will love you.'[886]

Imam 'Ali describes how the Prophet did without: he scorned the world, belittling and despising it. He knew that Allah had withdrawn it from him out of preference for him and had given it freely to others out of disdain for them. The Prophet had turned away from the world with his heart, removed remembrance of it from his soul, and desired that its beauty disappear from his eyes, so that he might not take of its wealth nor desire from it influence and authority.'[887]

The Prophet stayed in the Qubbaa mosque one Thursday while he was fasting. When evening came he said, 'Do you have anything to drink?' A man got up and gave him a cup of milk mixed with honey; as soon as he had tasted it, the Messenger withdrew it from his mouth saying, 'These are two rich foods, and one of the two is enough. I will not drink it, but I am not forbidding it; rather, I humble myself to my Lord, for whoever humbles himself to Allah, He will raise, and whoever is haughty He will bring low; whoever lives within his means, Allah will provide for, and whoever is wasteful Allah will withhold from;

---

885   ibid.,114.
886   ibid.
887   *Nahj al-Balaaghah*,II,336.

whoever increases his remembrance of Allah, Allah will provide for.'[888]

It is related on the authority of Abu Ayyub al-Ansaari that the Messenger of Allah said to `Ali, 'Allah has given you a beauty more beloved of Allah, and longer lasting, which He has given to no other of his slaves: it is doing without in this world. Allah has given you this, [He] has not allowed the world to reach you in any way and has given you a mark by which you are recognized.'[889]

The Prophet said, 'A man will not find sweetness of faith until he is heedless of the fruits of this world.'[890]

'Longing for this world brings worry and sadness, doing without in this world brings ease to the heart and body.'[891]

Imam `Ali said, 'Contented are those who do without in this world and who are desirous of the next – they are the people who take the world as their carpet and its earth as a rug, its water as a perfume and love of the Qur'an as their distinguishing quality. There is no better kind of doing without than abstaining from forbidden things.'[892]

Referring to doing without, Imam `Ali said, 'Behavior which is most helpful in one's religion is doing without in this world.'[893]

He also said, 'Doing without in the world is restricting one's expectations, being grateful for every blessing and scrupulously avoiding everything which Allah has forbidden.'[894]

Al-Saadiq reported that Imam `Ali said, 'The mark of the person desirous of the reward of the next world is his doing

---

888   al-Haakim,II,221.
889   *Mishkaat al-Anwaar*,113-116.
890   ibid.
891   *al-Khisaal*,73.
892   *Nahj al-Balaaghah*,IV,679.
893   al-Tabarsi,113-115.
894   ibid.

without in the temporal beauty of this world.'[895]

Imam `Ali also said, 'Doing without is wealth, and scrupulousness is the Garden; the best kind of doing without is to conceal it. Doing without perfumes the body, revives hope, brings one's destiny closer and removes longing and desire. Whoever attains it exhausts himself to the utmost, and whoever does not wears himself out. There is no greater nobility than piety, no trade better than righteous action, no scrupulousness better than that of avoiding anything suspect and no better doing without than abstaining from what is forbidden. The meaning of doing without is contained in a few words: he who does not regret the past and does not rejoice in what is to come has grasped the meaning of doing without in all its aspects. O people, moderation is to restrict one's expectations, to express gratitude for blessings and to abstain from the forbidden. If you are unable to attain this, then do not allow what is forbidden to overcome your patience, and do not forget to express your thanks for any blessings you enjoy.'[896]

Imam Zayn al-`Abideen was asked about doing without in this world and he replied, 'Doing without is of ten degrees: the highest degree of doing without is the lowest degree of scrupulousness, the highest degree of scrupulousness is the lowest degree of certainty, and the highest degree of certainty is the lowest degree of contentment; indeed doing without is referred to in the book of Allah: "So that you may not grieve for what has escaped you, nor be exultant at what He has given you"[57:23].'[897]

Imam al-Saadiq was asked about doing without in the world, and he replied, 'It is to leave what is permissible for fear of being

---

895   al-Haakim,II,221.
896   *Mishkaat al-Anwaar*, 113-115.
897   ibid.

taken to account for it, and to abstain from the forbidden for fear of being punished for it.'[898]

Al-Saadiq said, 'Doing without in the world does not mean getting rid of one's wealth, nor making forbidden what is permissible; rather, doing without in the world means that you are less certain of that which is in your own hand than of what is in the hand of Allah.'[899]

He also said, 'If a person does without in the world, Allah will plant wisdom firmly in his heart, and by it will give expression of his tongue, will make him realize the shortcomings of the world, its illness and its cure, and will bring him safely from the world to the realm of peace.'[900]

'If Allah wishes good for a slave He will cause him to do without in this world, will make him respectful and knowledgeable of the laws, and will make him realize his own faults. Whoever is given this has been given the good of this world and the next.'[901]

Doing without basically means a lack of desire:-whoever does without something has not desired that thing. This meaning is made clear in the Book of Allah when He talks about the brothers of Yusuf: 'And they sold him for a small price, a few pieces of silver, and they showed no desire for him (wa kaanu fihi min al-zaahideen)' [12:20]. Allah describes them as having no desire because they wanted to turn the attention of their father to themselves – and this they preferred over their brother, and so they sold him and had no desire for him.

When considered in its specific sense, doing without refers to a state of mind which belittles the world and the ephemeral things contained therein, and prevents one from seeking or desiring them. Thus it may be that the man of immense wealth does without and the poor man who possesses nothing is

---

898	ibid.
899	ibid.
900	ibid.
901	ibid.

full of desire; it is this that is referred to by the person who said, 'The man who does without is not he who possesses nothing but rather the man who is possessed by nothing.[902]

What causes one to turn to the way of doing without — apart from nobility of character — is the penetrating insight of the intellect, which reveals the inferiority of the world and its many shortcomings. This insight teaches one that the world merits only scorn, and that one should live abstemiously, pleasing Allah rather than the world.[903]

The way of doing without is perfected only by taking on certain qualities: the cleansing of the self from worldly greed, purification of the heart from its dirt and squalor, intimacy with remembrance of Allah, and love of Allah. Cleansing of the self and purification of the heart may be attained only by abstaining from the demands of the passions, and intimacy and love are perfected only by increasing remembrance and being in a constant state of reflection.[904]

Good Actions towards Others

Allah says in His Book of Wisdom:

☼ On the day that every soul shall find present what it has done of good. (3:30)

☼ Whoever does good, whether male or female, and is a believer, We will most certainly make him live a happy life. (16:97)

☼ Allah has promised to those who believe and do good deeds [that] they shall have forgiveness and a mighty reward. (5:9)

☼ And [as for] those who believe and do good deeds, We will make them enter Gardens. (4:57)

---

902 al-`Amili, *Nur al-Ḥaqiqah*, 121.
903 ibid.
904 al-`Inaathi, I, 116.

☼ Those who do evil shall not be rewarded [for] aught except what they did. (28:84)

The Messenger said, 'There is much good, but those who do good are few.'[905]

Al-Baaqir relates how a man came to the Messenger and said, 'Teach me, O Messenger of Allah!' He replied, 'Renounce what is in the hands of others, for this is real wealth. If you intend to undertake something, then ponder on the consequences – if there is good and integrity in it, then go ahead, and if there is error, then abandon it.'[906]

Al-Saadiq tells how the Messenger said, 'The intention of a believer is better than his action, and the intention of the evil-doer is worse than his action – and everyone who acts does so according to his intention.'[907]

Al-Saadiq also quotes the Messenger as saying 'Whoever takes care in making his ablution, performs his prayer well, pays the *zakaat* from his wealth, restrains his anger, controls his tongue, seeks forgiveness for his wrong actions and shows good will towards the household of the Prophet, has perfected true faith, and the doors of the Garden are open for him.'[908]

Imam `Ali said, 'Speak words of goodness and you will be known for your goodness; do good, and you will be among the people of goodness.'[909]

Abu Basir said that al-Saadiq told him this, 'O Abu Muhammad, be scrupulous, strive hard, speak truthfully, guard

---

905   al-Khisaal,I,30.
906   Mishkaat al-Anwaar,144-147.
907   ibid.
908   ibid.
909   ibid.

whatever is entrusted to you, be good company for whoever keeps your company and stay long in prostration, for it is the practice of those before you."[910]

`Abd Allah ibn Ziyaad tells the following, 'We greeted al-Saadiq in Mina and I said to him, "O son of the Messenger of Allah, we are a people who are going through hard times and are unable to be in your presence as often as we would wish; so give us some directives." He replied, "I advise you to fear Allah in your actions, to speak truthfully, to guard whatever is entrusted to you, to be good companions for those who keep your company, to return the greeting, to feed people, to pray in their mosques, to visit their sick and to follow their funeral processions. My father related to me that our followers amongst the Household were the best of them – if he were a man of jurisprudence then he was one of them, if he were a muezzin then he was one of them, if an Imam then he was one of them, if the guardian of an orphan then he was one of them, if he were trusted by others then he was one of them, and if entrusted with something then he was one of them – so be like them".'[911]

Contentment (qanaa`ah)

Al-Baaqir relates that the Messenger said, 'Whoever desires to be the richest of people should be more certain of what is in the hands of Allah than in the hands of others.'[912]

Al-Saadiq relates that the Messenger said, 'The world is a series of changes in fortune: such benefit you may draw from it comes to you despite your frailty, and what is to your disadvantage will afflict you without your being able to ward it off. Anyone

---

910	ibid.
911	ibid.
912	ibid.,130-132.

who ceases to long for what has passed him by finds peace of mind, and whoever is content with what Allah has provided him will find coolness for his eyes.'[913]

He also relates that the Messenger said, 'Whoever asks of us we give to him, and whoever manages and is satisfied Allah will make rich.'[914]

The Messenger said, 'Contentment is a wealth which never dries up,'[915] and, 'Contentment is an inexhaustible treasure.'[916]

Al-Saadiq relates on the authority of his forefathers that a man said in the presence of the Prophet, 'O Allah, make me independent of all Your creation.' The Prophet then said, 'Never say such words, but rather say, "O Allah, make me independent of the worst of your creation," for the believer cannot do without his brothers.'[917]

Ibn Mas'ud relates that the Messenger said, 'The sacred spirit has revealed to my heart that a person never dies until the provision allotted to him has reached him – so be courteous in your demands.'[918]

The Messenger also said, 'Be scrupulous and you will be the strongest of slaves in worship; be content and you will be the most grateful of people; and when you desire for others what you want for yourself you will be a believer.'[919]

Imam 'Ali said, 'It is enough that a man has contentment as his possessions and good character as his ease and comfort.'[920]

913	ibid.
914	ibid.
915	ibid.
916	ibid.
917	ibid.
918	al-Ashtari,I,163.
919	ibid.
920	*Nahj al-Balaaghah*,IV,708.

When Imam `Ali was asked about Allah's words, 'We will most certainly make him live a happy life' [16:97], he replied, 'This refers to contentment.'[921]

Imam `Ali said, 'If a man is content with what satisfies him of the world, the least of things will be enough for him, but if a man is not content with what would suffice him of the world, there will never be anything which would be sufficient for him.'[922]

Al-Baaqir said, 'Take care that your eyes do not covet what is beyond you – Allah says to His Apostle: "Let not then their property and their children excite your admiration" [9:55], and, "Do not strain your eyes after what We have given certain classes of them to enjoy" [15:88]. If any of these things does enter your heart then remember the life of the Prophet: his bread was made from barley, his sweets were dates and his fuel was palm fronds, if he could find them.'[923]

Al-Saadiq said, 'The greatest of riches is contentment.' The advice he gave one man was: 'Be content with what Allah has allotted you; do not look to what others possess, and do not wish for what you have not obtained. He who is content always has enough, and whoever is not content will never be surfeited. Take your pleasure from your life in the next world.' He also said, 'Whoever desires to be free of his self, yet has not rid himself of his anger, dies in a state of grief.'[924]

Abu `Ubaydah al-Hadhdhaa' tells how he asked al-Saadiq, 'Pray to Allah for me so that He does not place my wealth in the hand of His slaves.' Al-Saadiq replied, 'Allah has willed that my wealth and that of the slaves be distributed amongst you by yourselves; so ask rather of Allah that He may place your

---

921	ibid.
922	al-Kulayni,II,138-140.
923	ibid.
924	*Mishkaat al-Anwaar*, 130-132.

provision in the hands of the best of His creation, for this is true prosperity, and that He not place it in the hands of the worst of His creation, for this is true hardship."[925]

Imam al-Zaahid Abu al-Husayn Warraam al-Ashtari has said in his work Al-Majmu`ah:

'Poverty is laudable, but the poor man should be content and cut off all desires for creation; he should not be attracted by what is in the hands of others, and should not yearn after any kind of wealth. He will be capable of this only if he is content with the food, drink and clothing which is necessary for his needs, and if he does not long after abundance and have excessive expectations – for this is not contentment, rather, it is dishonor. There is no place for covetousness and the disgrace of greed, for they bring with them discourteous behavior and lead to the committing of evil actions which destroy honor and manhood. Man, however, has been created with the qualities of covetousness and greed, and by his nature lacks contentment.'[926]

Trust (amaanah)

☼ Surely We offered the trust to the heavens and the earth and the mountains, but they shrank from bearing it, and were afraid of it. And man assumed it. Truly he has proved a tyrant and a fool. (33:72)

☼ If one of you trusts another, then he who is trusted should deliver his trust. (2:283)

☼ Surely Allah commands you to make over trusts to their owners. (4:58)

☼ Be not unfaithful to Allah and the Apostle, nor be unfaithful to your trusts. (8:27)

---

925   ibid.
926   al-Ashtari,I,163.

☼ And those who are keepers of their trusts and their covenant. (23:8)

The Messenger said, 'Whoever breaks trust is not of us.'[927]

He also said, 'Do not look to how much they pray, fast and go on the Hajj, their kindly actions and their murmuring of prayers in the night, but rather look to their telling the truth and guarding what is entrusted to them.'[928]

Imam `Ali said, 'As for maintaining trust, whoever does not possess this quality is lost. This trust was offered to the heavens and the earth, but they refused it and feared the punishment; they thus realized something that someone weaker than them had failed to realize, namely man.'[929]

Al-Saadiq said, 'There are three things which one must carry out at all costs: maintaining the trust placed in you by both righteous and evil persons, keeping to one's promise, whether it be to a righteous or an evil person, and treating one's parents with kindness, whether they be righteous or evil.'[930]

Al-Saadiq also said, 'The most beloved slave of Allah is the man who speaks the truth and maintains prayer, and who preserves the trust which Allah has placed in him. If a person is entrusted with something and fulfills the trust, then a thousand fetters of fire are released from his neck – so strive to maintain the trust placed in you.'[931]

`Abd Allah ibn Sinaan relates the following: 'I went in to see al-Saadiq. He had just prayed the afternoon prayer and was sitting

---

927   *Mishkaat al-Anwaar*, 52-53.
928   ibid.
929   *Nahj al-Balaaghah*,II,459.
930   *Mishkaat al-Anwaar*,52-53.
931   ibid.

in the mosque facing the direction of Makkah. I said to him, "O son of the Messenger of Allah, some of the sultans entrust us with their wealth, but do not pay the *khums* tax. Should we return what has been entrusted to us?" "By the Lord of this *qiblah*" he replied, "even if ibn Muljim, my father's assassin, had entrusted me with something I would have returned it to him".'[932]

Imam al-Kaazim said, The people of the earth are treated with mercy as long as they love each other, fulfil the trust placed in them, and carry out their work with sincerity.'[933]

Al-Saadiq said, 'Never has Allah sent a messenger without him speaking the truth and fulfilling the trust placed in him.'[934]

Al-Saadiq said to one of his companions, 'Look at what `Ali was taught in the presence of the Prophet and how he kept to it – surely he was taught to speak the truth and to fulfil people's trust in him; and this he taught to others.'[935]

The Keeping of Secrets (kitmaan al-sirr)

The Messenger of Allah said, 'The good man comes with good news and the bad man with bad news.'[936]

Al-Saadiq relates that the Prophet said, 'Happy is the lot of the slaves who are unknown to the people and known to Allah: they are lights of guidance and springs of knowledge; all oppressive difficulties pass them by, they have few words to say and have none of the coarseness of the hypocrites.'[937]

It is reported that Imam `Ali said, 'If a man restrains himself

---

[932] ibid.
[933] ibid.
[934] ibid.
[935] al-Kulayni,II,104.
[936] al-Tabarsi,323-324.
[937] al-Kulayni,II,222.

from revealing his innermost thoughts, then that is because he chooses secrecy. Any conversation which is transmitted beyond two people [who were conversing, is something that] has been divulged.'[938]

A man told Imam Zayn al-'Abideen that someone was accusing the Imam of being led astray and of being an innovator. He replied, 'You have not honored the company of that man by transmitting to us what he said, and you have not respected me by informing me of something about a brother I knew nothing of. Surely death comes to us all. The Resurrection will be our gathering together; outstanding on the final day is our appointment with Allah, and He will judge between us. Beware of backbiting, for it is the food of dogs, the inhabitants of the fire.'[939]

Al-Baaqir said, 'By Allah! The most beloved of my companions are the most scrupulous, the most knowledgeable in matters of the law and those who best refrain from telling others of our conversation; the worst and most hated of them for me are those who if they hear the conversation, ascribe it to us and narrate it as coming from us.'[940]

Al-Saadiq said, 'People have been ordered to adopt two qualities, but they have abandoned them and they now amount to nothing: patience and the keeping of secrets.'[941]

Al-Kaazim said, 'If there is something in your hand, then try not to know it if you are able to.'[942]

'Do not allow people to lead you by the neck and so

---

938   *Mishkaat al-Anwaar*,323-324.
939   ibid.
940   al-Kulayni,II,222-226.
941   ibid.
942   ibid.

humble you.'943

Kindness to Parents (birr al-waalidayn)

Allah has said:

> ☼ ... And dutiful to his parents, and he was not insolent, disobedient. (19:14)

> ☼ And We have enjoined man in respect of his parents. (31:14)

> ☼ And that ye be kind to your parents... Say not to them [so much as] 'Fie' nor chide them, but speak to them a generous word. (17:23)

> ☼ ... And dutiful to my mother, and He has not made me insolent, unblessed. (19:32)

A man came to the Messenger asking for instruction. He replied, 'Do not associate partners with Allah in any way – even if you were burning in fire or being tortured – except if your heart was at peace in the certainty of faith; obey and be kind to your parents, whether they be alive or dead; and if they command you to leave your family and wealth, then do it, for this is true faith.'944

A man asked the Messenger, 'What right does the father have over the son?' He replied, 'He should not call his father by name, nor walk or sit in front of him, and he should not revile him.'945

A man came to the Apostle, saying, 'O Messenger of Allah, whom should I treat kindly?' 'Your mother,' he replied. 'And

---

943   ibid.
944   ibid.,II,157-160.
945   ibid.

then whom?' 'Your mother.' 'And then whom?' 'Your mother.' 'And then whom?' 'Your father.'[946]

Al-Saadiq relates that a man came to the Apostle, saying, 'O Messenger of Allah, I desire and feel ready to fight in the way of Allah.' The Prophet then said to him, 'Then fight in the way of Allah, for if you are killed you will be living with Allah and will be provided for, and if you die then your reward will be due from Allah; if you return, then you will return as free from wrong action as the day you were born.' The man said, 'O Messenger, I have two elderly parents who claim that they are so fond of me that they do not want me to leave.' The Messenger replied, 'Then stay with your parents, for by the One who has my soul in His hand, their fondness for you – be it only a day and night – is better than fighting for a whole year.'[947]

When `Abd Allah ibn Mas`ud asked the Messenger which acts Allah loved best he replied, 'The prayer performed at its proper time, kindness towards one's parents, and fighting in the way of Allah.'[948]

A man asked Imam al-Saadiq what goodness meant in the words of Allah: 'And goodness (*ihsaan*) to your parents' [17:23]. He replied, 'Goodness is to be good company for them, and not burdening them by allowing them to ask for something they need, even if they are capable of obtaining it themselves. Does not Allah say, "By no means shall you attain to righteousness until you spend benevolently out of what you love" [3:91]. As for Allah's words, "If either or both of them reach old age with you, say not to them [so much as] 'Fie' or chide them": if they annoy you, do not say "Fie" to them and do not chide them if they hit you. The meaning of "and speak to them a generous

---

946 ibid.
947 ibid.
948 *al-Khisaal*,I,163.

word" is that if they hit you, you should say to them, "May Allah forgive you" – these are the words of generosity.'[949]

Al-Saadiq said, 'There are three actions which one must at all costs perform: fulfilling the trust placed in one, whether on the part of a good or evil man, keeping of one's promise, whether to a good or evil man, and being kind to one's parents, whether they be good or evil.'[950]

'Be kind to your parents and grandparents, and your children will be kind to you; keep your eyes lowered in the presence of women, and others will lower their eyes in the presence of your women.'[951]

'Whoever desires that Allah relieve the torment of death should maintain close ties with his relations and treat his parents with kindness. If he does this, Allah will lighten the torment of death and he will never be afflicted by poverty during his lifetime.'[952]

'If a person looks with hatred at his parents even though they have caused him wrong, then his prayer will not be accepted.'[953]

Maintaining Family Ties and the Courtesies of Social Intercourse

The Education of Children

Allah has said:

☼ And when Luqman said to his son, while he admonished him: O my son! Do not associate aught with Allah; most

---

949	al-Kulayni, II, 157.
950	*Mishkaat al-Anwaar*, 158-165.
951	ibid.
952	ibid.
953	ibid.

surely association of others with Allah [polytheism] is a grievous iniquity. And We have enjoined man in respect of his parents – his mother bears him in weakness upon weakness, and his weaning takes two years – saying: Be grateful to Me and to both your parents. (31:13-14)

☼ O my son! Keep up the prayer and enjoin the good and forbid the evil, and bear patiently that which befalls you; surely these acts require courage. And do not turn your face away from people in contempt, nor go about in the land exulting overmuch; surely Allah does not love any self-conceited boaster. (31:17-18)

☼ O People! Guard against [the punishment of] your Lord and dread the day when a father shall not avail his son, nor shall the child avail his father. (31:33)

The education of children begins at birth. Imam al-Saadiq relates how the Messenger said, 'Whoever has a new born child should say the call to prayer (*aadhaan*) in his right ear and the call to start the prayer (*iqaamah*) in his left – this is a protection against the accursed Satan.'[954]

`Abd Allah ibn Fadala quotes Abu Ja`far al-Baaqir as saying: 'When a child becomes three years old, one should tell him to recite *laa ilaaha illa'Llaah* (there is no god but Allah) seven times; then you should leave him until he reaches the age of three years and seven months, when you should tell him to recite seven times *Salla'Llaahu `alaa Muhammad wa aalihi* (May Allah bless Muhammad and his family). Then you should leave him until he is five years old, when you should ask him, "Which is your right hand and which is your left?" If he knows this, then turn his face in the direction of the Ka`bah and tell him to prostrate himself.

---

954   *al-Muhajjah al-Bayda'*, III, 120-121.

Then you should leave him until he is seven years old, when you should tell him to wash his face and hands. When he has washed them, tell him to perform the prayer. Then you should leave him until he reaches the age of nine, when you must teach him the ablution, coercing him to it. If he learns the ablution and the prayer, then Allah will forgive his parents – if Allah wills.'[955]

Al-Saadiq said, 'Leave your child to play for seven years. Teach him how to behave for seven years, and keep him with you for seven years, so that he may prosper. If he does not, then he is of those in whom there is no good.'[956]

He also said, 'A young boy should play for seven years, learn the Book for seven years, and learn what is allowed and forbidden for seven years.'[957]

Imam 'Ali said, 'Teach your children to swim, to throw and to shoot.'[958]

Al-Saadiq said, 'Endeavor to converse with your children, lest others who transgress and disobey get to them before you.'[959]

Maintaining Good Family Relations

Allah has said:

☼ And those who join that which Allah has bidden to be joined. (13:21)

☼ Those who break the covenant of Allah after its confirmation and cut asunder what Allah has ordered to be joined, and make mischief in the land; these it is that are

---
955   ibid.
956   al-Kulayni, VI, 46.
957   ibid.
958   ibid.
959   ibid.

the losers. (2:27)

The Apostle said, 'Maintaining good family relations increases one's numbers and wealth, gives life to one's people, and is a staff for the weak at the time of death.'[960]

Al-Baaqir relates that the Messenger said, 'Instruct those present and those absent from my *ummah*, and those in the loins of men and the wombs of women until the Last Day, that they maintain good family relations – even if it means journeying for a year – for this is part of the *Deen*.'[961]

The Messenger said, 'No crime merits Allah's swift punishment in this world and the storing up of punishment for the next world more than committing injustice and the breaking off of family relations.'[962]

Al-Baaqir relates that the Messenger said, 'Kindness to parents and the maintaining of close family ties lighten the reckoning.' Then he recited the verse, 'And those who join that which Allah has bidden to be joined' [13:21].[963]

The Messenger relates how Allah said to Gabriel, 'I am the Beneficent (*al-Rahmaan*) and have caused the womb (*al-rahm*) to derive from My name: if anyone joins with others related by birth, I will join with him; and if anyone breaks off such relations, I will break with him.' The Messenger also said, 'If any man is approached by a cousin asking him for something he has plenty of, and he refuses him, then Allah will deny him of His plenty on the Last Day.' Furthermore, he said, 'Maintain good relations with your family even if it is by a mere greeting: Mercy

---

960	al-'Amili,*Nur al-Ḥaqiqah,*142.
961	al-Kulayni,II,151.
962	al-Ashtari,I,283-285.
963	*Mishkaat al-Anwaar*,166.

will not descend on those who break off ties of kinship.'⁹⁶⁴

Abu Dharr relates that he heard the Messenger of Allah say, 'On the Last Day kinship and trust will line the Path (*al-siraat*): when the man who has maintained the ties of kinship and fulfilled the trust placed in him passes along it, he will be brought by them to the Garden; but when the man who has broken the trust placed in him, and who has broken the ties of kinship passes by, no action of theirs can save him – and the Path will throw him into the Fire.'⁹⁶⁵

The Messenger said, 'The action most quickly rewarded is that of maintaining ties of kinship.'⁹⁶⁶

He also said, 'There are people who are evil, who are not righteous in any way except that they maintain the ties of kinship, so their wealth increases and they live to a good age – how would it be, then, if they were righteous and upright?'⁹⁶⁷

Al-Saadiq said, 'B€eware of *haaliqah*, for it means death to man. 'When asked what *haaliqah* was, he replied, 'Abandoning the ties of kinship.'⁹⁶⁸

He also said, 'The first organ to speak on the Last Day will be the womb. It will say: "O my Lord, whoever has joined the ties of kinship, then join him with You; and whoever has broken off the ties, then break off the ties between him and You".'⁹⁶⁹

'Maintain the ties of kinship even if it is by giving just a drink of water; the best means of maintaining these ties is to refrain from causing them harm.'⁹⁷⁰

964	ibid.
965	al-Kulayni,II,152-155.
966	ibid.
967	ibid.
968	al-Ashtari,II,283.
969	al-Kulayni,II,151.
970	*Mishkaat al-Anwaar*,166-167.

'I strive to maintain the ties of kinship even before they ask for a gift or a favor from me.'[971]

The Courtesies of Marriage and what is Obligatory for the two Spouses

Allah has said:

☼ And when souls are united. (81:7)

☼ And [that] He created pairs, the male and the female. (53:45)

☼ And of everything We have created pairs in order that you may be mindful. (51:49)

☼ He it is Who created you from a single being, and of the same [kind] did He make his mate. (7:189)

☼ Keep your wife to yourself and be careful of [your duty to] Allah. (33:37)

☼ And one of His signs is that He created mates for you from yourselves that you may find rest in them. (30:21)

Al-Baaqir relates how the Messenger said that Allah said, 'If I wished to give a Muslim all the good in this world and the next, I would make his heart humble, his tongue full of remembrance, his body patient in times of trial, and I would give him a believing wife, who fills him with delight when he looks at her, and protects herself and his wealth when he is away.'[972]

The Messenger went on to the *minbar* (pulpit) and said, 'O people, Gabriel came to me from the Subtle (*al-Latif*), the Aware

---

971 ibid.
972 al-Shiraazi, 187-190.

(*al-Khabir*) and said, "Virgins are like the fruits of the tree: if they ripen and are not picked, they will rot in the sun and be dispersed in the winds. If virgins reach the maturity of women, then they should marry; if they do not, then they will not be secure from degradation, for they are human".[973]

Abraham complained to Allah about Sara's discourteous behavior, and Allah revealed: 'The likeness of a woman is that of a curved rib: if you try to straighten it you will break it, but if you let it be, you may take your pleasure in it – so be patient with her.'[974]

`Abd Allah al-Nawfali tells how he went to see Abu `Abd Allah al-Saadiq, who said, 'Tell my helpers that I guarantee them the Garden as long as they avoid seven kinds of people: the man addicted to wine or games of chance, the man who refuses a favor or present, the man who is haughty with the believer, the man who prevents the believer from obtaining what one needs, the man who does not help the believer who comes to him in need or the man who does not give his daughter in marriage to the believer who comes to seek her hand.'[975]

The husband should practice moderation and be courteous in twelve matters: the wedding feast (waleemah), times of companionship, conviviality, maintaining balance, jealousy, financial support, during instruction, when sharing [between wives], in disciplining in the case of recalcitrance, sexual intimacy, birth and divorce.

The wedding feast is desirable (*mustahabb*), for the Prophet said, 'Feasts should be held on four occasions: a wedding, when an animal is slaughtered for the birth of a child, circumcision, and when a man returns from a journey and invites his brothers

---

973 ibid.
974 ibid.
975 Mishkaat al-Anwaar, 101.

after his absence.'[976]

Imam al-Kaazim relates that the Prophet forbade the holding of a feast to which only rich people had been invited and the poor had been left out.[977]

Concerning companionship in marriage, Allah has said, 'And treat them [i.e. wives] kindly' [4:19].

Allah demands respect for the rights of the wives when He says, 'And they have made with you a firm covenant' [4:21].

The last instructions given by the Messenger before his death were: 'Allah, Allah, as for women, they are your helpers and [are] in your hands; you have taken them according to Allah's covenant and you have made sexual intercourse with them licit by saying the word "[in the name of] Allah".'[978]

Concerning conviviality, he said, 'The believer with the most perfect faith is he who is the most courteous and kind with his family.'[979]

'The best of you are those who treat their wives best, and I am the best of you in the way I treat my wives.'[980]

Regarding the way of balance and moderation: this means not exceeding the bounds of kindness and courtesy and not ceding to one's wife's desires if it threatens to corrupt her behavior and violate her honor, but maintaining moderation in kindness and courtesy. The Apostle said, 'It is wretched to be the slave of one's wife,' and, 'Obedience to one's wife is full of regret.'[981]

About moderating one's jealousy, the Prophet said, 'There is

976	*al-Muhajjah al-Bayda'*, III, 96-128.
977	ibid.
978	ibid.
979	ibid.
980	ibid.
981	ibid.

a kind of jealousy which is hateful to Allah and His Messenger: it is the jealousy of the man for his wife without just cause.' This is suspicion, which Allah has forbidden: 'For surely suspicion in some cases is a sin' [49:12].[982]

Jealousy in the proper place is inevitable, and even praiseworthy. The Prophet said, 'Allah becomes jealous as does the believer – and the jealousy of Allah is His care and concern when a believing man does something which Allah has forbidden him.'[983]

Al-Saadiq said, 'Allah is vigilantly caring and loves concern in others; this is because of His concern that He has forbidden all kinds of abominations, both inner and outer.'[984]

Concerning support for one's wife, moderation in what one gives out is laudable – one should neither be wasteful nor niggardly with her. The Apostle said, '[Out of] the dinar you spend on your family, the dinar you spend in the way of Allah, the dinar you spend to free a slave, the dinar you give in charity to a destitute person, the dinar which carries the greatest reward is the one spent on your family.'[985]

As far as instruction is concerned, the husband should teach his wife the obligations of the prayer, and which prayers she should make up and which she does not need to make up during her period. This is because he has been commanded to protect her from the Fire by Allah, Who says, 'Protect yourselves and your family from the Fire' [66:6]. He should also instill fear of Allah in her if she becomes lax in matters of the *Deen*, and if his knowledge is deficient then he acts on her behalf by asking one who is knowledgeable and sound of judgment. Regarding being

---

982   ibid.
983   ibid.
984   ibid.
985   ibid.

fair to each of one's wives, the Messenger said, 'Whoever has two wives and does not treat them equally will arrive on the Last Day with half of his body hanging awry.'[986]

As to equal treatment in respect of what you give them and how you house them, if a man has been away on a journey and he wishes to be with one of his wives, then he should cast lots between them, just as the Apostle used to do. As for the way a man loves or has sexual intercourse, then that is not something over which he has control. Allah says, 'And you have it not in your power to do justice between wives even though I may wish [it]' [4:129].

The Messenger would both house and give to his wives equally, and would say, 'O Allah, this is my striving, in so far as I am the owner, but I have no power over what You own and I do not own.' Here he is referring to love.[987]

Regarding discipline, if hostility breaks out between them, and the dispute cannot be resolved, then two arbitrators must be appointed, one from his family and the other from hers, to look into and settle the matter.

About the courtesies of sexual intercourse, the Messenger said, 'No one should mount his wife like an animal: let there be communication between them.' When asked what that communication was, he replied, 'Kissing and talking.'[988]

It is a weakness on the part of the man if he approaches his wife and enters her before talking intimately and lying with her – that is, fulfilling his own need of her before she fulfills her need of him.

Imam al-Saadiq relates that Imam `Ali said, 'If one of you

986	ibid.
987	ibid.
988	ibid.

has sexual relations then say, "In the name of Allah and by Allah, O Allah! Keep Satan far from me and far from what you have provided me with"."[989]

A man should not enter his wife while she is menstruating and not even after the menses has finished before she has made the great ablution – this is forbidden by a text from the Qur'an. He may, however, take his pleasure in all parts of the body of the menstruating woman, fondling is permitted, he may enjoy what is below the loins as long as there is no coition. Al-Saadiq has related that he was asked what was permitted for the husband in respect of his menstruating wife, and he replied, 'Everything, except her sexual organ.'[990]

The courtesies on the occasion of a birth are four in number:

1. A man should not feel happier at the birth of a boy and sadder at the birth of a girl. The Messenger said, 'Boys are wealth and girls are like good actions, and Allah takes one to account for the wealth and rewards good actions.[991]

2. The call to prayer should be said in the right ear of the new born. Abu Raafi` relates how he saw the Messenger make the call to prayer in Hasan's ear after Fatimah had given birth to him.[992]

3. He should be given a good name. The Messenger said, 'When you name someone, then use names which indicate worship.'[993] Al-Saadiq said, 'The most fitting names are those which contain the word `abd (slave of)

989	ibid.
990	ibid.
991	ibid.
992	ibid.
993	ibid.

and the best of names are those of the prophets.'[994]

4. Slaughter of an animal (`aqiqah`). The Messenger said, 'When a baby boy is born an animal should be slaughtered – it strengthens his blood and removes harm from him.'[995] Imam al-Ridaa said, 'When a boy is born, then an animal is slaughtered for him, his head is shaved and a measure of silver equal in weight to his hair is given to charity; the midwife is given the leg and the haunch, a party of Muslims are invited to eat, they make a prayer for the boy and he is named on the seventh day.'[996]

Divorce is permitted but it is the most hated of the permitted things with Allah; it is permitted as long as it is not an evil without valid cause. Allah has said, 'Then if they obey you, do not seek a way against them' [4:34]. In other words, do not seek an excuse for divorce.

Al-Saadiq said, 'Allah loves the house in which there is a wedding and hates the house in which there is divorce; and there is nothing more hateful to Allah than divorce.'[997]

If a woman asks her husband for divorce without just cause then she is a wrongdoer, and is forbidden the Garden. The Messenger said, 'Women who have divorced at their own insistence are hypocrites.'[998]

994	ibid.
995	ibid.
996	ibid.
997	ibid.
998	ibid.

The Duties of the Wife and the Rights of the Husband over his Wife

The Messenger said, 'Any woman who dies and her husband is satisfied with her will enter the Garden.'[999]

'If a woman prays five times a day, fasts for the month of Ramadan, is chaste and obeys her husband, she will most likely enter the Garden.'[1000]

Imam al-Baaqir relates that the Messenger passed some women on the day of sacrifice (*yawm al-nahr*) whereupon he stopped near them and said, 'O women, be charitable with your husbands and obey them, for indeed, most of you are in the Fire.' When they heard this they wept; then one of them went up to him saying, 'O Messenger of Allah, are we in the Fire with the unbelievers? By Allah, we are neither unbelievers nor of those who are bound for the Fire.' The Messenger then replied, 'You are in denial (*kufr*) in relation to your husbands' rights over you.'[1001]

Among her duties are that she should not squander her husband's wealth, rather, she should protect it for him. The Apostle said, 'It is not permissible for her to feed someone from his house except with his permission, or when there is a possibility that the fresh dates will go bad if not given away; if she feeds someone with his permission, then she has a similar reward to his, but if she feeds someone without his permission, then he receives the reward and she the consequence.'[1002]

It is her duty to be righteous and modest, to obey him without being rebellious, to fast only with his permission, not to prevent him from fasting, and not to leave his house without his permission.

999	ibid.,III,131-137.
1000	ibid.
1001	ibid.
1002	ibid.

Imam al-Baaqir said, 'If a woman retires for the night when her husband is angry with her for a just reason, then her prayer will not be accepted from her until he is satisfied with her. If a woman perfumes herself for someone other than her husband, her prayer will not be accepted until she washes that perfume off herself, just as she would wash herself during the major ablution after intercourse.'[1003]

In relation to the laws of marriage, if the husband dies then the wife must wait for four months and ten days before she may remarry: she is in mourning for this period, avoiding perfume and finery, but she is not to mourn for longer than this. The Messenger said, 'It is not permitted to a woman who believes in Allah and the Last Day that she mourn for a dead person more than three day s, except for her husband, the period of mourning for whom is four months and ten days.'[1004]

The Courtesies of Social Relations

Jaabir ibn `Abd Allah al-Ansaari relates that the Messenger said, 'It is part of the good behavior of the prophets and the truthful that when they see each other they are filled with joy, and when they meet they shake hands. The man who visits for the sake of Allah has a right over the person he visits – namely, that he be treated generously.'[1005]

It is related by Abu Hurayrah that the Prophet said, 'If a slave visits his brother for the sake of Allah, a voice calls from the sky: "Good fortune is yours and excellent are your actions – an abode has been built for you in the Garden".'[1006]

1003	ibid.
1004	ibid.
1005	al-Ashtari,I,29.
1006	ibid.

The Prophet relates that Allah has said, 'Those who love each other for My sake are worthy of My love, and those who visit each other for My sake are also worthy of My love.'

'Every part of the believer is enviable: his honor, his wealth and his blood.'[1007]

'Do not look for the faults of the believers. Whoever seeks after the faults of his brother, then Allah will seek after his faults; and whoever Allah looks for in search of his faults then He will discover, even if he is hidden in his house.'[1008]

Imam 'Ali said, 'It is preferable to me that I help to reconcile two people than to give away two dinars in charity.'[1009]

'Beware of the jester, for he generates resentment and ill will.'[1010]

He said to his son Hasan, by way of disciplining him, as he entered, 'Stand up for your masters.'[1011]

'To display a friendly mien is the foundation of a loving friendship; and tolerance is the graveyard of faults.'[1012]

Al-Saadiq said, 'Allah loves charity. Help to reconcile people if relations between them have soured and to bring them together if they have become estranged.' He also said, 'There is not a believer but that he has a sense of humor.' When asked what this sense of humor was, he replied, 'His good-natured banter.'[1013]

Imam al-Saadiq said, 'The believer has seven rights over his

[1007] *Mishkaat al-Anwaar*,190-192.
[1008] ibid.
[1009] al-'Inaathi,I,67.
[1010] *Mishkaat al-Anwaar*,190-192.
[1011] ibid.
[1012] ibid.
[1013] al-Ashtari,I,31.

fellow believer. Just as they are rights, they are also obligations on him. If he does not fulfill them, then he is departing from the law of Allah and disobeying Him; there will be nothing of benefit in this from Allah.'

'The easiest of these obligations is that he should love for his brother what he loves for himself, and hate for his brother as he hates for himself.

The second is that he should strive after his needs, seek his contentment and not argue with him.

The third is that he join with him by means of his self, his wealth, his hand, his foot and his tongue.

The fourth is that he be the eye of his brother, his guide, his mirror and his robe.

The fifth is that he should not eat his fill while his brother is hungry, nor clothe himself while he is naked, nor drink his fill while he is thirsty.

The sixth is that if you have a wife and a servant when your brother has neither, then you should send your servant to wash his clothes, prepare his food and make his bed – all this is an investment between you and him.

The seventh is that you keep his oath, accept his invitation, attend his funeral, visit him when he is sick. You should stand in for him whenever necessary, you should not allow him to want something so that he asks you for it, but rather you should strive to see to his needs before they occur. If you do this, then you are joining your friendship to his and your friendship to the friendship of Allah.'[1014]

Mu'awiyah ibn Wahab relates how he once asked al-Saadiq, 'How should we be amongst ourselves, and how should we be

---

1014   *Mishkaat al-Anwaar*, 189-203.

between ourselves and the people we mix with?' He replied, 'Fulfill the trust they place in you, testify for and against them, visit their sick and attend their funerals.' He also said, 'Go with your people to the mosques and love for the people what you love for yourself; anyone of you should feel shame if his neighbor knows his right over him when he does not know the right of his neighbor.'[1015]

Al-Saadiq said, 'Whoever restrains his hand from [doing evil to] people has restrained only one hand; but they will restrain many hands from him.'[1016]

Commenting on Allah's words, 'Surely we see you to be the doers of good' [12:36]. He also said, 'He [the doer of good] would make room for someone to sit down, lend to someone in need and help the weak.'[1017]

'Beware of apologizing, for surely the believer does not offend, and does not need to excuse himself, while the hypocrite offends every day and apologizes.'[1018]

Commenting on Allah's words, 'And say to the people words of kindness' [2:83], al-Baaqir said, 'Say to the people kinder words than you yourself would like to hear, for Allah hates those who curse much, who insult and defame the believers, the profligate and the obscene in speech, and the one who molests with his questioning; but He loves the modest, the gentle, the chaste and the abstemious.'[1019]

Al-Saadiq said, 'If there is a group of three believers, then two of them should not converse together without involving the

---

1015   al-Kulayni,II,635.
1016   al-Khisaal,I,7.
1017   Mishkaat al-Anwaar,189-203.
1018   ibid.
1019   ibid.

third, for this would cause him sorrow and pain.'[1020] He also said, 'Talk about your brother when he is out of your sight as you would like him to talk of you when you are out of his; leave him alone at those times when you would like to be left alone, and act like the one who knows that he is rewarded for good actions and punished for bad.'[1021]

Courtesy when meeting people is part of Islam, and is more important than presenting a gift. Moreover, a joyful mien is preferable to a good deed. It has been related in a Prophetic tradition, 'If two Muslims meet, then be the most beloved of them in the eyes of Allah, and the best of them by your more joyful encounter with your companion; when two Muslims shake hands, then Allah makes a hundred mercies descend on them, ninety of them being for the one who began the handshake.'[1022]

In expounding on this, one of the scholars has said, 'The believer possesses an aura of faith, [with] its respect, brilliance and beauty. The most joyful of them [i.e. of the two Muslims] is the most understanding and perceptive of the two, in that his intellect comprehends what Allah has blessed him with, and he demonstrates this knowledge of Allah, and the fact that He is bestowing this on his slave, by His joy.'[1023]

Another scholar has said that the foundation of companionship is based on four things: agreement, sympathy, preferring the other to oneself and service. Moreover, among the courtesies of intimate relationships are speaking kindly and listening when spoken to. The best and most noble kind of companionship is to maintain relations with a bad-mannered person until he reforms.[1024]

1020	ibid.
1021	ibid.
1022	ibid.
1023	Unknown; the print version doesn't provide a reference for this footnote number.
1024	Unknown; the print version doesn't provide a reference for this footnote number.

Greeting People with the Greeting of 'Peace'

Allah has said:

> ☼ And when you are greeted with a greeting, greet it with [a] better [greeting] than it or return it. (4:86)

> ☼ And peace be on him the day he was born, and the day he dies, and the day he is raised to life [again]. (19:15)

> ☼ And when those who believe in Our communications come to you, say: Peace be on you. (6:54)

> ☼ ... And shall be met therein with greetings and salutations. (25:75)

> ☼ And they shall call out to the dwellers of the Garden: Peace be on you. (7:46)

> ☼ He is Allah, besides Whom there is no god; the King, the Holy, the Bestower of Peace. (59:23)

The Messenger said, 'When you meet, then greet each other with the greeting of peace and shake hands; and if you part company with each other, then seek forgiveness at your parting.'[1025]

'It is part of the good behavior of the prophets and the truthful that they are joyful of mien when they see each other, and shake hands when they meet; the man who visits for the sake of Allah has a right over the one he visits, in that the latter must treat him generously.'[1026]

'If one of you gets up from a gathering, then you should bid them farewell with the greeting of peace.'[1027]

1025   al-'Inaathi,I,27.
1026   ibid.
1027   ibid.

Al-Saadiq said, 'The Messenger used to greet women, and they would answer his greeting; Imam `Ali would greet women and they would answer him, but he disliked greeting young women, saying, "I fear lest her voice attracts me and more enters my heart than I expected".'[1028]

Imam `Ali said, 'The greeting of peace is equal to seventy good deeds – sixty-nine of them for the one who began the greeting and one for the person who answered.'[1029]

Imam `Ali said, 'Do not be the first to greet the people of the Book, and if they greet you with "Peace be on you," then say, "And on you".'[1030]

Al-Baaqir said, 'Spread the peace of Allah by using the greeting, for the peace of Allah will not reach the oppressors.'[1031]

He also said, 'If one of you makes the greeting, then let him say it out loud. He should not say, "I have made the greeting and they did not reply," for it may be he greeted them but they did not hear. If one of you replies to a greeting, then he should say it out loudly: the Muslim does not say, "I made the greeting and they did not reply to me".'[1032]

Al-Baaqir said, 'Do not get angry, greet people, speak kind words, pray during the night while people are asleep, and you will enter the Garden with peace.' Then he recited the words of Allah, 'The Giver of Peace, the Granter of Security, Guardian over All (al-Salaam, al-Mu'min, al-Muhaymin).'[1033]

Al-Saadiq said, 'It is part of humility that you greet those you meet.' He also said, 'The miser is he who is miserly with his

---

1028 ibid.
1029 ibid.
1030 ibid.
1031 ibid.
1032 ibid.
1033 ibid.

greeting.' Elsewhere, 'The one mounted should greet the one walking, the one walking should greet those sitting; if a group of persons meets another group, then the smaller group should greet the larger, and if a single person meets a group he should greet the group.'[1034]

Al-Saadiq said, 'If one man from a group gives a greeting this suffices for the others, and if he greets a group of people it is enough that one of them return the greeting.' He also said, 'Whoever says, "Peace be upon you", has the reward of ten good actions; whoever says, "The peace and mercy of Allah be upon you", earns the reward of twenty good actions; and whoever says, "The peace, mercy and blessing of Allah be upon you", has the reward of thirty.'[1035]

Al-Saadiq was asked, 'What is the prayer [greeting] for the Jew and the Christian?' He replied, "May Allah bless you in this world of yours".'[1036]

Shaking Hands and Kissing

The Messenger said, 'If two Muslims meet, the most beloved of them with Allah is the one who shows the most joy at meeting his companion. If they shake hands, then Allah causes a hundred mercies to descend on them, ninety for the one who began the handshake.'[1037]

'If one of you meets his brother then he should greet and shake hands with him, for Allah has bestowed this on the angels – so do as the angels do.'[1038]

1034	ibid.
1035	ibid.
1036	ibid.
1037	*Mishkaat al-Anwaar*, 196-201.
1038	al-'Inaathi, I, 67.

Al-Saadiq said, 'Never has the Messenger of Allah shaken his hand with a man and withdrawn it before the other man has withdrawn his.'[1039]

He also said, 'He [the Prophet] would dislike a man shaking hands with a woman, even if she were middle-aged.'[1040]

Al-Saadiq said, 'In your shaking of hands there is a reward like that of those who have emigrated [in the way of Allah].'[1041]

Abu `Ubaydah al-Hadhdhaa' tells the story, 'I was accompanying Abu Ja`far. Whenever he dismounted for any reason and then returned to his mount, he would shake my hand. 'It is as if you regard this as particularly important,' I said, 'Yes,' he replied, 'if the believer shakes the hand of another believer they part from each other free of sin.'[1042]

He also said, 'If a man shakes the hand of his companion, then the one who is constant in this will have a greater reward than the one who is lax in this matter; indeed, the sins rub off from each other until not a sin is left.'[1043]

A man called Ishaaq asked al-Saadiq about the reward for those believers who embraced each other when they met. He replied, 'When they embrace they are showered with mercies, and if they keep company with each other – not desiring anything by it but the face of Allah, nor wanting any of the goods of this world – then they are told they have been forgiven and may begin again with a fresh reckoning. If they come up against a problem, then the angels will say to each other, "Turn away from them, for they have a secret and Allah has confided in them".'

Ishaaq then said, 'So they do not record their words? Has not

---

1039	ibid.
1040	ibid.
1041	ibid.
1042	ibid.
1043	ibid.

Allah said, "He utters not a word but there is by him a watcher at hand" [50:18]?' Then the descendant of the Prophet [al-Saadiq] breathed deeply and wept until his beard became wet with tears, saying, 'O Ishaaq, Allah has commanded the angel to withdraw from two believers when they meet out of respect for them – even if the angel does not record their words and does not know what they are saying, Allah the Knower of the Secrets and that which is even more hidden knows it and is observing them.'[1044]

Al-Saadiq said, 'The speed with which hearts join when the righteous meet – even though they do not display any affection in their speech – is like the speed with which the water from the sky mixes with the water of the rivers; and the distance between the hearts of the evil when they meet – even if they display affection in their speech – is like the distance between animals, even if they have been well fed over a long period of time at the same trough.'[1045]

'Truly you possess a light by which you are known in this world; if one of you meets his brother, he may kiss him on the place of light on his forehead.'[1046]

'One should not kiss anyone on the mouth – except one's wife or a small child.'[1047]

A man once kissed his [al-Saadiq's] hand, whereupon he said, 'This is fitting only for the Prophet.'[1048]

Zariq relates that al-Saadiq said, 'Shaking hands with a believer is equal to a thousand good actions.'[1049]

The two sisters of Muhammad ibn Abi `Umayr, Sa`idah

[1044] ibid.
[1045] ibid.
[1046] ibid.
[1047] ibid.
[1048] ibid.
[1049] ibid.

and Aymanah, tell how they went in to see al-Saadiq and asked, 'Should a woman visit a sick brother for the sake of Allah?' 'Yes,' he replied. They then asked, 'And should they shake hands?' 'Yes,' he said, 'as long as there is some cloth between them.'[1050]

Imam al-Kazaim said, 'There is nothing wrong with kissing someone you are related to, nor kissing a brother on the cheek and kissing the Imam between his eyes.'[1051]

The Courtesies of Sitting

Al-Saadiq said, 'The Messenger would usually sit facing the direction of the Ka`bah.'[1052]

'Whenever the Messenger entered a house he would sit in the nearest suitable place.'[1053]

'When a man is content to sit without distinction and honors in company, Allah and His angels bless him until he rises.'[1054]

The Messenger said, 'Three qualities describe a man's love for his brother: he has a joyful mien on meeting him, he makes room for him if he comes to sit by him, and he calls him by his favorite names.'[1055]

The Messenger said, 'The place where the believer sits is his mosque, and his house is his place of spiritual seclusion.'[1056]

He also said, 'Do not make your brother get up from a company to make room for you to sit down ... If you come to sit with a teacher or attend gatherings of religious knowledge, then

---

1050	ibid.
1051	ibid.
1052	*Mishkaat al-Anwaar*, 192-203.
1053	ibid.
1054	ibid.
1055	ibid.
1056	ibid.

come close and let each one of you sit behind the other; do not sit apart from each other, like the people of the *jaahiliyyah*.'[1057]

In his instructions to Abu Dharr, the Messenger said, 'Whoever desires that men should remain standing in his presence is building his abode in the Fire!'[1058]

'There are three kinds of people sitting with whom causes the heart to die: the depraved, women and the rich.'[1059]

'If a group of people begins to sit down, and a man requests his brother for a place and he grants it, then he should take it – this is an honor for him on behalf of his brother. If he does not make room for him, then he should look for the best place he can find and sit down there.'[1060]

'It is better for you to make room for your brother at a gathering than to free a slave.'[1061]

'One should only make room for someone on three conditions: when the person is of similar age, knowledge and authority.'[1062]

'A man who sits and listens to the wisdom of others and only talks of the bad he has heard in their company is like a man who comes to a shepherd saying, "Give me one of your sheep," and the shepherd says, "Go and take the best one" – so he takes the [sheep] dog by the ear.'[1063]

'Sitting with people of religion means eminence in this world

---

1057	ibid.
1058	ibid.
1059	ibid. [or, due to an error in the printed version, it could be from *Mishkaat*, 189.]
1060	ibid.
1061	ibid.
1062	ibid.
1063	ibid.

and the next.'[1064]

Al-Saadiq was asked about Allah's words, 'Surely We see you to be the doers of good,' and he replied, 'He would make room for someone to sit down, lend money to the one in need and help the weak.'[1065]

The Courtesies of Asking Permission

Allah has said:

> ☼ Do not enter houses other than your own houses until you have asked permission and saluted their inhabitants. (24:27)

> ☼ Then do not enter them until permission is given to you, and if it is said to you: Go back, then go back; this is purer for you. (24:28)

> ☼ So when you enter houses, greet your people with a salutation from Allah, blessed [and] goodly. (24:61)

When the Messenger came to someone's door he would not enter until the greeting of peace had been made three times, giving him permission to enter.[1066]

Jaabir ibn `Abd Allah said, 'The Messenger of Allah went to see Faatimah when I was with him. When we came to the door he placed his hand on it and pushed it ajar, saying "Peace be upon you." Faatimah replied, "And on you be peace, O Messenger of Allah." "Shall I enter?" he asked. She replied, "Enter, O Messenger of Allah." "Should I and the person with me enter?"

1064   ibid.,203-206.
1065   *al-Khisaal*,I,5.
1066   ibid.,194-196.

Then she said, "There is no veil on my head." "O Faatimah," he said, "Wrap the fold of your cloak to veil your head." This she did and then he said, "Peace be upon you." "And on you be peace, O Messenger of Allah." He said, "Shall I enter?" "Yes, O Messenger of Allah." "I and the man with me?" "And the man who is with you," she replied.'[1067]

Imam `Ali said, 'If one of you comes to his room then he should give the greeting – it will dispel Shaytaan's companion; and if one of you enters his house, then he should say the greeting. Blessing will cover him and the angels will keep him close company.'[1068]

Al-Saadiq said, 'If you go into your house, then say, "In the name of Allah and by Allah," and greet your family. If there is no one in the house then say, "In the name of Allah and peace be on His Messenger and on the family of his household, and peace be on us and on the upright slaves of Allah." If he says this, Allah will make Satan flee from his house.'[1069]

He also said, 'A man should greet his family when he enters the house; he should make a noise with his shoes and cough discreetly in order to alert them of his arrival, and so that he will not see anything he dislikes.' Commenting on Allah's words, 'Until you have asked for permission and saluted their inmates,' [24:27] he said, 'Asking for permission means making the greeting and stamping with the shoes.'[1070]

'If one of you seeks permission, then begin with the greeting of peace, for it is one of the names of Allah. He should ask from behind the door before looking into the house itself, for you have been commanded to ask permission because of the

---

1067	ibid.
1068	ibid.
1069	ibid.
1070	ibid.

evil eye. Permission should be sought three times; if someone bids you to enter, then enter, and if they tell you to keep out, then keep out. The first time is for the people of the house to hear, the second is to warn them, and the third is to allow them to choose – if they wish, they may give permission and if they wish they may refuse.'[1071]

Al-Saadiq said, 'Let those whom your right hand possesses and those of you who have not attained puberty ask permission three times as Allah has commanded. Whoever has attained puberty should not enter the presence of his mother, sister or the like except by their permission; and they should not give permission until he has given the greeting of peace. The greeting of peace means obedience to Allah, as we know from His words, "O you who believe! Let those whom your right hands possess and those of you who have not attained to puberty ask permission of you three times" [24:58].'[1072]

There is a narration which says that `Ali would seek permission, even from the people of the Book.[1073]

The Giving of Gifts

The Messenger said, 'It is a mark of respect for a fellow Muslim when you accept a gift from him that you present him with something of your own and do not obligate him with anything.' And, 'I do not like those who obligate others.'[1074]

Al-Baaqir tells how the Messenger would use gifts but not charity, and would say, 'Give each other gifts, for a gift will remove hatred, rancor and malice.'[1075]

1071	ibid.
1072	ibid.
1073	ibid.
1074	ibid.,219-220.
1075	ibid.

Al-Ridaa transmits from his father and his grandfather the *hadith* that the Prophet used to love gifts, found delight in them, urged people to give them and repaid in kind those who gave them.[1076]

The Prophet said, 'If I were given a sheep's foot I would accept it, for this is part of the *Deen*. If a non-believer or a hypocrite were to give me a load of corn I would not accept it – and this is also part of the *Deen*. Allah has refused me the cream and the food of the idol-worshippers and hypocrites.'[1077]

Muhammad ibn Muslim relates that al-Saadiq said, 'Those who keep company with a man are those who share gifts with him.'[1078]

He [al-Saadiq] also said that there are three kinds of gift: the gift which is rewarded, the gift of conciliation and the gift for the sake of Allah.[1079]

Al-Saadiq also said that the most blessed of actions is to make a gift in a time of need.[1080]

'Make gifts to each other and love each other, for surely gifts remove malice and spite.'[1081]

The Adoption of Brothers

Allah has said:

> ☼ The believers are but brethren, therefore make peace between your brethren. (3:103)

1076 ibid.
1077 ibid.
1078 ibid.
1079 ibid.
1080 *al-Khisaal*,I,27.
1081 ibid.

☼ Then He united your hearts so that by His favor you became brethren. (49:10)

☼ And We shall root out whatever of rancor is in their breasts – [they shall be] as brethren, on raised couches, face to face. (15:47)

The Messenger said, 'Sitting with the people of the *Deen* means honor in this world and the next.'[1082]

'After faith in Allah the height of intellect is to endear oneself to people.'[1083]

'The believer is as a mirror to his brother, and he removes harm from him.'[1084]

'If a man exposes his fellow Muslim, it is as if he has mauled his face.'[1085]

'When a slave establishes someone as a brother in Allah, a station for him is established in the Garden.'[1086]

'The likeness of brothers is the likeness of two hands washing each other: just as the two hands help each other for one purpose, so do brothers.'[1087]

Imam `Ali said, 'That I give twenty dirhams to a brother is preferable to me than if I were to give a hundred dirhams away to the poor.' He also said, 'That I prepare a measure of food and gather together the brothers in Allah is preferable to me than freeing a slave.'[1088]

1082   ibid.,I,15.
1083   ibid.
1084   *Mishkaat al-Anwaar*,187-189.
1085   ibid.
1086   ibid.
1087   al-`Inaathi,I,72-73.
1088   ibid.

'Keep with the brothers, for surely they are the means to this world and the next. Have you not heard the words of the people of the Fire: "So we have no intercessors, nor a true friend"? Even if a man were to stand in prayer at night, fast during the day, and make a sacrifice between the corner of the Ka`bah and the station of Ibrahim, Allah will not raise him up except with the ones he loves, obtaining whatever they have attained. If it is the Garden, then so be it; if the Fire, then so be it.'[1089]

Imam Husayn ibn `Ali once said to a man, 'Would one of you put his hand into the pocket or bag of his brother and take what he wanted without permission?' 'No,' replied the man. 'Then you are not brothers,' he said.[1090]

Imam al-Baaqir said, 'It is incumbent on the believer to give advice to the believer.'[1091]

'It will be said to the believer on the Last Day, 'Let the faces pass in review one by one – whoever has given you to drink, or food to eat, or has done something for you, take him by the hand and bring him to the Garden.'[1092]

'When a person is generous to the believer it is as if he is generous with Allah, and whenever a man prays for his fellow believer, Allah will avert affliction from him and will make his provision plentiful.'[1093]

Al-Baaqir said, 'Whoever supports and defends a fellow believer who is slandered in one's presence, Allah will help in this world and the next; whoever does not support or defend him when he is capable of this, Allah will fill him with fear in this

---

1089   *Mishkaat al-Anwaar*,187-189.
1090   al-`Inaathi,I,73.
1091   *Mishkaat al-Anwaar*,187-189.
1092   ibid.
1093   ibid.

world and the next.'[1094]

Al-Saadiq said, 'Do not cheat people, for you will find yourself without a single friend.'[1095]

'A believer is a brother to the believer; he does not oppress him, abandon him or cheat him, nor does he slander him, betray him or lie to him.'[1096]

'Do not destroy the decorum between you and your brother, for if decorum is destroyed, then so is modesty, and if decorum remains, then courtesy and manhood will remain.'[1097]

'Whoever honors the religion of Allah honors the rights of his brothers, and whoever treats his religion lightly is treating his brothers lightly.'[1098]

'If one of you is in difficulties, then his brother should be aware of it, so that he is not alone in facing the difficulties.'[1099]

'If anyone is asked for help by a fellow believer who is in need through loss or injury, and he refuses him money when he is capable of giving it (either from himself or by securing the help of others), then Allah will have him stand in the assembly on the Last Day with his hands tied to his neck, until He has finished taking Creation to account.'[1100]

'Whoever walks with his brother Muslim who is in need and does not counsel him, has betrayed Allah and His Messenger.'[1101]

1094	ibid.
1095	ibid.
1096	ibid.
1097	ibid.
1098	ibid.
1099	ibid.
1100	ibid.
1101	ibid.

Respect for Elders

Imam `Ali relates that the Messenger of Allah said, 'Reverence for Allah demands the honoring of three types of person: elderly Muslims, those who act justly, and those who have learnt the Qur'an by heart and are neither offensive nor excessive.' He also said, 'When a young man honors an old man for his years, Allah will send someone to honor him when he grows old.' The Messenger also said, 'Truly Allah feels shy at punishing the man advanced in years.'[1102]

Ibn `Abbas relates that the Messenger said, 'Whoever does not have mercy on our young and does not honor our elderly is not one of us.'[1103]

The Messenger also said, 'Treat the elderly with deference, for deference to the elderly is honoring Allah, and whoever does not treat them with deference is not one of us.'[1104]

The Messenger also said, 'Shall I tell you who are the elite among you? Those of you who live the longest if they are sound and proper.'[1105]

Al-Saadiq relates on the authority of his grandparents that two men came to the Prophet, one elderly and the other a youth, and the youth spoke before the elderly man, whereupon the Prophet exclaimed, 'The elder! The elder!'[1106]

He also relates that the Messenger said, 'If anyone recognizes the excellence of an elder man because of his age, and honors him, then Allah will protect him from the terror of the day of Final Judgment.'[1107]

1102	ibid.,168-170.
1103	ibid.
1104	ibid.
1105	ibid.
1106	ibid.
1107	ibid.

Al-Saadiq relates that the Messenger said, 'When a man reaches fifty years of age, Allah lightens the reckoning for him; when he reaches sixty, He grants him repentance; if he reaches seventy, then Allah and the inhabitants of the heavens love him; if he reaches eighty, Allah commands that his good actions be recorded and his bad be ignored; if he reaches ninety, Allah forgives him the wrong he has committed and the wrong he will commit, and he is reckoned as one of Allah's captives on earth.'[1108]

The Messenger also said, 'The elder man amongst his people is like the Prophet and his nation. If a man reaches forty years of age and his good actions have not yet gained ascendancy over his bad, Satan kisses him between the eyes and says, "This face will not prosper".'[1109]

The Messenger also said, 'Whoever lives to be more than forty, and whose good actions have not triumphed over his bad, should prepare himself for the Fire.'[1110]

Al-Saadiq said, 'Husayn would never walk in front of Hasan nor would he begin the conversation when they met, out of respect for him.'[1111]

Al-Saadiq also said, 'An old man will be brought forward on the day of Final Judgment; he will be given his book, plain to see for the people following him, with nothing but bad actions to be seen. This lasts a long time for him and he says. "O Lord, are you ordering me to the Fire?" The Powerful One then says, "O you who are advanced in years, I am loath to torment you, for you used to pray in the abode of the world – take this slave of mine

---

1108 ibid.
1109 ibid.
1110 ibid.
1111 ibid.

to the Garden".'[1112]

'Abd Allah ibn Abaan relates that al-Ridaa said, "O 'Abd Allah, have respect for the elderly amongst you and maintain your ties of kinship. There is no better way of maintaining ties with them than refraining from troubling them.'[1113]

The Rights of the Neighbor

The Messenger said, 'Do you know the rights of the neighbor? Methinks you know but little. Surely a man does not believe in Allah and the Last Day if he does not protect his neighbor from harm. If he asks for a loan then he should lend it to him; if something good happens to him he should congratulate him; if something evil, he should console him. He should not construct a high building in such a way as to cut off the wind except with his permission. If he desires fruit, then he should be given it, for if the fruit is taken in secrecy and neither he nor his children are given any of it then they will be vexed. There are three types of neighbors: those who have three rights – the rights of Islam, the right of being a neighbor, and the right of kinship; those who have two rights – the rights of Islam and that of the neighbor; and those who have one right – the unbeliever who has the right of the neighbor.'[1114]

'He is not a believer who satiates his hunger while his next door neighbor goes hungry.'[1115]

'Whoever causes harm to his neighbor, Allah will deprive of the wind of the Garden; his abode will be hell, and he will have a terrible end. Whoever does not fulfill the rights of his neighbor

---

1112   ibid.
1113   al-Kulayni,II,165.
1114   *Mishkaat al-Anwaar*,212-215.
1115   ibid.

is not one of us.'[1116]

'Gabriel instructed me about the neighbor to such an extent that I thought he was going to give him the right of inheritance.'[1117]

'Whoever refrains from causing harm to his neighbor, Allah will consider as having undone his offences on the day of Final Judgment; whoever abstains from excessive food and drink will be felicitous and a king, and whoever frees a believing soul will have a house built for him in the Garden.'[1118]

Al-Saadiq tells how a man complained to the Messenger of Allah about his neighbor, and the Messenger turned away from him; he then returned, but again the Messenger turned away from him; when he returned again, the Messenger said to `Ali, Salmaan and al-Miqdaad, 'Go and call for the curse of Allah and the Angels to be on those who cause trouble to their neighbors.'[1119]

During the battle of Tabuk the Messenger said, 'Anyone who has caused trouble to his neighbor should not accompany us.'[1120]

'Whoever believes in Allah and the day of Final Judgment should not cause harm to his neighbor.'[1121]

'Whoever dies with three neighbors all pleased with him is forgiven.'[1122]

Al-Saadiq relates that the Messenger said, 'I seek refuge with Allah from having an evil neighbor in one's place of residence: his eyes see you and his heart observes you; if he sees you well,

---

1116	ibid.
1117	ibid.
1118	ibid.
1119	al-Kulayni,II,666.
1120	*Mishkaat al-Anwaar*,212-215.
1121	ibid.
1122	ibid.

this displeases him, and if he sees you in difficulties this makes him happy.'[1123]

Al-Baaqir relates that he read in the book of 'Ali that the Messenger had prescribed for the emigrants from Makkah, the *ansaar* and those who joined them from the people of Yathrib, that 'the neighbor is like the person who causes no harm or injury, and the veneration of one neighbor for another should be like his veneration for his mother.'[1124]

Certain people told the Messenger that there was a woman who fasted during the day, stood in prayer at night, gave in charity but vexed her neighbor by her words. He said, 'There is no good in her and she is destined for the Fire.'[1125]

'Good neighborliness means increase in one's years and prosperity in the homes.'[1126]

'The law of neighborliness is not just abstaining from causing trouble, but rather, your patience in the face of trouble from your neighbor.'[1127]

Al-Saadiq said, 'The prayers of the man against his neighbor are not answered. Allah has given him the means to sell his house and move from the neighborhood.'[1128]

'Know that the man who does not deal kindly with his neighbors is not one of us.'[1129]

1123	ibid.
1124	al-Kulayni,II,666.
1125	*Mishkaat al-Anwaar*,212-215.
1126	ibid.
1127	al-Kulayni,II,667.
1128	*Mishkaat al-Anwaar*,214.
1129	al-Kulayni,II,668.

Helping the Believers

Al-Saadiq relates that the Messenger was asked who were the most beloved of Allah, and he replied, 'Those who help others the most.'[1130]

The Messenger also said, 'The believer has seven rights over the believer which have been imposed by Allah: esteem for him in his eyes, love for him in his breast, help for him from his wealth, that he should respect him in his absence, visit him when he is sick, follow his coffin to the grave and speak only good of him after his death.'[1131]

'Whoever is troubled by his bad actions and made happy by his good [ones] is a believer.'[1132]

'Allah will remove seventy-three difficulties from the man who aids a believer: one from this world and seventy-two from the day of great difficulties – the day when each is too worried about himself.'[1133]

Al-Saadiq relates that the Messenger said, 'Creation is the family of Allah, therefore the most beloved of creation to Allah is whoever helps the dependants of Allah and brings happiness to the Family of the Household.'[1134]

The Apostle said, 'By the One Who has my soul in His hand, you will not enter the Garden until you believe; you will not believe until you love each other; and you will not love each other until you give the greeting of peace to each other.'[1135]

Imam `Ali said, 'Among the things which expiate the

1130   ibid.,II,164.
1131   *Mishkaat al-Anwaar*,77 & 87.
1132   ibid.
1133   al-Kulayni,II,199,164,169.
1134   ibid.
1135   *Mishkaat al-Anwaar*,82-84.

major wrong actions are helping the unfortunate and relieving someone's affliction.'[1136]

Al-Saadiq said, 'Among the rights the believer has over his fellow believer is that he should feed him if he is hungry, conceal his private parts, alleviate his affliction, pay his debts and if he dies, assume responsibility for his family and sons.'

Al-Baaqir said, 'Love your brother Muslim; love for him what you love for yourself and hate for him what you would hate for yourself. If you are in need ask of him and if he asks of you then give to him. Do not store any food and deprive him of it, for he would not store it up and deprive you of it; be a support for him just as he is a support for you. If he is absent then protect his good name, and if he is present then visit him, honor him and be generous to him, for he is of you and you are of him. If he has rebuked you, then do not leave him until you have gently removed his resentment and anything else he harbors within himself. If good comes to him then praise Allah for him, and if he is afflicted then help and find a pretext to distract him.'[1137]

Imam al-Baaqir also said, 'Allah possesses a Garden which is entered by only three kinds of people: the man who rules himself in a proper manner, and the man who visits his fellow believer for the sake of Allah, and the man who prefers his fellow believer above himself for the sake of Allah.'[1138]

Al-Saadiq said, 'The Muslim is the brother of the Muslim: he is his sight, his mirror, and his guide. He does not betray him, cheat him, oppress him, lie to him or slander him, nor does he promise him something and then go back on his promise.'[1139]

1136	ibid.
1137	ibid.
1138	al-Khisaal,I,131.
1139	al-Kulayni,II,166.

'If a man deprives a Muslim of his right, Allah forbids him the Garden and decrees the Fire for him – even if it is [on account of] depriving him of a tooth-stick from the Arak tree.'[1140]

Al-Saadiq said, 'To see to the needs of a believer is better than the acceptance of a thousand pilgrimages performed with all its rites and freeing a thousand slaves for the sake of Allah.'[1141]

'Serve your fellow Muslim, but not if he seeks to have himself served.'[1142]

Al-Saadiq said, 'The best of you are the most generous of you, and the worst the most miserly of you; among the most correct of actions is kindness to your fellow Muslims and striving to see to their needs. To do this is to spite Satan, to move away from the Fire and to enter the Garden.' He said, 'O Jameel, tell this *hadith* to the noblest of your companions.' Jameel said, 'My I be your sacrifice, who are the noblest of my companions?' 'Those who do good in both easy and harsh times,' he replied. Then he again said, 'O Jameel, it is easy for those who possess much, but Allah has praised those who possess little: "And prefer [others] before themselves though poverty may afflict them, and whoever is preserved from the niggardliness of his soul, these it is who are the successful ones" [59:9].'[1143]

'No believer abandons his brother while being in a position to save him but that Allah abandons him in this world and the next.'[1144]

'On the Last Day, the man who has been ordered to the Fire will pass those of you who are believers, saying, "O such and such a person, save me! For I did you a good turn in the world."

1140	*Mishkaat al-Anwaar*,82-84.
1141	ibid.
1142	al-Ashtari,II,249.
1143	*Mishkaat al-Anwaar*,82-84.
1144	ibid.

The believer will say to the angel, "Let him go." Allah will then order the angel to let him go.'[1145]

Al-Saadiq was asked what was the least of the rights of a believer over his brother. He replied, 'That he should not keep for himself that of which the other has more need.'[1146]

Love of Men who are Righteous

The Messenger said, 'You will not enter the Garden until you believe, you will not believe until you love each other, and you will not love each other until you greet each other with the greeting of peace.'[1147]

'Whoever loves us, the Family of the Household, should praise Allah for the first of blessings.' He was asked what was the first of blessings, and he replied, 'Good birth — only those of good birth love us.'[1148]

'A slave does not believe until I am more beloved to him than his self, my family are more beloved to him than his own family, my kin more beloved to him than his kin, and my being is more beloved to him than his own being.'[1149]

'Whoever Allah bestows with a love of the Family of my House has been given the good of this world and the next, and there is no doubt that he is in the Garden. Those who love the Family of my Household possess twenty qualities: ten of them in this world and ten in the next. The ten qualities in this world are as follows: doing without, love of knowledge, scrupulousness in religion, desire for worship, turning to Allah before death,

---

1145	ibid.
1146	al-Khisaal,I,8.
1147	Mishkaat al-Anwaar,70-84.
1148	ibid.
1149	ibid.

constancy in standing in prayer at night, renunciation of what is in the hands of others, maintaining Allah's commands and prohibitions, dislike of this world and the next, and generosity.'

'As for the next world, no tribunal and no balance will be set up for him; he will be given his book in his right hand, and exemption from the Fire will be prescribed for him; his face will be made white and he will be clothed with the ornaments of the Garden; he will be an intercessor for a hundred of his family and Allah will look to him with mercy; he will be crowned with one of the crowns of the Garden and he will enter the garden without being called to account. Happy therefore is the lot of those who love the Family of my Household.'[1150]

Al-Saadiq said, 'The most beloved of Allah's slaves are those who are truthful in speech, who maintain the prayer and whatever Allah has made incumbent on them – including fulfilling the trust.'[1151]

Salmaan al-Faarisi said, 'My friend the Messenger of Allah advised me to love and be close to the poor, to tell the truth even if it be bitter, to maintain the ties of kinship – even if it is for a slave-girl.'[1152]

Al-Baaqir said, 'Love your Muslim brother, love for him what you would love for yourself, and hate for him what you would hate for yourself; if you are in need, then ask him; if he asks you, then give to him, and do not store up some good thing he needs, for he would not store up something of which you were in need.'[1153]

Al-Saadiq said, 'Love for other people what you yourselves

1150 ibid.
1151 ibid.
1152 ibid.
1153 ibid.

would like for yourselves.'[1154]

'Part of man's love of his religion is his love for his brothers.'[1155]

'Among the strongest ties to Islam are a man's loving for the sake of Allah, hating for the sake of Allah, giving for the sake of Allah and denying [someone something] for the sake of Allah.'[1156]

'Fear Allah in your actions, love each other, visit each other, maintain ties with each other, be merciful with each other and be devoted brothers.'[1157]

Visiting Each Other

The Messenger said, 'If a slave visits his brother for the sake of Allah, a voice calls from Heaven, "Prosperous are you and prosperous your steps; a house has been built for you in the Garden".'[1158]

'It is part of the good character of the prophets and men of truth that they have joy in their faces when they see each other, and shake each other's hand when they meet; the man who visits another for the sake of Allah has a right to be treated generously.'[1159]

The Messenger said to Abu Dharr, 'Do not forsake your brother – actions are not accepted from the one who forsakes another. If you feel obliged to leave him, then do not cut him off for more than three full days. If a man dies having cut off

---

1154   ibid.
1155   al-Khisaal,I,3-7.
1156   ibid.
1157   Mishkaat al-Anwaar,84.
1158   al-Ashtari,I,29.
1159   ibid.

his brother, then the Fire is the most fitting thing for him.'[1160]

Imam `Ali said, 'The coming of Friday means visiting and beauty.' When he was asked what he meant by beauty he said, 'The carrying out of what is incumbent upon you and visiting each other.'[1161]

'In your visiting each other you have the reward of those who go on pilgrimage.'[1162]

Al-Baaqir said, 'Whoever visits his brother for the sake of Allah is a visitor of Allah; when he shakes hands with him he will not ask Allah for something whether religious or spiritual, but that it will be given to him.'

'Allah possesses a Garden which only three kinds of people will enter: the man who has mastered his self in a correct way, the man who has visited his fellow believer for the sake of Allah, and the man who prefers his fellow believer to himself for the sake of Allah.'[1163]

Al-Saadiq said, 'No two men separate and break off relations with each other without one of them deserving disavowal and a curse; often both of them merit this.' Mu`tab then said to him, 'That is clear for the wrong-doer, but what about the person who was wronged?' He replied, 'That is because he does not call his brother to make up their differences, nor does he turn a blind eye to what he has said. I have heard my father saying that if two people quarrel, then one should assist the other, and the one who has been wronged should go back to the one who wronged him and say, "O brother, I was in the wrong," so that he makes up the break in relations between them. Allah is a just arbiter and He will take from the one who did wrong for the sake

---

1160 *Mishkaat al-Anwaar*, 203-212.
1161 ibid.
1162 ibid.
1163 ibid.

of the wronged.'[1164]

'Relations are maintained between brothers by visiting each other when they are resident in one place, and by writing to each other when they are travelling.'[1165]

'If the slave goes out to visit his brother for the sake of Allah he does not come back without his wrong actions being forgiven, and his needs in this world and the next being fulfilled.'[1166]

'Visit each other in your houses, for in it is life for this affair of ours; Allah has mercy on the slave who gives life to our affair.'[1167]

Al-Ridaa tells how Hasan and Husayn argued with one another. Muhammad ibn al-Hanifah came to Husayn and said, 'O Abu `Abd Allah, are you not going to Abu Muhammad? He is the elder.' Then Husayn replied, 'I have heard my grandfather, the Messenger of Allah, saying that there are no two persons who argue with one another and one of them takes up the greeting again but that the one who began will be the first of them to enter the Garden – but I did not want to arrive at the Garden before him.' Then Muhammad went to Hasan and informed him of this and Hasan said, 'Abu `Abd Allah has spoken the truth – let us go to see him.'

Kindness and Compassion (rifq) towards People

Kindness is being of a gentle disposition, compassionate, avoiding harshness and rudeness in one's actions and words with people at all times.

1164   ibid.
1165   ibid.
1166   ibid.
1167   al-Khisaal,I,22.

The Messenger said, 'Kindness is prosperity and offensiveness is misfortune.'[1168]

'Never was kindness placed on something but that it beautified it, and never was it removed but that it marred it.'[1169]

'In kindness there is increase and blessing; whoever withholds kindness withholds goodness.'[1170]

'If kindness were a visible creation, nothing which Allah has created would be more beautiful than it.'[1171]

'No two persons keep company with each other but that the one with the greatest reward and the most beloved of Allah is the one who is the most kind to his companion.'[1172]

Imam `Ali said, 'Joyous is the one who becomes intimate with people and they with him out of obedience to Allah.'[1173]

Imam al-Baaqir said, 'For everything there is a lock and the lock of faith is kindness.'[1174]

'Whoever has been given a portion of kindness has been given a portion of faith.'[1175]

'Allah is kind (*rafeeq*) and He loves kindness; He gives for kindness what He does not give if someone is harsh.'[1176]

'A cheerful welcome and a joyous face produce love and nearness to Allah; and a frowning face and a cold welcome produce the hate of Allah and distance from Him.'[1177]

1168	al-Kulayni,II,119-120.
1169	ibid.
1170	ibid.
1171	ibid.
1172	ibid.
1173	*Mishkaat al-Anwaar*,180.
1174	al-Kulayni,II,120.
1175	ibid.
1176	ibid.
1177	*Mishkaat al-Anwaar*,179-180.

Al-Saadiq said, 'The smile of one believer to another believer is a fine action rewarded by Allah.'[1178]

'Allah is liberal with the provision of a household which gives its fair share of kindness.'[1179]

'Whoever is kind in his affairs will obtain what he wants from people.'[1180]

Imam Musa al-Kaazim said, 'Kindness is half of life.'[1181]

Accompanying the Corpse to the Grave

The Messenger was asked who were the most abstemious of people and he replied, 'Those who have not forgotten the corpse in the grave and its decomposition, who avoid the superfluous beauty of the world, who prefer what is eternal to what is temporal, those who do not reckon tomorrow as one of their days, and who reckon themselves as people of the grave.'[1182]

The Messenger also said, 'If a man undertakes four actions Allah will make flow for that person a river in the Garden: the man who begins his day by fasting, who visits the sick, who accompanies the coffin (*janaazah*) to the grave, and who gives charity to the poor.'[1183]

'I have not seen a more profound sight than the grave.'[1184]

The Messenger said to Abu Dharr, 'Visit graves and thereby remember the next world; wash the dead, for doing this is rewarded and it is a profound lesson; pray over the dead that

---

1178	ibid.
1179	ibid.
1180	al-Kulayni,II,120.
1181	ibid.
1182	al-Ashtari,I,283-288.
1183	ibid.
1184	ibid.

it may make you grieve, for the one who grieves is under the protection of Allah.'[1185]

He said in another *hadith*, 'Visit your dead, pray over them and greet them, for in this there is a lesson.'[1186]

Imam al-Saadiq would often come to the graves at night and say, 'O people of the graves, how is it that when I call you do not reply?' Then he would say, 'By Allah! I am preventing them from replying; it is as if I am like them.' Then he would face in the direction of Makkah until the sun rose.[1187]

Al-Saadiq said, 'A Muslim has rights over another Muslim: he greets him on meeting him, visits him if he is sick, wishes him well when he is absent, accepts when he invites him and accompanies his coffin to the grave when he dies.'[1188]

In another *hadith* he said, 'If he is absent, then he looks after his affairs, and if he dies he visits his grave.'[1189]

Imam al-Zaahid Warraam al-Ashtari said, 'There is a lesson for the man of reflection in following the coffin to the grave, and there is also a warning and a reminder. The forgetful do not gain anything from this spectacle except hardness, because they think that they will always be looking at other people's burials and do not reckon with their being carried to the grave themselves. Thus a slave should not look at a burial without realizing that he himself will soon be carried there too.'[1190]

Some have reported that whenever they saw a burial they would say, 'Go ahead! We are close behind.'[1191]

1185	ibid.
1186	ibid.
1187	ibid.,II,109.
1188	ibid.,I,284.
1189	al-Kulayni,II,169-171.
1190	ibid.
1191	ibid.

Visiting the Sick

The Messenger said, 'The believer is like newly mown grass which is tossed this way and that by the winds, as the believer is tossed by pain and sickness; while the hypocrite is like the stiff rod – nothing affects it until death comes and shatters it to pieces.'[1192]

'If a man undertakes four actions, Allah will make a river flow for him in the Garden: he begins his day fasting, visits the sick, follows the coffin to the grave, and gives in charity to the poor.'[1193]

Al-Saadiq said, 'Visit your sick and comfort them with prayer, for surely this is equal to the prayer of the angels. If anyone falls sick at night and accepts it with a total acceptance, then Allah will record for him the equivalent of seventy years of worship.' When asked what was the meaning of acceptance, he replied, 'That he does not complain to anyone of what has afflicted him, and when he wakes in the morning he praises Allah for what the night has brought.'[1194]

Mu`ali ibn Khanees relates how he asked Abu `Abd Allah al-Saadiq what were the rights of the Muslim over the Muslim. He replied, 'There are seven rights, all of them without exception obligatory.' When he had enumerated six rights he came to the seventh, saying, 'The seventh right is that you accept his oath, accept his invitation, visit him when sick, and follow his coffin to the grave; and if you learn that he has some need you endeavor to see to that need and do not oblige him to ask for it.'[1195]

`Ali ibn `Uqbah relates that al-Saadiq said, 'Among the rights that a Muslim has over his brothers is that he greets him when

---

1192   *Mishkaat al-Anwaar*, 280.
1193   al-Ashtari, II, 109.
1194   *Mishkaat al-Anwaar*, 281.
1195   al-Kulayni, II, 169-171.

he meets him, visits him when sick, wishes him well when he is absent, prays for him if he sneezes, accepts his invitation and follows his coffin if he dies.'[1196]

'Abd Allah ibn Sinaan relates that he heard Abu 'Abd Allah al-Saadiq say, 'I instruct you to fear Allah in your action, and not to carry people on your shoulders and so humble yourselves. Allah says, "And say to the people words of kindness".' Then he said, 'Visit your sick, attend their burial, testify for them and pray with them in their mosques.'[1197]

Keeping Company with People and Assisting them

The Messenger said, 'Whoever assists the poor and is just with people of his own accord is a true believer.'[1198]

'Recognize your limits in doubtful matters, and overlook the shortcomings of the generous — except those who become angry.'[1199]

'There are three types of hand: the one which asks, the one which gives and the one which takes, and the best of them is that which gives.'[1200]

'Your help to the weak is the greatest of charities.'[1201]

'My Lord has ordered me to keep the company of people, just as He has ordered me to perform the obligatory duties.'[1202]

'You will never be able to meet the demands of the

1196 ibid.
1197 al-Barqi,*al-Mahaasin*,18.
1198 *al-Khisaal*,I,47.
1199 *Mishkaat al-Anwaar*,219-220.
1200 ibid.
1201 ibid.
1202 ibid.

people with your wealth, so meet them with your courtesy and manners.'[1203]

'The person with the best faith is he who is the best mannered; the most righteous of them is the one who is most beneficial to the people, and the best of people is he who is the most useful to them.'[1204]

The Messenger said, 'O `Ali, need is Allah's trust placed with his creation – whoever keeps it to himself, Allah will give the reward of the one who prays, and whoever discloses it to someone who is capable of meeting this need but does not meet it, then it is as if he has cursed him.'[1205]

The Messenger said to Husayn ibn `Ali, 'Perform the obligatory duties of Allah and you will be among the most pious of people. Be content with what Allah has apportioned you and you will be among the richest of people, and abstain from what Allah has forbidden and you will be among the most scrupulous of people. If you maintain good relations with your neighbors, you are a believer, and if you are good company for your companions, then you are a Muslim. Keeping company with the people of religion is an honor in this world and the next.'[1206]

Al-Baaqir relates that the Messenger said, 'The most fortunate of my friends is the man who is amiable, serious, devout in his worship when hidden from people, unknown amongst people, content with his provision and patient with it; when he dies he bequeaths little, and few are his mourners.'[1207]

Hasan ibn `Ali was asked about honor and manhood, and he replied, 'It consists in maintaining one's religion, acting to

---

1203   ibid.
1204   ibid.
1205   ibid.
1206   ibid.
1207   ibid.

bring about righteousness in the country, disputing justly, giving the greeting, uttering gentle words and showing love to the people.'[1208]

Al-Sukuni tells how he said to Abu Ja`far, 'Often I have apportioned something between my companions and corrupted them [by it]; so how should I give to them?' He replied, 'Give them in accordance with their migration (*hijrah*), their religion, their knowledge of the laws and their excellence.'[1209]

Al-Saadiq, commenting on the meaning of Allah's words, 'Surely we see you to be one of the doers of good,' said, 'He made room for a person to sit down, lent to the person in need and helped the weak.'[1210]

He also said, 'To conceal one's need is one of Allah's treasures.' And again, 'If a believer complains of his need to a non-believer or to someone who opposes him in his religion, then it is as if he has complained about Allah; and if anyone complains of his need to a believer, then it is as if he has taken his complaint to Allah.'[1211]

'To resolve a problem afflicting a Muslim yields a greater reward than your fasting and your prayer, and it is the best means whereby the slaves may come close to Allah.'[1212]

Al-Baaqir said, 'Do not keep company or establish brotherhood with these four kinds of person: the foolish, the mean, the cowardly and the untruthful. The foolish man wishes to be of benefit to you, but harms you; the mean person will take from you and not give to you; as for the coward, he will flee from you and his parents; and the untruthful will be given credence

---

1208 ibid.
1209 ibid.
1210 ibid.
1211 ibid.
1212 ibid.

but will not be telling the truth.'[1213]

Al-Saadiq said, 'Come closer to Allah by assisting your brothers.'[1214]

'The Muslim is a brother to the Muslim; he neither oppresses him, forsakes him, nor betrays him; Muslims should strive to unite in friendship and to help each other, to have goodwill towards each other, to assist those in need and to be sympathetic to each other until they are as Allah has ordered them to be:

☼ "Compassionate among themselves" [48:29].'[1215]

'Among the most beloved acts in the eyes of Allah are bringing happiness to the believer, stilling his hunger, relieving his hardship and paying off his debt.'[1216]

VICES AND BLAMEWORTHY BEHAVIOR AND CHARACTERISTICS

Vices

Oppression

Allah has said:

☼ So woe to those who were unjust because of the chastisement of a painful day. (43:65)

☼ That it may warn those who are unjust and as good news for the virtuous. (46:12)

☼ And [as for] those who are unjust from among these, there shall befall them the evil [consequences] of what they earn. (39:51)

1213 ibid.
1214 *al-Khisaal*,I,8.
1215 al-Kulayni,II,174 &192.
1216 ibid.

☼ And whoever among you is unjust We will make him taste a great chastisement. (25:19)

☼ But whoever repents after his iniquity and reforms [himself], then surely Allah will turn to him [mercifully]. (5:39)

The Messenger said, 'If anyone seizes part of a Muslim's wealth with his right hand, Allah will forbid him the Garden.'[1217]

Imam al-Ridaa relates on the authority of his father and Imam `Ali that the Messenger said, 'Beware of oppression for it ruins your hearts.'[1218]

The Prophet said, 'Whoever walks with an oppressor in order to help him, knowing that he is an oppressor, has left Islam.'[1219]

'The warding off of something forbidden by a believer is equal to seventy accepted pilgrimages in the eyes of Allah.'[1220]

'If a morsel of forbidden food falls into the belly of the slave, all the angels of the heavens and the earth curse him.'[1221]

'If admonition from Allah comes to a slave concerning his religion, then it is a blessing from Allah; if he accepts it, then he is expressing gratitude; and if not, then this is proof for Allah that He should increase His anger against him.'[1222]

'To act justly for an hour is better than the worship of seventy years, standing in prayer at night and fasting during the day; to act unjustly for an hour is a worse crime and more grievous with

---

1217 al-Ashtari,I,53.
1218 *Mishkaat al-Anwaar*,315-317.
1219 ibid.
1220 ibid.
1221 ibid.
1222 ibid.

Allah than the acts of disobedience of sixty years.'[1223]

'If anyone spends the morning without desiring to oppress anyone, then Allah will forgive his crimes.'[1224]

Jaabir ibn `Abd Allah relates that the Messenger said, 'Protect yourselves from oppression, for surely oppression means darkness on the Last Day; and protect yourselves from miserliness, for surely miserliness has caused those before you to perish, to shed blood, and to take delight in that which was forbidden to them.'[1225]

The Prophet said, 'The people who will receive the greatest punishment on the Last Day will be those who associate others with Allah's sovereignty, and who are unjust in their governance.'[1226]

Imam `Ali said, 'That I spend the night on the thorns of the Si`daan bush without sleep, and that I be dragged bound in chains is preferable to me than meeting Allah and His Messenger on the Last Day as an oppressor of some of His slaves, or as someone who has unlawfully seized something of this world. Why would I oppress anyone? Man is hastening to decay in his returning, and lies long in the earth in his place of rest. Surely your world means less to me than a leaf in the mouth of a locust as he chews it up – what is it to `Ali? The blessings of this world disappear and pleasure does not last.'[1227]

Imam `Ali also said, 'Whoever fears the reprisal refrains from oppressing people.'[1228]

Imam al-Baaqir relates that, as his father `Ali ibn al-Husayn was dying, he clasped him to his breast, saying, 'O son! I give

---

1223 ibid.
1224 ibid.
1225 al-Ashtari,I,56.
1226 ibid.
1227 ibid.
1228 al-Kulayni,II,331.

you the same advice as my father gave me when he was dying, and which was the same as the advice his own father gave him: O my son, beware of oppressing those who have no help but that of Allah.'[1229]

Al-Saadiq said, 'Whoever restrains his hand from harming people is restraining one single hand, but they [the people] will restrain many hands from him.'[1230]

'If a man excuses an oppressor from the guilt of his oppression then Allah will have people rule over him and oppress him; if he makes a prayer, then it will not be answered, and Allah will not protect him from His darkness.'[1231]

Miserliness

Allah has said:

☼ And whoever is preserved from the niggardliness of his soul these it is who are the successful ones. (59:9)

☼ And let not those who are miserly in giving away that which Allah has granted them out of His grace, deem that it is good for them; nay, it is worse for them; they shall have that whereof they were niggardly made to cleave to their necks on the Day of Resurrection. (3:180)

☼ Those who are niggardly and bid people to be niggardly and hide what Allah has given them out of His grace. (4:37)

☼ And as for him who is niggardly and considers himself free from need [of Allah], and rejects the best, We will facilitate for him an adverse end. (92:8-10)

1229   *al-Khisaal*,I,16-17.
1230   ibid.
1231   al-Kulayni,II,334.

The Messenger said, 'Protect yourselves from miserliness, for surely miserliness has caused those before you to perish, to shed blood, and to take delight in that which was forbidden to them.'[1232]

'No miser, impostor, betrayer, ill-behaved person, tyrant or begrudger of something given will enter the Garden.'[1233]

'Three [kinds of people] are doomed to perish: the man advanced in years who fornicates, the begrudging miser and the arrogant head of a family.'[1234]

'O Allah, I seek refuge in you from miserliness, I seek refuge in you from cowardliness and I seek refuge in you lest I be brought back to a life of baseness.'[1235]

'I swear by Allah, by His glory, His might and His majesty that neither the miser nor the avaricious man will enter the Garden.'[1236]

'Avarice and faith are never to be found together in the heart of a slave.'[1237]

'Two qualities should never be found in a Muslim: miserliness and bad behavior.'[1238]

'The food of the generous person is a cure, and the food of the miserly person an affliction.'[1239]

'The miser is far from Allah, far from people, far from the Garden and close to the Fire.'[1240]

1232	al-Ashtari,I,171-172.
1233	ibid.
1234	ibid.
1235	ibid.
1236	ibid.
1237	Mishkaat al-Anwaar,231-232.
1238	ibid.
1239	ibid.
1240	ibid.

Giving advice to Abu Dharr, the Messenger said, 'Be more avaricious for your life than for your dirhams and dinars.'[1241]

'Love of position and wealth causes hypocrisy to flourish in the heart just as water causes green plants to flourish.'[1242]

Imam `Ali said, 'Miserliness is a disgrace and cowardliness is a deficiency. Be aware of how much you spend, but do not be niggardly.'[1243]

'I am amazed at the miser – he quickly brings to himself the very poverty from which he is fleeing and he misses the riches which he is seeking so he lives the life of a poor man in the world and he will be taken to account in the next world as the rich are taken to account. Miserliness comprises all kinds of grievous deficiencies and is the bridle which leads a man to all kinds of evil.'[1244]

'Miserliness is a disgrace and cowardliness is a deficiency; poverty renders the alert person mute regarding his case; the needy is a stranger in his country; and incapacity is a blight; patience is courage; doing without is wealth, and scrupulousness is the Garden.'[1245]

'Miserliness comprises all kinds of disgraces.'[1246]

Lying

Allah has said:

☼ Who is then more unjust than he who utters a lie against Allah and [he who] gives lie to the truth when it

---

1241 al-Ashtari,I,52.
1242 *al-Haqaa'iq*,I,119.
1243 *Mishkaat al-Anwaar*,231-232.
1244 ibid.
1245 ibid.
1246 al-`Amili,*Nur al-Ḥaqiqah,*157.

comes to him. (39:32)

☼ Who is then more unjust than he who forges a lie against Allah? (10:17)

☼ [They are] listeners of a lie, devourers of what is forbidden. (5:42)

☼ And if he be a liar, on him will be his lie. (40:8)

The Messenger said, 'Beware of lying, for it belongs with the depraved, and they are both in the Fire.'[1247]

'Lying is one of the doors of hypocrisy.'[1248]

'Great is the betrayal if you speak to your brother and he believes you while you are lying to him.'[1249]

'As long as the slave continues to lie and pursue lies he is recorded with Allah as a liar.'[1250]

'There are three kinds of people whom Allah will not talk to or look at on the Last Day: the one who begrudges something given, the one who sells his goods with a false oath, and the one who [through pride] wears a loincloth that trails along the ground.'[1251]

'Woe to the one who speaks and lies to make people laugh – woe to him! Woe to him! Woe to him!'[1252]

`Abd Allah ibn Jaraad relates how he asked the Prophet, 'O Prophet of Allah, May Allah bestow His blessings upon you, does a believer commit fornication?' 'It may be,' he replied.

1247	al-Ashtari,I,113-114.
1248	ibid.
1249	ibid.
1250	ibid.
1251	ibid.
1252	ibid.

'O Apostle of Allah, does a believer lie?' 'No,' he replied, then continued, '[but] He may trump up a lie against those who do not believe.'[1253]

The Apostle said, 'Whoever errs by swearing an oath that he will unjustly deprive a Muslim of wealth, will meet Allah on the Day of the Encounter; and He will be angry with him.'[1254]

'All qualities and traits are contained in the believer except those of betrayal and lying.'[1255]

Giving instruction to Abu Dharr, the Messenger said, 'A man who speaks about everything he hears is not better than a liar.'[1256]

'O Abu Dharr, nothing merits imprisonment more than the tongue.'[1257]

Imam `Ali said, 'A slave will not taste faith until he stops lying – whether it be in jest or in earnest.'[1258]

'A Muslim should avoid being a brother to a liar, for the liar will persist in his lies until one day he tells the truth – but then he is not believed.'[1259]

Imam Zayn al-`Abideen said, 'Protect yourself from lying, whether it be a small or big lie, whether serious or in jest; for if a man tells a small lie, then he will venture to tell a big lie. You have heard what the Messenger said: "As long as the slave tells the truth, Allah will record him as being a truthful person; and as long as the slave lies, Allah will record him as being a liar".'[1260]

Al-Baaqir said, 'Allah has placed locks over evil and made

1253	ibid.
1254	ibid.
1255	ibid.
1256	ibid.,II,61-62.
1257	ibid.
1258	al-Kulayni,II,338-340.
1259	ibid.
1260	ibid.

drinking [alcohol] one of the keys – and lying is worse than drink.'[1261]

Al-Saadiq said, 'Lying about Allah and His Messenger is one of the major sins.'[1262]

Hypocrisy

Allah has said:

☼ Allah has promised the hypocritical men and the hypocritical women and the unbelievers the fire of Hell. (9:68)

☼ So Allah will chastise the hypocritical men and the hypocritical women and the polytheistic men and the polytheistic women. (33:73)

☼ Surely the hypocrites strive to deceive Allah, but it is He who deceives them. (4:142)

☼ O Prophet! Strive hard against the unbelievers and the hypocrites and be unyielding to them. (9:73)

The Messenger said, 'O `Ali, the ruin of this *ummah* is in the hands of every hypocrite who is eloquent of speech.'[1263]

'Whatever increases the humility of the body over and above that of the heart is hypocrisy in our eyes.'[1264]

Imam `Ali describes the hypocrites in one of his discourses: 'I advise you, O slaves of Allah, to be in awe of Allah, and beware of hypocrites, for they are astray and lead astray, and

---

1261   ibid.
1262   ibid.
1263   al-*Khisaal*,I,69.
1264   al-Kulayni,II,396.

they have erred and cause others to err. They take on all sorts of hues and beguile people with their speech. They are envious of ease, compound difficulties and lead to despair. They exchange praise and vie with each other in their expectation of reward. If they ask, they importune; if they mediate, they expose; and if they govern, they slander. They have prepared for every truth a falsehood, for every upright one a disputant, for every living one a killer, for every door a key, and for every night a lamp.'[1265]

Al-Baaqir said, 'The worst slave is the two-faced, duplicitous slave: he praises his brother when he is present, and backbites him when absent; if his brother is given something he is envious, and if his brother is afflicted by something he deserts him.'[1266]

'There are four kinds of heart: the heart in which there is hypocrisy and faith (believing in some of what the Prophet brought and denying some); the inverted heart; the defiled heart and the resplendent heart. The defiled heart is that of the hypocrite; the resplendent heart that of the believer – if he is given something he is grateful, and if tested is patient; and the inverted heart is that of the one who associates others with Allah.'[1267]

Al-Saadiq said, 'Whoever is two-faced and duplicitous when meeting the Muslims will appear on the Last Day with two tongues of fire.'[1268]

'Allah never grants a pleasing aspect, understanding or good behavior to the hypocrite or the corrupt person.'[1269]

'You find one man never pronounces a letter wrongly and is eloquent and strong of voice, but his heart is blacker than the

---

1265   *Nahj al-Balaaghah*,II,444.
1266   al-Kulayni,II,343.
1267   ibid.,II,423.
1268   ibid.,II,343.
1269   *al-Khisaal*,I,127.

darkest night; and you find another who cannot express with his tongue what is in his heart, but his heart is as radiant as the shine of a lamp.'[1270]

Anger

Allah has forbidden anger and praises those who restrain their anger:

☼ And those who restrain [their] anger and pardon men; and Allah loves the virtuous. (3:134)

☼ And know that Allah is Forgiving, Forbearing. (2:235)

It is related that a man asked the Messenger of Allah to command him to accomplish an action which would not overburden him. 'Do not become angry,' he replied. 'Do not become angry.'[1271]

The Messenger said, 'Strength is not physical combat, but rather controlling oneself when angry.'[1272]

'If one of you becomes angry he should say, "I seek refuge from the accursed Satan", for anger comes from Satan.'[1273]

'If one of you becomes angry, then he should perform the ablution with water, for anger comes from fire.'[1274]

'Anger is from Satan, Satan is from fire, and water extinguishes fire.'[1275]

Abu Sa`eed al-Khudri relates that the Messenger said, 'Surely anger is a live coal in the heart of the son of Adam – do you

---

1270 al-Kulayni,II,396.
1271 al-Ashtari,I,122-126.
1272 ibid.
1273 ibid.
1274 ibid.
1275 ibid.

not see the redness of his eyes and his swelling jugular veins? So whoever finds any of this in himself should press his cheek to the earth.' This seems to refer to prostration and a fixing of the noblest part of the body to the lowliest of places, the dust, to fill the self with humility and to remove the pride and conceit which causes anger.[1276]

'Never does a slave swallow something in which there is as great a reward as when he swallows his anger, restraining it for the sake of Allah.' He also said, 'If you become angry, then hold your tongue.'[1277]

'Allah loves the kind, modest, prosperous and chaste person, and hates the lewd, the obscene, the beggar and the person who importunes.'[1278]

'When all of creation is gathered on the Last Day a voice will call out, "Where are the people of excellence?" Some people will stand up, but they will be few; then they will move quickly to the Garden and the angels will meet them saying, "We see you hastening to the Garden," They will say, "We are the people of excellence (*fadl*)." "What was your excellence?" They will reply, "If we were wronged, then we forgave; if we were treated badly, then we overlooked it; and if people behaved foolishly towards us, we put up with it." Then they are told, "Enter the Garden – blessed is the reward of those who acted in this way".'[1279]

'Oh that one of you cannot be like Abu Damdam!' When asked who Abu Damdam was, he replied, 'He was someone before you who would say on rising, "O Allah! I give my honor as charity to the person who does wrong to me".'[1280]

1276	ibid.
1277	ibid.
1278	ibid.
1279	ibid.
1280	ibid.

'By the One Who has my soul in His hand! There are three things you should swear commitment to: charity will not deplete wealth, so give in charity; a man does not forgive for the sake of Allah the one who has wronged him but that Allah increases him by it on the Last Day; and a man does not open up the possibility of resolving a problem but that Allah grants him victory over poverty.'[1281]

'Humility only increases a slave in rank, so be humble and Allah will raise you in rank; forgiving will only increase a slave in honor, so forgive and Allah will increase you in honor; and giving in charity will only increase one's wealth so give and Allah will have mercy on you.'[1282]

'Allah's love will inevitably fall on the person who responds with kindness when [they are] the object of someone's anger.'[1283]

Imam `Ali said, 'The intellect which is chained by anger and desire does not benefit from wisdom.'[1284]

'Good does not lie in an increase in your wealth or children, but rather in that you increase your actions and kindness, and that you vie with people in worship of your Lord: if you are correct, then praise Allah, and if you act wrongly, then seek the forgiveness of Allah. The first effect of someone's forbearance is that everyone assists him in overcoming the ignorant.'[1285]

It is related that a man insulted Zayn al-`Abideen, [whereupon] the latter threw his cloak over the man and ordered him to be given a thousand dirhams. In commentary on this it has been said that he combined three qualities in this action: forbearance, removal of the injury, and freeing the man from

---

1281 ibid.
1282 ibid.
1283 *Mishkaat al-Anwaar*,309.
1284 al-Kulayni,II,305.
1285 ibid.

what distanced him from Allah.[1286]

A man said to al-Saadiq, 'A dispute has occurred between myself and another person over a certain matter and I wish to let him off but people say that to do this is an abasement.' Al-Saadiq replied, 'It is the one who did wrong who is abased.'[1287]

Al-Saadiq said, 'Anger is the key to all evil.'[1288]

'Whoever controls his self when he desires, or when he fears, or when he yearns for something or when he becomes angry, or when content or vexed, Allah will forbid his body the Fire.'[1289]

'Whoever restrains his anger, then Allah will conceal his faults.' This is because a man's shortcomings manifest during anger.[1290]

'Anger means ruin for the heart of the wise: whoever does not control his anger has no control over his intellect.'[1291]

'If a man refrains from getting angry with people, Allah will remove from him the punishment of the Last Day.'[1292]

Backbiting

Allah says in His Book:

☼ And do not spy nor let some of you backbite others. Does one of you like to eat the flesh of his dead brother?

1286	ibid.
1287	Unknown; the print version doesn't provide a reference for this footnote number.
1288	Unknown; the print version doesn't provide a reference for this footnote number.
1289	Unknown; the print version doesn't provide a reference for this footnote number.
1290	al-Haqaa'iq,69-73.
1291	ibid.
1292	ibid.

But you abhor it. (49:12)

Thus Allah proclaims the blame in backbiting and compares the one who practices it to the one who eats dead flesh.

The Prophet said, 'Everything of the Muslim is inviolate for the Muslim – his blood, his wealth and his honor – and backbiting is a violation of honor.'[1293]

'Do not be envious of one another, nor hate one another, and do not let some of you backbite others. Be worshippers of Allah, and [be] brothers.'[1294]

Jaabir and Abu Sa`eed relate that the Messenger said, 'Beware of backbiting, for surely backbiting is worse than fornication. A man may fornicate and then turn [to Allah] for forgiveness, and Allah will turn to him; but the one who backbites will not be forgiven until the person whom he slandered forgives him.'[1295]

Anas relates that the Messenger said, 'On the night I was taken on the night journey I passed some people who were scratching their faces with their nails. I asked Gabriel who they were and he replied, "Those who used to backbite people and attack their honor".'[1296]

Saleem ibn Jaabir relates how he went to the Messenger and asked him to teach him a good action by which Allah would benefit him. He replied, 'Do not despise doing the least act of kindness, even if it is to empty your jar into the cup of a man craving for water; when you meet your brother, then meet him with a cheerful face, and if he leaves, then do not backbite

---

1293	al-Ashtari,I,115-122.
1294	ibid.
1295	ibid.
1296	ibid.

him.'[1297]

Al-Baraa' relates how the Messenger of Allah gave a speech, and continued until he brought it to the hearing of the young girls in their houses, saying, 'O all you who believe with your tongues and not with your hearts! Do not backbite the Muslims and do not seek out their faults, for if a man looks for the faults of his brother, then Allah will look for his faults; and in whomsoever Allah looks for faults he will disclose them, even if he is in the depths of his house.'[1298]

Anas relates how the Messenger made a speech in which he mentioned increase of wealth through usury, and how serious it was, saying, 'The best increase is the honor of a Muslim.'[1299]

Mujaahid relates that the Messenger, commenting on Allah's words, 'Woe to every slanderer, defamer' said, 'The slanderer is the one who criticizes people and the defamer is the one who backbites people [lit. eats their flesh].'[1300]

It is related that in the time of the Messenger people did not consider perfection of worship to be in fasting or prayer, but rather in abstaining from giving offence to people's honor.[1301]

The Messenger was asked what the expiation for backbiting was, and he replied, 'You seek Allah's forgiveness for the one you have been backbiting against every time you remember him.'[1302]

The Messenger asked if they knew what backbiting was, and they replied, 'Allah and His Messenger know best.' He said, 'Mentioning your brother in a way which he would dislike.' Someone asked, 'What if there truly exists in my brother the

---

1297	ibid.
1298	ibid.
1299	ibid.
1300	ibid.
1301	ibid.
1302	al-Kulayni,II,357.

thing I accuse him of?' He replied, 'If what you say about him is true, then you are backbiting him, and if not, then you are defaming him.'[1303]

Just as it is forbidden to backbite with the tongue, it is also forbidden to backbite by making signs, signals or other movements. `A'ishah said, 'A woman came to see us; when she turned round I indicated with my hand that she was small, and the Prophet said, "You are backbiting her," and he forbade me to do anything like this.'

The Messenger said, 'The one who remains silent is an associate of the slanderer,' and also, 'The one who listens is one of the two slanderers: the listener is not free of the offence of backbiting unless he abjures it by speech, and if he is afraid, then with his heart. If he is able to get up or interrupt the conversation by broaching another subject but he does not do it, then of necessity he is following the conversation.'[1304]

'If anyone defends the honor of his brother from backbiting, then it is incumbent upon Allah to defend his honor on the Last Day.' He has also said, 'If anyone defends his brother's honor from backbiting, it is incumbent on Allah to free him from the Fire.'[1305]

Al-Saadiq said, 'Whoever meets the Muslims with one face and backbites them with another will come on the Last Day with two tongues of fire.'[1306]

'The worst slave is the one who has two faces and two tongues: he praises his brother-in-Allah when he is present, and backbites him when absent; if the brother is given something he

---

1303	al-Ashtari,I,115-122.
1304	ibid.
1305	ibid.
1306	al-Khisaal,I,38.

is envious, and if afflicted by anything he forsakes him.'[1307]

'Backbiting is to talk about your brother in a way which he would dislike – whether it be a defect in his body, lineage, character, actions, religion, his worldly affairs or even his dress. As for his body, you might say, for example, that he is one-eyed, short, bald, black or yellow. As for lineage, you might say he is Indian, Nabatean, profligate, despicable or something he would dislike. As for character, you might say, for example, that he is arrogant, mean or foolhardy. As for religion, you might say he is a thief, a liar, lax in his prayer or unkind to his parents. As for his worldly affairs, you might say he is badly behaved, speaks and eats too much or is dirtily dressed.'[1308]

Defamation or Slander

Allah says:

☼ ... Defamer, going about with slander, forbidder of good, outstepping the limits, sinful. (68:11-12)

☼ If an evil-doer comes to you with a report, look carefully into it, lest you harm a people in ignorance. (49:6)

The Messenger said to Abu Dharr, 'The slanderer will find no relief from the punishment of Allah in the next world.'[1309]

The Messenger also said, 'Shall I not inform you of the worst of you?' He continued, 'Those who revile others with slander and those who separate friends.'[1310]

1307   ibid.
1308   al-Ashtari,117.
1309   ibid.,II,51.
1310   *al-Khisaal*,I,183.

Giving advice to Abu Dharr, he said, 'Calumniators will not enter the Garden.' When asked who the calumniators were, he replied, 'The slanderers.'[1311]

Imam ʿAli said, 'The worst of you are those who revile others with slander, separate friends from each other, wrong the innocent and always find faults.'[1312]

Imam al-Saadiq said, 'The Garden is forbidden to those who calumniate and revile others with slander.'[1313]

'Three kinds of person will not enter the Garden: he who spills blood, he who drinks wine, and he who reviles with slander.'[1314]

Dissemblance

Allah says:

☼ They do it only to be seen of men and do not remember Allah save a little. (4:142)

☼ So woe to the praying ones who are unmindful of their prayers, who wish only to be seen, and withhold acts of kindness. (107:6-7)

Allah also says, 'We only feed you for Allah's sake; we desire from you neither reward nor thanks' [76:9] – thereby praising the sincere and rejecting any intention other than the face of Allah, dissembling being the opposite of sincerity.

Allah also says, 'Therefore whoever hopes to meet his

1311	al-Ashtari,II,65.
1312	*al-Khisaal*,I,180.
1313	al-Kulayni,II,369.
1314	ibid.

Lord, he should do good deeds, and not associate anyone in the worship of his Lord' [18:110] – revealing it for those who seek reward and praise for their acts of worship and actions.

The Messenger said to a man who asked him in what lay salvation, 'That the slave not perform acts of worship of Allah for the sake of being seen by people.'[1315]

'The thing I most fear for you is the smaller of the two kinds of "association of another with Allah" (*shirk*).' They asked what this minor form of association was, and he replied, 'Dissembling – Allah will say on the Last Day as he is requiting the slaves for their actions, "Go, all of you, to those you acted in front of in order to be seen and look to see if you find reward with them".'[1316]

'Allah will not accept an action in which there is an atom's weight of dissemblance.'[1317]

'Those who dissembled will be called on the Last Day: "O corrupter! O traitor! O dissembler! Your actions have come to naught, and you have lost any reward. Go and take your reward from the one for whose sake you were acting, for I do not accept an action which is tainted in any way by the world and its people".'[1318]

The following *hadith* of the Messenger of Allah is related: 'There are three kinds of person who will never be rewarded: the man killed in the way of Allah, the man who gives his wealth in charity, and the man who recites His Book. Allah will say to each one of them, "You lied, and wanted people to say of you 'that person is generous'; you lied, and you wanted people to say, 'that person is courageous'; you lied and you wanted people to say,

---

1315	al-Ashtari, I, 163-187.
1316	ibid.
1317	ibid.
1318	ibid.

'that person recites"'.' The Messenger declares that they would never be rewarded for these actions.[1319]

On the authority of al-Ridaa, his father and grandfather, Imam `Ali, `Ali said, 'The world is all ignorance, except for the places of knowledge; and all knowledge is an argument against you, except what you put into action; and all action is dissembling, except that which is sincere; and sincerity is at risk, until the slave sees how his actions are sealed.'[1320]

'Act for Allah without dissembling, nor for love of reputation – anyone who acts for other than Allah, Allah will leave to his actions.'[1321]

Imam `Ali said, 'Three actions typify the dissembler: he becomes active when people see him, lazy when he is alone, and loves to be praised in all his affairs.'[1322]

Al-Saadiq said, 'All dissembling is associating others with Allah. Whoever acts for the people has his reward from the people and whoever acts for Allah has his reward from Allah.'[1323]

'If the person who allows his good actions to be seen and hides the bad would consult his self, then he would find it should not be like this, and that Allah has said, "Nay! Man is evidence against himself, though he puts forth his excuses" [75:15]. If the inner self is correct, then it strengthens the manifest, outer self.'[1324]

'Fear Allah and act for Him, for whoever acts for Allah is in need of Him, and whoever acts for other than Allah, Allah will

---

1319	ibid.
1320	*Mishkaat al-Anwaar*,311-312.
1321	ibid.
1322	al-Kulayni,II,295.
1323	*Mishkaat al-Anwaar*,311.
1324	al-Kulayni,II,295.

leave to the one he acted for.'[1325]

'Make this affair of yours Allah's affair, not the affair of people. If it is for Allah, then it belongs to Allah; and if it is for people, then it will not reach Allah. Do not dispute with the people over your religion, for argument is a sickness of the heart. Allah says to his Apostle, "Surely you cannot guide whom you love, but Allah guides whom He pleases" [28:56], and "Will you then force men until they become believers?" [10:99].'[1326]

Commenting on Allah's words, 'And do not utter your prayer with a raised voice, nor be silent with regard to it' [17:110], Hasan al-Basri said, 'Do not raise your voice because of dissembling, and do not be silent out of modesty.'[1327]

Flattery

Allah says:

☼ So do not yield to the rejecters. They wish that they should be pliant so they [too] would be pliant. (68:8-9)

☼ Do you then hold this announcement in contempt? (56:81)

Imam `Ali said, 'Do not sit with a scholar, unless he calls you [away] from three things towards three others: from pride to humility, from flattery to keeping one's distance from guile, and from ignorance to knowledge.'[1328]

'The word "enemy" (`aduww) is derived from the verb "to transgress" (ya`du): whoever beguiles you by flattering your faults

---

1325 Mishkaat al-Anwaar, 311-312.
1326 ibid.
1327 al-`Amili, Nur al-Haqiqah, 57.
1328 Nahj al-Balaaghah, II, 388.

is the enemy.'¹³²⁹

'Whoever protects you from your faults and criticizes you in your absence is the enemy, so beware of him.'¹³³⁰

'May the person you like best be the one who presents your faults to you in your presence.'¹³³¹

'He who makes you aware of your faults is giving you advice.'¹³³²

'He who praises you is slaughtering you.'¹³³³

`Umar ibn al-Khattaab asked Hudhayfah ibn al-Yamaan, 'You know the Messenger of Allah's secret thought concerning the hypocrites – do you see in me any signs of hypocrisy?' He replied, 'You know your own state; the one who avoids flattery has few friends, but is ennobled; so inform people of their faults, and do not let a friend who is envious or someone who wants something consider a fault as other than a fault, or let them hide from you some of your faults through flattery.'¹³³⁴

Blameworthy Behavior

Pride

Allah severely criticizes pride in many places in the Qur'an:

☼ I will turn away from My Revelations those who are unjustly proud in the earth. (7:146)

☼ ... And whoever disdains His service and is proud. (4:172)

1329 al-Haakim,I,157-158.
1330 ibid.
1331 ibid.,265-266.
1332 ibid.
1333 ibid.
1334 al-Ashtari,I,198-199.

☼ Today you shall be recompensed with an ignominious chastisement because you spoke other than the truth concerning Allah, and [because] you scorned His Revelations. (6:93)

☼ So certainly evil is the dwelling place of the proud. (16:29)

☼ Thus does Allah set a seal over the heart of every proud, haughty one. (40:35)

☼ And every insolent opposer was brought to naught. (14:15)

The Messenger said, 'No one who has a mustard-seed's weight of pride will enter the Garden, and no man will enter the Fire who has a grain of faith in his heart.'[1335]

The Messenger relates that Allah said, 'Pride is my cloak, and might My robe, so whoever disputes over any one of these with Me, I will throw into *Jahannam*.'[1336]

'The haughty will not enter the Garden.'[1337]

'The worst of slaves is the one who is arrogant, and transgresses and forgets the Supreme Compeller (*al-Jabbaar al-A`laa*); the worst of slaves is the one who is arrogant and self-important, and who forgets the One of Grandeur (*al-Kabeer*) and Sublimity (*al-Muta`aali*); the worst of slaves is the one who is negligent, careless, who forgets the graves and putrefaction of bodies; and the worst of slaves is the one who molests and commits outrage, and forgets the Beginning and the End.'[1338]

1335   al-Kulayni,II,310.
1336   al-Ashtari,I,198.
1337   ibid.
1338   ibid.

Pride is a result of vanity and is produced from hatred, envy or dissemblance – or from all three of them. The Messenger said. 'The most beloved of you with us and the nearest to us in the next world are those who have the best behavior; the most hated of you by us and the most distant from us are the garrulous, the fast talkers and those who claim to be learned.' 'O Messenger of Allah,' they said, 'May Allah bestow His Blessing on you! We know of the garrulous and the fast talkers, but who are those who claim to be learned?' 'The proud,' he replied.[1339]

'The haughty and the proud will be assembled on the Last Day like tiny particles, estranged from the people because of their contempt for Allah.'[1340]

'There is not one of you who is proud and haughty but that he finds abasement in his self, and truly, there is for the proud a valley in *Jahannam* called *Saqar*, about which they complain to Allah because of its terrible heat.'[1341]

'Whoever feels self-important and is overbearing in his gait will meet Allah and He will be angry with him.'[1342]

'If you see people full of pride, then act proudly towards them, for surely it will abase and belittle them.'[1343]

'Allah has commanded the master of His creatures – may peace be upon him – to be humble: "And be kind to him who follows you of the believers" [26:215].'[1344]

'No one humbles himself to Allah but that Allah raises him.'[1345]

1339	ibid.
1340	al-Kulayni,II,311.
1341	*al-Haqaa'iq*,85.
1342	al-Ashtari,I,199.
1343	*al-Haqaa'iq*,86.
1344	ibid.
1345	ibid.

The Apostle said to some of his companions, 'Why is it that I do not see any sign of sweetness of worship with you?' They replied, 'And what is sweetness of worship?' 'Humility,' he said.[1346]

In his *Al-Qaasi`ah* speech, Imam `Ali inveighs against pride and the accursed Satan as being the leader of the proud: 'Do you not see how Allah has belittled him by His greatness, abased him by His ascendancy, made him an outcast in this world, and has prepared the flaming fire for him in the next world?'[1347]

'Resolve to place abasement on your heads, to cast honor and power beneath your feet, and to strip pride from your necks.'[1348]

'If Allah had allowed any of His slaves to have pride He would have allowed it in His prophets and His friends, but He has made haughty airs repulsive to them and humility pleasing to them; He has brought their cheeks close to the earth, has covered their face with dust and has made them kind to the believers – and they were people who were weak and oppressed.'[1349]

Al-Saadiq said, 'Humility is the origin of all great honor and exalted rank.'[1350]

Vanity

Allah says:

☼ I have greater wealth than you, and am mightier in followers. (18:34)

☼ Let not their property and their children excite your

1346 ibid.
1347 *Nahj al-Balaaghah*, II, 419 & 424.
1348 ibid.
1349 ibid.
1350 *al-Haqaa'iq*, 86.

admiration. (9:55)

☼ And certainly a believing bondswoman is better than an idolatrous woman. (2:221)

☼ Allah also says, 'O you who believe! Do not make your charity worthless by reproach and injury' [2:264]. Reproach here is a result of deeming one's action great, which is conceit.

Allah has said, 'There are among my believing slaves the man who has a high degree of obedience to Me and I love him, but I remove this from him, so that he does not feel vain at his acts (of worship); there are also among My believing slaves the man for whom only poverty is fitting, and if I were to change his state to riches, he would perish.'

The Messenger said, 'There are three things which cause ruin and three which bring salvation: those which bring salvation are fear of Allah in secret and in the open, resolution in poverty and wealth, and justice in anger and containment. Those which bring ruin are yielding to niggardliness, following one's desires, and feeling self-important.'[1351]

Imam `Ali said, 'There is no honor better than humility and no loneliness worse than vanity – I am amazed at the proud man who yesterday was a sperm and tomorrow will be a corpse.'[1352]

Imam `Ali said, 'A wrong action which dismays you is better than a good action which pleases your vanity.' He also said, 'A man's conceit with himself is a kind of envy on the part of his intellect.'[1353]

1351   ibid.,91-92.
1352   *Mishkaat al-Anwaar*,312-314.
1353   ibid.

He also said, 'The worst kind of loneliness is the loneliness of vanity.'[1354]

'Whoever is pleased at his own opinions will be overcome by his enemies.'[1355]

'Giving instruction to his son Hasan, he said, 'There is no loneliness and no solitude worse than vanity.'[1356]

'Ignorance is enough for you if you are pleased with your own knowledge.'[1357]

'Vanity ruins the intellect.'[1358]

'If a man is vainly pleased with his actions then his intellect will be afflicted.'[1359]

Giving advice to his son he said, 'O son, know that vanity is contrary to what is correct, and is the blight of the intellect.'[1360]

'With the first conceit of a man comes the ruin of his intellect.'[1361]

'The self-complacency of a man is proof of the weakness of his intellect.'[1362]

'Get rid of your airs, bring low your pride and remember your grave.'[1363]

Imam al-Saadiq said, 'Vanity prevents one from seeking knowledge, and invites one to disdain and ignorance.'[1364]

1354	ibid.
1355	al-Haakim,I,157.
1356	ibid.
1357	al-Hurr,I,79.
1358	al-Haakim,I,157-158.
1359	ibid.
1360	al-Haakim,I,158.
1361	ibid.
1362	ibid.
1363	*Nur al-Ḥaqiqah*,91.
1364	al-Haakim,I,157.

'There is no ignorance worse than conceit.'[1365]

'Whoever does not recognize excellence in others is the one who is conceitedly pleased with his own opinions.'[1366]

Imam al-Haadi said, 'When a man is pleased with himself then those who are displeased with him will multiply in number.'[1367]

Love and Greed for this World

Allah says:

☼ Whoever desires the reward of this world, [let him know that] with Allah is the reward of this world and the Hereafter. (4:134)

☼ And the life of this world is nothing but a provision of vanities. (3:185)

☼ Say: The provision of this world is short, and the Hereafter is better for him who guards [against evil]; and you shall not be wronged [by so much as] the husk of a date stone. (4:77)

☼ And this world's life is naught but play and idle sport. (6:32)

☼ And surely what comes after is better for you than that which has gone before. (93:4)

The Messenger reproaches the world, saying, 'The world is a prison for the believer and a paradise for the non-believer.'[1368]

1365	ibid.
1366	ibid.
1367	ibid.
1368	al-Ashtari, I, 128.

'Whoever loves this world is harming his afterlife, and whoever loves his afterlife harms his world – so prefer that which abides to that which disappears.'[1369]

'Love of the world is the source of all faults.'[1370]

'The world is a dwelling for the man who has no dwelling in the next life, and the man who amasses wealth and property for this world has no intellect.'[1371]

'What is the world to me? I am to the world like a rider who sleeps a little beneath a tree on a summer's day, then departs and leaves it far behind.'[1372]

'Oh, what can be more astonishing than the man who confirms the continuance of life after death while striving after the world of deceptive illusion?'[1373]

'Surely Allah has not created anything more hated by Him than the world.'[1374]

The Messenger of Allah passed a dead sheep and said, 'Do you see this sheep has died unnoticed by its owner? By the One Who has my soul in His hand, the world is more insignificant to Allah than this is for its owner.'[1375]

It is related that the Messenger of Allah stood at a pile of garbage and said, 'Come to this world!' and he took hold of a ragged strip of cloth from the rubbish, together with some decomposing bones, saying, 'The world and these things are an indication that the world's beauty will fade like this worn cloth, and the bodies you see will likewise become like these rotten

---

1369   ibid.
1370   ibid.
1371   *al-Haqaa'iq*,102.
1372   ibid.
1373   al-Ashtari,I,128-129.
1374   ibid.
1375   ibid.

bones.'¹³⁷⁶

He also said, 'Truly the thing I most fear for my *ummah* is illusory desire and excessive expectation, for desire bars one from the truth and expectation makes one forget the next world. This world is receding, but the next world is approaching; and each of them has sons. If you are able to be among the sons of the next world and not of the sons of this world then be of them, for surely today you are in the abode of action which is not accounted for, and tomorrow you will be in the abode of account and not of action.'¹³⁷⁷

Imam `Ali said, 'There are two kinds of people most likely to perish: those who fear poverty and those who seek opulence.'¹³⁷⁸

Imam `Ali wrote to some of his companions giving them advice: 'I instruct you and myself to have fear of Allah, I instruct him who does not make disobedience of Him a lawful thing and who does not hope for anyone but Him – and there are not riches nor independence but by Him. If a man fears Allah, then He strengthens, feeds, waters, and raises his intellect far from the people of this world. His body remains with the people of this world, while his heart and intellect are manifest in the next world. With the light of his heart he extinguishes what his eyes see of love of this world, rejects such of it as is forbidden, distances himself from ambiguous matters except for those from which there is no escape – a chunk of bread to strengthen his back, and some clothes of the thickest and coarsest cloth. Moreover, in these matters of necessity he has no certainty of trust or hope, since he places his trust in the Creator of these things.'¹³⁷⁹

He also said, 'Reject the world, for surely love of this world

---

1376   ibid.
1377   *al-Khisaal*,I,51 & 69.
1378   ibid.
1379   *al-Haqaa'iq*,102-103.

blinds, deafens, makes dumb and abases the necks of people.'[1380]

Describing the world he said, 'What should I describe of an abode whose beginning is all trouble, and whose end is extinction? In what is lawful there is a reckoning and in what is forbidden there is a punishment. If a man distances himself from it, then it comes to him; if a man reflects upon it, then it enlightens him; and if a man looks towards it, it will blind him.'[1381]

'Whoever begins the morning with sadness is beginning the morning angry with what Allah has decreed; and whoever begins by complaining of something which has afflicted him is complaining against his Lord.'[1382]

Imam al-Baaqir said, 'A man greedy for the world is like a silkworm: the more the worm spins the thread around itself, the more difficult it is for it to get out, and so it dies, completely enveloped.'[1383]

Al-Saadiq said, 'If anyone spends the morning and the evening with the world as his greatest concern, then Allah will place poverty between his eyes, and will make his life dispersed, and he will not get anything of the world but that which has been apportioned to him. If anyone spends the morning and the evening with the next world as his greatest concern, then Allah will place riches and independence from the world in his heart and will bind his life together.'[1384]

'Love of the world is the crown of all troubles.'

'The slave is the furthest he could possibly be from Allah

1380	ibid.
1381	ibid.
1382	*Nahj al-Balaaghah,* IV, 708.
1383	al-Kulayni, II, 316.
1384	al-Ashtari, I, 130.

when he is only interested in his stomach and his sex.'[1385]

'Whoever attaches his heart to the world is attaching his heart to three things: anxiety, which will never cease; hopes, which will never be realized; and expectations which can never be met.'[1386]

Luxury

Allah says:

> ☼ ... [Those] who disbelieved and called the meeting of the Hereafter a lie, and whom We had given plenty to enjoy in this world's life. (23:33)

> ☼ And when We wish to destroy a town, We send Our commandment to the people of it who lead easy lives, but they transgress therein. (17:16)

> ☼ And We never sent a warner to a town but those who led lives of ease in it said: We are surely disbelievers in what you are sent with. (34:34)

Giving advice to `Abd Allah ibn Mas`ud and his people, the Messenger said, 'Look to Allah's words, "And were it not that all people had been a single nation, We would certainly have assigned to those who disbelieve in the Beneficent [to make] of silver the roofs of their houses and the stairs by which they ascend, and the doors of their houses and the couches on which they recline and [other] embellishments of gold; and all this is naught but provision of this world's life, and the Hereafter with your Lord is only for those who guard [against evil]" [43:33-35]. O Ibn Mas`ud, whoever yearns for the Garden makes

---

1385   al-Kulayni,II,319-320.
1386   ibid.

haste to do good actions, and whoever fears the fire abandons desire; whoever is always watchful of death turns away from the pleasure of the senses, and whoever does without in the world will find afflictions easier to bear.'

'O Ibn Mas`ud, recite the words of Allah, "The love of desires, of women and sons and hoarded treasures of gold and silver and well-bred horses and cattle and tilth is made to seem fair to men" [3:13]. O Ibn Mas`ud, how can the one who delights in the pleasures of this world gain if he will be forever in the fire?

'They know the outward of this world's life, but of the Hereafter they are absolutely heedless' [30:7] – they build houses and erect palaces, and cover the mosques in ornamentation, their only concern being for the world, to which they are attached and on which they are completely reliant. Their god is their stomach. nothing prevents them from seeking what they desire, whether it be lawful or unlawful. Allah says, 'And they rejoice in this world's life, and this world's life is nothing compared with the Hereafter but a temporary enjoyment' [13:26].

'O Ibn Mas`ud, beware of the world, its pleasures, desires, beauty and anything forbidden, gold, silver and women.'[1387]

The Messenger said, 'There will come after you a people who will eat from every kind of delicacy on earth, marry the most beautiful women of every hue, wear the softest of clothes in every shade and ride the swiftest of horses of every color. They will have stomachs that are not satisfied with a little, and characters which are not content with much. They are attached to the world and have taken it as a god – forgetting their God – and as a lord – forgetting their Lord.'[1388]

1387 *Makaarim al-Akhlaaq*,447.
1388 al-Ashtari,I,155.

Play and Idle Sport

Allah says:

☼ And this world's life is naught but play and idle sport. (6:32)

☼ ... Who take their religion for idle sport and play, and this life's world deceives them. (7:51)

☼ Know that this world's life is only sport and play and gaiety and boasting among yourselves. (57:20)

☼ And when they see merchandise or sport they break up for it. (62:11)

Giving instruction to `Ali, the Apostle said, 'Three things harden the heart: listening to idle talk, seeking after booty and petitioning at the door of the Sultan.'[1389]

Giving instruction to `Abd Allah ibn Mas`ud and his people, the Messenger said, 'Do not let the world and its desires distract you – surely Allah has said, "What! Did you then think that We had created you in vain and that you shall not be returned to Us?" [23:115]'.[1390]

Giving instruction to Abu Dharr, he said, 'Beware of laughing a lot, for surely it kills the heart and takes away light from the face.'[1391]

The Messenger used to say, 'I jest, but I say nothing but the truth.' Some have asked why – if it had been reported that the Messenger used to jest – he used to forbid it. The answer is that if you are able to do what the Messenger did, namely to jest, not

---

1389   Makaarim al-Akhlaaq, 446-454.
1390   ibid.
1391   ibid.

saying anything but the truth, nor disturbing anyone's heart, nor going to excess, then there is no objection to it.[1392]

'Abd al-Waahid ibn al-Mukhtaar relates that when he asked Imam al-Baaqir about the game of chess, he replied, 'Believers are too busy to play games.'[1393]

When asked who were the basest of people, al-Saadiq replied, 'They are those who drink wine and play the drum.'[1394]

It is reported that al-Saadiq asked some of his students what they had learned from him. One of them replied, 'Eight matters, O master. I have seen the amusement and entertainment of the people and have heard the words of Allah: "And as for him who fears to stand in the presence of his Lord and forbids the soul from low desires, then surely the Garden – that is the abode" [79:40]. So I strove to remove desire from myself until I became constant in my worship of Allah.'[1395]

'As for laughing at others or making fun of them and mocking them, this is forbidden. Allah says, "Let not [one] people laugh at [another] people, perchance they may be better than they" [49:11].'[1396]

Excessive and constant joking are also forbidden; occasional joviality is permissible, but to be habitually in this state is reprehensible because, carried to excess, it leads to excessive laughter, kills the heart, causes rancor, destroys esteem and honor and indicates neglect of the Hereafter.[1397]

1392 ibid.
1393 *al-Khisaal*,I,26.
1394 ibid.
1395 *al-Ashtari*,I,303.
1396 ibid.,I,111.
1397 ibid.

Greed and Covetousness

Allah says:

☼ And call on Him fearing and hoping. (7:56)

☼ And I adjusted affairs for him with ease; and yet he desires that I should add more! (74:14-15)

☼ ...Lest he in whose heart is a disease yearn [for you, O wives of the Prophet]. (33:32)

Longing for many material goods and having excessive expectation is the opposite of contentment, and leads to greed and the ignominy of covetousness. Greed and covetousness lead to bad qualities of behavior and the committing of evil acts, which destroy manhood and honor. Man has been created with greed and covetousness and a lack of contentment.

The Messenger said, 'There are two insatiable cravings: in the seeker of knowledge and in the one who vies for wealth.'[1398]

'Riches are not to be found in the ephemeral things of the world but rather in contentment of the self.'[1399]

'The one who is modest in his spending is never needy.'[1400]

'Correct management is half way to a means of living.' He also said, 'Whoever is modest in his spending, Allah will enrich; whoever is wasteful, Allah will impoverish, and whoever remembers Allah, Allah will love.'[1401]

'If you want something, then you should be patient until Allah grants you respite or a way out; to be unhurried in one's

---

1398	ibid.,I,163-187.
1399	ibid.
1400	ibid.
1401	ibid.

spending is most important.'[1402]

'The son of Adam becomes senile and decrepit, but two kinds of people become youthful in their excitement: the man greedy for wealth and the man covetous for his life.' In another tradition he said, 'The son of Adam becomes senile and decrepit and afterwards two things remain of him: greed and expectation.'

Some have said that greed is poverty and renunciation is riches, and that whoever renounces what other people have, becomes free of them. Whoever wants the honor of contentment should close the doors of greed on himself as far as he is able, and direct his self to what is strictly essential. Whoever becomes excessively greedy and spends lavishly will not achieve contentment. Surely moderation in one's economy is the root of contentment.[1403]

Imam `Ali said, 'Be independent of whomever you like and you will be their equal, ask of whomever you wish and you will be their captive, and be kind to whomever you wish and you will be their emir.'[1404]

Imam al-Saadiq said, 'I have seen that all goodness resides in removing man's desire for what is in the hands of others.'[1405]

Imam al-Baaqir said, 'The worst of slaves is he who is guided by a craving, and the worst of slaves is he who has a desire that humiliates him.'[1406]

Sa`daan relates that he asked al-Saadiq what it was that established faith in the slave. 'Scrupulous caution,' he replied. 'And what destroys faith?' 'Greed.'[1407]

1402	ibid.
1403	*al-Khisaal*,I,73.
1404	al-Ashtari,I,169.
1405	al-Kulayni,II,320.
1406	ibid.
1407	ibid.

Envy

Allah says:

☼ ... And from the evil of the envious when he envies.' (113:5)

☼ Or do they envy the people for what Allah has given them of His grace? (4:54)

☼ Many of the People of the Book long that they could turn you back into unbelievers after your faith, out of envy ... (2:109)

The Messenger said, 'There is no envy [permissible] except in two matters: the man who has been given wealth by Allah, and spends it throughout the night and day, and the man who has been given the Qur'an by Allah, and he stands reciting it throughout the night and day.'[1408]

'Envy consumes good actions just as fire consumes wood.'[1409]

'Do not envy each other, do not hate each other, do not backbite each other, and be slaves of Allah and brothers. Envy means disliking seeing the blessing of the person envied, and wanting to remove it from him. As for the man who does not desire it to be removed, and does not mind that the blessing continue for that person, but rather desires the same for himself, then this is called pleasure and also aspiration – Allah says, "And for that let the aspirers aspire" [83:26]. Exultation in another's fortune is allowed in the world and is encouraged for spiritual reasons.'[1410]

1408	al-Khisaal,I,76.
1409	al-Kulayni,II,306.
1410	al-Haqaa'iq,76-77.

'The believer exults and the hypocrite envies.'[1411]

'O `Ali, put an end to three despicable qualities: envy, lying and greed.'[1412]

He also said, 'To whomever guarantees me five things, I will guarantee the Garden: sincerity to Allah, to his Messenger, to the Book of Allah, to the religion of Allah and to the community of the Muslims.'[1413]

'Do not show joy at your brother's misfortune, lest Allah have mercy on him and tests you with affliction.'[1414]

'Poverty can lead to disbelief, and envy can be like challenging the divine decree.'[1415]

Imam al-Saadiq said, 'The blight of religion is envy, conceit and boasting.'[1416]

'The envious harms himself before he harms the person envied – just as Iblees brought the curse upon himself by his envy, so for Adam he brought preference, guidance and elevation to the rank of the elite. Be among the envied and not among those who envy, for surely the balance of the envious is light [in goodness] in comparison with the balance of the envied. Provision has already been allotted, so what good is envy to the envied, and what harm does envy cause to the envied? The origin of envy is blindness of the heart and a rejection of the bounty of Allah, and these are two aspects of disbelief: it is because of envy that the son of Adam falls into eternal loss and comes to ruin with no chance of salvation. There is no repentance for the one who envies because there is no changing him: he believes

---

1411 ibid.
1412 *Mishkaat al-Anwaar*,310.
1413 ibid.
1414 ibid.
1415 al-Kulayni,II,307.
1416 ibid.

in it and is characterized by it. Envy manifests itself without obvious cause and grows unchecked. It is an innate characteristic which does not change from its original form, even if treated.'[1417]

'When Noah came down from the ship Iblees came to him saying, "There is not a man on the earth more benevolent to men than you. You have called on Allah against those corrupt people and have thus freed me of them. Shall I not advise you in two matters? Beware of envy, for that was placed for me, and beware of greed for that was what was placed in Adam.'[1418]

'A man in whom there is niggardliness, envy and cowardliness is not a believer, and the believer is neither a coward, nor greedy nor niggardly.'[1419]

Blameworthy Characteristics

Hopelessness and Despair

Allah says:

☼ Indeed they despair of the Hereafter as the unbelievers despair of those in tombs. (60:13)

☼ And if We make man taste mercy from Us, then remove it from him, most surely he is despairing, ungrateful. (11:9)

☼ And despair not of Allah's mercy; surely none despairs of Allah's mercy except the disbelieving people. (12:87)

☼ And if evil touch him, then he is despairing, hopeless. (41:49)

☼ And if evil befall them for what their hands have already wrought, lo! they are in despair. (30:36)

1417 *al-Haqaa'iq*,76-77.
1418 *Mishkaat al-Anwaar*,309.
1419 Ibid.

☼ And who despairs of the mercy of his Lord but the erring ones? (15:56)

☼ Do not despair of the mercy of Allah; surely Allah forgives all sins. (39:53)

☼ And He it is Who sends down the rain after they have despaired, and He unfolds His mercy. (42:28)

Imam al-Kaazim relates on the authority of his forefathers that the Prophet said, 'On the final day Allah will raise those who have despaired with their faces covered – that is, the whiteness of their faces is covered over by blackness – and it will be said to them that they are the ones who despaired of the mercy of Allah.'[1420]

Imam `Ali said, 'And you have asked Him to provide from His stores of mercy, no other being able to give increase in years nor in health of body, nor in amplitude of provisions; then He has placed in your hand the keys to His stores, in that He has permitted you to ask to be given from them. Thus whenever you wish you may cause the doors of His blessings to open by your prayer, and bring showers of His mercy down. But do not despair that the response is slow in coming, for surely the giving is in proportion to the intention.'[1421]

Imam al-Baaqir reports that Imam `Ali said, 'Shall I not tell you who is the true man of jurisprudence? Whoever does not make people despair of the mercy of Allah, whoever does not make them feel they are safe from the punishment of Allah, whoever does not destroy their hope in the Spirit of Allah, and whoever does not give them leave to disobey Allah.'[1422]

'I am amazed at the one who despairs when he is able to turn

1420   al-Haakim,I,403.
1421   ibid.,I,402-404.
1422   ibid.

for forgiveness.'[1423]

Imam al-Sajjaad said in his prayer, 'Do not allow me to despair of the hope I have in You, lest despondency overcome me instead of Your mercy.'[1424]

Imam al-Saadiq said, 'A believer is well, at ease, and covered with Allah's mercy as long as he does not try to hurry up affairs, despairs and abandons prayer.' I said to him, 'How does he hurry things up?' He replied, 'The believer says, "I have been praying since such and such a time and I do not see the response."'[1425]

Imam al-Saadiq said that he had read in certain books that Allah said, 'Even if the inhabitants of the heavens and the earth were all to have hopes and expectations, and I were to give each one of them what all of them had hoped for, it would not decrease My kingdom by an atom. How should My kingdom decrease when I am its Maintainer? O what misery for those who despair of My mercy, and O what misery for those who disobey Me and do not fear Me.'[1426]

Excessive Hope

Allah says:

☼ Until when the Hour comes upon them all of a sudden they shall say: O our grief for our neglecting it! (6:31)

☼ So when the Doom is come they cannot put it off for an hour, nor can they advance it. (7-34)

☼ And the matter of the Hour is but as the twinkling of an eye or it is nearer still. (16:77)

1423	ibid.
1424	ibid.
1425	ibid.
1426	al-Shiraazi,480.

☼ ... And because the Hour is coming, there is no doubt about it. (22:7)

The Messenger said, 'O people, have you no shame before Allah?' They said, 'How is that, O Messenger of Allah?' He replied, 'You amass what you do not use, you hope for that which you cannot obtain, and you erect buildings which you do not live in.'[1427]

Abu Sa`eed al-Khudri relates, 'Usaamah ibn Zayd brought something for a hundred dinars by means of a one-month loan, and I heard the Messenger of Allah say, "Are you not surprised at Usaamah buying something he wants to pay for after a month? Surely Usaamah has excessive expectations! By the One in Whose hand is my soul, I do not blink my eyes but that I think that Allah will take my spirit before my eyelids met again; I do not raise my glance but that I think Allah will take me before I lower it and I do not take a morsel but that I think I will choke to death before I swallow it. O sons of Adam! If you reflect, then prepare yourselves for your deaths – by the One in Whose Hand is my soul, surely what you have been promised is coming, and there will be no escape for you.'[1428]

'The son of Adam gets older, but two things fill him with youthful energy: greed and hope.'[1429]

'When the son of Adam stands upright, beside him are ninety-nine desires: he ages as his desires are unfulfilled.'[1430]

'The most I fear is that you take on two qualities: you yield to your desires, and you have excessive expectations. Following

---

1427   al-Ashtari,I,270-272.
1428   ibid.
1429   ibid.
1430   ibid.

desire turns one away from the truth; and excessive expectation makes one love the world. Allah gives the things of the world to those whom He loves and hates, and if Allah loves a slave, then He gives him faith. Surely religion has sons and the world has sons; so be among the sons of religion, and not among the sons of the world. Surely the world is fleeing from its followers and the Hereafter is approaching.'[1431]

'When the morning comes, do not busy yourself thinking of the evening; and when the evening comes, do not busy yourself with the morning. Take from your world for your Hereafter, from your life for your death and from your health for your sickness; for surely you will not know what tomorrow will bring.'[1432]

'Do all of you wish to enter the Garden? Then contain your expectation, fix the appointed time of your death in your sights, and be truly modest before Allah.'[1433]

'Whoever begins his morning full of sadness is beginning the day angry with his Lord; whoever complains of something which has afflicted him is complaining to his Lord, and for any poor man who humbles himself to a rich man for the sake of his worldly affairs, a third of his religion departs. Whoever begins the morning concerned with any other than Allah is not of Allah; whoever does not fear Allah is not of Allah, and whoever does not concern himself with the Muslims is not of them.'[1434]

Imam `Ali relates that the Prophet said, 'Surely the worst of my *ummah* are those who are generous out of fear of the evil of others; whoever are generous in order to guard against their evil are not of me.'[1435]

1431	al-Haqaa'iq,313.
1432	ibid.
1433	al-Ashtari,I,273.
1434	al-Shiraazi,451-454.
1435	al-Khisaal,I,14.

'If a man praises a sultan in return for reward, and is over-respectful and servile because he desires to obtain something from him, then his soul is in the fire.' Allah said, "And do not incline to those who are unjust, lest the fire touch you" [11:113].'[1436]

'Whoever pleases a sultan while causing Allah to be angered has gone outside the religion of Allah.'[1437]

'If anyone seeks to please people while incurring the anger of Allah, then Allah will cause the one who lauded the people to be rebuked by the people; whoever prefers obedience to Allah while incurring the anger of the people, Allah will protect from the enmity of every enemy, from the envy of every envier and from the error of every transgressor, and Allah will be his ally and supporter.'[1438]

Al-Saadiq said, 'The one who gives allegiance to someone who disobeys Allah has no religion.'[1439]

Love of Reputation

Allah says:

☼ [As for] that future abode, We assign it to those who have no desire to exalt themselves in the earth nor to make mischief, and the good end is for those who guard [against evil]. (28:83)

☼ Whoever desires this world's life and its finery, We will pay them in full their deeds therein, and they shall not be made to suffer loss in respect of them. These are they for

---

1436   al-Ashtari,II,259.
1437   al-Kulayni,II,273.
1438   ibid.
1439   ibid.

whom there is nothing but fire in the Hereafter, and what they wrought in it shall go for nothing, and vain is what they used to do. (11:15-16)

The Messenger said, 'Many a disheveled and dusty man, clothed in tatters, unheeded by people, I would acquit if he gave oath by Allah.'[1440]

'Shall I not show you the inhabitants of the Garden? All the weak and the chaste: when they give oath by Allah I acquit them. As for the inhabitants of the Fire, they are all the proud and arrogant.'[1441]

'Surely the inhabitants of the Garden are all the disheveled, the dusty and unnoticed of men: if they seek permission from the emirs they are not given it; if they seek the hand of a woman they do not succeed in marrying her; and if they speak they are not listened to. Their cares agitate in their breast, but when His light is apportioned on the Last Day, it will cover them liberally.'[1442]

'It is enough of a trial for a man that people point at him with their fingers in matters of religion or the world.'[1443]

'Two voracious wolves sent into a sheepfold are no less destructive than love of position and wealth for the religion of a Muslim.'[1444]

'People are ruined by following their desires and by their love of praise.'[1445]

1440 al-Ashtari,I,182.
1441 ibid.
1442 ibid.
1443 *Mishkaat al-Anwaar*,320.
1444 al-Kaashaani,119.
1445 ibid.

'Love of wealth and prestige causes hypocrisy to flourish in the heart, just as water causes green plants to flourish.'[1446]

'Give generously, do not become famous, and do not elevate your own person so that you are remembered for your knowledge. Keep hidden and silent: you will be protected; it will gladden the righteous and enrage the corrupt.'[1447]

Imam Hasan said, 'Whoever wears the robe of fame, Allah will clothe with a robe of fire on the Last Day.'[1448]

Imam al-Saadiq said, 'Truly Allah hates two kinds of renown: renown for one's clothes and renown for one's prayer.'[1449]

'Reputation, both good and bad, means the Fire.'[1450]

Disdain of Others

Allah says:

☼ Let not a folk deride a folk who may be better than they. (49:11)

`A'ishah said, 'I mimicked someone and the Messenger rebuked me for it, saying, "I do not like to mimic anyone".'[1451]

The Messenger said, 'Whoever criticizes his brother for a sin he has turned away from will not die until he commits the same sin himself.'[1452]

'Whoever disdains a friend of mine is preparing for war with

1446 ibid.
1447 ibid.
1448 *Mishkaat al-Anwaar*,320-321.
1449 ibid.
1450 ibid.
1451 *Mishkaat al-Anwaar*,322.
1452 al-Ashtari,I,113.

me.'[1453]

Al-Saadiq said, 'On the Last Day, a voice will call out, "Where are those who opposed and made fun of My friend?" Then a people without flesh on their faces will rise, and it will be said, "These are the ones who tormented the believers, caused them distress, doggedly opposed them and treated them harshly because of their religion." Then they will be ordered to *Jahannam*.'[1454]

'Whoever is resentful towards a Muslim in need, Allah will continue to be resentful towards him until he ceases to be resentful to the Muslim.'[1455]

'If a man seeks to humiliate or disdain a believer because of his poverty or his lack of property, Allah will surely divulge his offences by proclaiming them over the heads of creation.'[1456]

'Whoever is respectful of the religion of Allah is respectful of the rights of his brothers.'[1457]

'Whoever sees to the need of a believer without looking down upon him will be given an abode in Paradise.'[1458]

Heedlessness

Allah says:

☼ They are as cattle, nay, they are in worse error; these are the heedless ones. (7:179)

☼ ... And those who are heedless of Our Revelations: [as

1453	ibid.	
1454	*Mishkaat al-Anwaar*,322.	
1455	al-Kulayni,II,351.	
1456	*Mishkaat al-Anwaar*,322-323.	
1457	ibid.	
1458	ibid.	

for] those, their abode is in the Fire. (10:7-8)

☼ These are they on whose hearts and their hearing and their eyes Allah has set a seal, and these are the heedless ones. (16:108)

☼ Their reckoning has drawn near to men, and in heedlessness are they turning side. (21:1)

The Prophet said to Abu Dharr, 'The one who remembers Allah amongst those who are heedless is like the one who fights as the others flee.'[1459]

Giving instruction to Abu Dharr, the Prophet said, 'Make an intention do a good deed – even if you do not do it you will not be recorded amongst the heedless.'[1460]

'All of goodness is contained in three states: one's looking, one's silence and one's speech. Any looking which is made without reflection is negligence, any silence in which there is no thought is heedlessness, and any speech which does not contain remembrance is idle talk. Fortunate are they whose looking is reflection, whose silence is thought and whose speech is remembrance, who weep over their mistakes and allow no evil to reach the people by their hand.'[1461]

Imam `Ali also said, 'How many a heedless man weaves cloth to dress himself in, and it turns out to be his shroud; and builds a house to live in and it becomes his place of burial.'[1462]

Rebuking the heedless and comparing them to cattle. Imam `Ali said in one of his speeches, 'O you heedless people, of

---

1459 ibid.
1460 al-Ashtari,II,61.
1461 ibid.
1462 *Mishkaat al-Anwaar*,55.

whom Allah is not heedless; O you who abandon what you have been commanded to, whose lives have been seized for their crimes: how is it I see you going away from Allah, yearning for another as if you are cattle being taken to pasture by the herder? O people! I do not urge you to obedience of Allah but that I strive to outstrip you to it myself; and I do not forbid you from acts of disobedience but that I myself desist from them before you.'[1463]

'I advise you to remember death and diminish your negligence of it. How is it that you are negligent of something which will not neglect you, and are avid for something which will grant you no respite?'[1464]

'Beware of heedlessness for it is the corrupter of excellence.'[1465]

'Heedlessness is loss.'[1466]

'Heedlessness is the most destructive of enemies.'[1467]

'The one who is heedless is slumbering, and heedlessness is deception.'[1468]

'Whoever slumbers in the face of the enemy is awakened by his stratagems.'[1469]

'Woe to the sleeper! How great is his loss – he is lacking in action and diminished will be his reward.'[1470]

While supplicating Allah, al-Sajjaad said, 'Awaken me from the inertia of the heedless, the sleep of the immoderate and the

---

1463	al-Haakim,I,179.
1464	ibid.
1465	ibid.
1466	ibid.
1467	ibid.
1468	ibid.
1469	ibid.
1470	ibid.

slumber of the vile. Do not inveigh against me as You would the one who has fallen from Your eye of care and concern. Do not resist me as You would those who have been covered in disgrace by You, but rather take me by the hand, away from the errors of those who are rejected, away from the terror of those who deviate, away from the mistakes of the deluded and the plight of those doomed to perish.'[1471]

Al-Saadiq said, 'Beware of heedlessness, for whoever is heedless is being heedless of himself; and beware of treating Allah's command with disdain, for whoever does this Allah will treat with disdain on the Last Day of Judgment.'[1472]

Obligation

Allah says:

> ☼ They think that they oblige you by becoming Muslims. Say: You are not obliging me by your Islam. Rather, Allah lays you under an obligation by guiding you to the faith. (49:17)

> ☼ And bestow not favors, seeking worldly gain. (74:6)

The Messenger relates that Allah said, 'The Garden has been forbidden those who lay others under obligation, the miserly and the backbiters.'[1473]

'If a man does an act of kindness for his brother and then makes him feel obliged for it, Allah will bring his action to nothing, will make him responsible, and will not be thankful for

---

1471 ibid.
1472 ibid.
1473 ibid.

his effort.'[1474]

Giving instruction to Imam `Ali he said, 'O `Ali, Allah hates for this *ummah* frivolity in prayer, the laying of obligations on others for charity given, and coming to the mosque in an impure state.'[1475]

`Ali relates that he said, 'O Allah, do not cause me to be in need from any of your creation.' Then the Messenger said, 'Never say it in that way – surely there is no one but that is in need of the people.' `Ali then said, 'O Messenger of Allah, what should I say?' He said, 'Say, "O Allah, do not cause me to be in need of the evil among Your creation." `Ali then said, 'O Messenger of Allah, who are the evil among His creation?' He replied, 'Those who, if they give, lay an obligation on those they gave to, and when they refuse to give are full of reproof.'[1476]

Imam `Ali said, 'There are three kinds of person hated by Allah: the one who makes others feel obligated for his charity, the one who is niggardly in his endeavor and the poor man who is wasteful.'[1477]

1474 al-Shiraazi,242.
1475 al-Akhlaaq,432.
1476 ibid.
1477 al-Ashtari,I,39.

Bibliography

Imam `Ali ibn Abi Taalib. *Nahj al-Balaaghah*,Sharh Muhammad `Abduh. 4 vols. Daar al-Ma`aarif li'l-Matbu`aat (Beirut, 1982).

al-`Amili, `Abd al-Husayn Sharaf al-Deen. *al-Muraaja`aat*. 18th ed. Daaral-Qur'an al-Kareem (Qum, 1978).

al-`Amili, `Izz al-Deen bin `Abd al-Samad al-Haarithi. *Nur al-Haqiqah wa Nur al-Hadiqah fi `Ilm al-Akhlaaq*. Matba`ah Muhr (Qum, 1983).

Al-Ashtari, Abi'l-Husayn Warraam. *Tanbeeh al-Khaweetir wa Nuzhat al-Nawaazir (Majmu`aat Warraam)*. 2 vols. Maktabat al-Faqih (Qum, 1956).

al-`Ayaashi, Muhammad bin Mas`ud. *Tafseer al-`Ayaashi*. 2 vols. al-Maktabah al-`Ilmiyyah al-Islaamiyyah (Tehran, 1380 AH).

al-Barqi, Abi Ja`far Ahmad bin Muhammad. *al-Mahaasin*. 2 vols. 2nd ed. Daar al-Kutub al-Islaamiyyah (Qum, 1326 AH).

al-Hakeem, Muhammad Ridaa, Muhammad `Ali. *al-Hayaat*. 2 vols. 2nd ed. (offset). Daar al-Tibaa`ah wa al-Nashr (Tehran 1981).

al-Hindi, `Alaa' al-Deen al-Burhaan Fawri. *Kanz al-`Ummaal fi Sunan al-Aqwaal wa al-Af`aal*. ed. Shaykh Bakri Hayaati. Vol 14 (n.d.).

al-Hurr, Muhammad bin al-Hasan. *Wasaa'il al-Shi'ite*. ed. `Abd al-Raheem al-Sheeraazi. 16 vols. Daar Ihya' al-Turaath al-`Arab (Beirut,n.d.).

al-`Inaathi, Muhammad. *Adab al-Nafs*. ed. Kaazim al-Musawi. 2

vols. al-Maktabah al-Radawiyyah (Iran, 1380 AH).

al-Irbilli, Abi'l-Hasan `Ali bin `Isaa. *Kashf al-Ghummah fi Ma`rifat al-A'immah.* 3 vols. Daar al-Kitaab al-Islaami (Beirut, 1981).

al-Kaashaani, Muhammad bin al-Murtadaa al-Fayd. *al-Haqaa'iq fi Mahaasin al-Akhlaaq.* 2nd ed. Daar al-Kitaab al-`Arabi (Beirut, 1979).

Qurrat al-`Uyun fi al-Ma`aarif wa'l-Hikam. 2nd ed. Daar al-Kitaab al-`ArabI (Beirut, 1979).

al-Muhajjah al-Baydaa' fi Tahdheeb al-Ihyaa'. 2nd ed. 4 vols. Daftar-e Enteshaaraat-e Islaami (Qum, 1383 AH).

al-Khuraasaani, Ibraahim bin Muhammad al-Juwayni. *Faraa'id al-Simtayn fi fadaa'il'il al-Murtadaa wa'l-Batul wa'l-Sibtayn.* 2nd vol. ed. and pub. al-Shaykh Muhammad Baaqir al-Mahmudi.

al-Kulayni, Muhammad bin Ya`qub. *al-Kaafi.* ed. `Ali Akbar Ghaffaari. 4th ed. Daar Sa`b wa Daar al-Ta`aaruf (Beirut, 1401 AH).

Ibn Maajah, Muhammad bin Yazeed al-Qazweeni. *Sunan Ibn Maajah.* ed. Muhammad Fu'aad `Abd al-Baaqi. Vol.2. Daar Ihyaa' al-Kutub al-`Arabiyyah (n.d.).

al-Mufeed, Muhammad bin al-Nu`maani al-Akbari. *al-Irshaad.* Maktabat Baseerati (Qum,n.d.).

al-Saduq, Muhammad bin `Ali al-Qummi. *al-Khisaal.* 2 vols. Manshuraat Jamaa`at al-Mudarriseen fi'l-Hawza al-`Ilmiyyah (Qum, 1983).

`Uyun Akhbaar al-Ridaa. ed. al-Sayyid Mahdi al-Husayni. 2 vols. Enteshaaraat Jehaan (Tehran, n.d.)

al-Tawheed. ed. Hasahim al-Husayni al-Tehraani. Maktabah al-Saduq. (Tehran, 1398 AH).

al-SheeraazI, Hasan bin Mahdi. *Kalimat Allah*. 1st ed. Daar al-Saadiq (Beirut, 1969).

al-Tabarsi, Abu'l-Fadl `Ali. *Mishkaat al-Anwaar*. 2nd ed. Daar al-Kutub al-Islaamiyyah (Qum, 1965).

al-Tabarsi, Radiy al-Deen al-Husayn bin al-Fasl. *Makaarim al-Akhlaaq*. 6th ed. Mu`assasat al-`Ilmi li al-Matbu`aat (Beirut, 1982).

al-Tusi, Abu Ja`far Muhammad bin al-Hasan. *al-Nihaayah fi Mujarrad al-Fiqh wa'l-Fataawi*. Daar al Kitaab al-`Arabi (Beirut, n.d.).

al-Amaali. 2nd ed. Mu'assasat al-Wafaa' (Beirut, 1981).

Other titles by this Author

Living Islam – East and West
Ageless and universal wisdom set against the backdrop of a changing world: application of this knowledge to one's own life is most appropriate.

The Elements of Islam/Thoughtful Guide to Islam
An introduction to Islam through an overview of the universality and light of the prophetic message.

The Qur'an & Its Teachings

Beams of Illumination from the Divine Revelations
A collection of teachings and talks with the objective of exploring deeper meanings of Qur'anic Revelations.

Commentary on Four Selected Chapters of the Qur'an
The Shaykh uncovers inner meanings, roots and subtleties of the Qur'anic Arabic terminology.

The Cow: Commentary on Chapters One and Two of the Holy Qur'an
The first two chapters of the Qur'an give guidance regarding inner and outer struggle. Emphasis is on understanding key Qur'anic terms.

The Family of `Imran
This book is a commentary on the third chapter of the Qur'an, the family of `Imran which includes the story of Mary, mother of `Isa (Jesus).

The Essential Message of the Qur'an
Teachings from the Qur'an such as purpose of creation, Attributes of the Creator, nature of human beings, decrees governing the laws of the universe, life and death. To obtain these titles in ebook or hard copy, please visit www.zahrapublications.com and www.sfhfoundation.com.

Heart of Qur'an and Perfect Mizan
Commentary on chapter Yasin. This is traditionally read over the dead person: if we want to know the meaning of life, we have to learn about death.

Journey of the Universe as Expounded in the Qur'an
The Qur'an traces the journey of all creation, seeing the physical, biological and geological voyage of life as paralleled by the inner spiritual evolution of woman.

Qur'an's Prescription for Life
Understanding of the Qur'an is made accessible with easy reference to key issues concerning life, and the path of Islam.

The Story of Creation in the Qur'an – A Sufi Interpretation
An exposition of the Qur'anic verses relating to the nature of physical phenomena, including the origins of the universe, the nature of light, matter, space and time, and the evolution of biological and sentient beings.

Sufism & Islamic Psychology and Philosophy

Beginning's End
This is a contemporary outlook on Sufi sciences of self-knowledge, exposing the challenge of our modern lifestyle that is out of balance.

Cosmology of the Self
Islamic teachings of Tawhid (Unity) with insights into the human self: understanding the inner landscape is essential foundation for progress on the path of knowledge.

a description of fasting in different faith traditions, its spiritual benefits, rules and regulations.

The Inner Meanings of Worship in Islam – A Personal Selection of Guidance for the Wayfarer

Here is guidance for those who journey along this path, from the Qur'an, the Prophet's traditions, narrations from the Ahl al-Bayt, and seminal works from among the Ahl al-Tasawwuf of all schools of thought.

Prophetic Traditions in Islam – On the Authority of the Family of the Prophet

Offers a comprehensive selection of Islamic teachings arranged according to topics dealing with belief and worship, moral, social and spiritual values.

The Wisdom (Hikam) of Ibn `Ata'allah – Translation and Commentary

These aphorisms of Ibn `Ata'Allah, a Shadhili Shaykh, reveal the breadth and depth of an enlightened being who reflects divine unity and inner transformation through worship.

The Sayings and Wisdom of Imām Ali

A selection of this great man's sayings gathered together from authentic and reliable sources. They have been carefully translated into modern English.

Transformative Worship in Islam: Experiencing Perfection

Uniquely bridges the traditional practices and beliefs, culture and language of Islam with the transformative spiritual states described by the Sufis and Gnostics.

The Lantern of the Path by Imam Ja'far al-Sadiq.

Imam Ja'far al-Sadiq was the founder of the Ja'fari School of Islamic Law and a renowned scholar of his age. The Imam shows in his ageless commentaries on the courtesies, practices

The Elements of Sufism/Thoughtful Guide to Sufism
Sufism is the heart of Islam. This introduction describes its origins, practices, historical background and its spread throughout the world.

Happiness in Life and After Death – An Islamic Sufi View
This book offers revelations and spiritual teachings that map a basic path towards wholesome living without forgetting death: cultivating a constant awareness of one's dual nature.

The Journey of the Self
After introducing the basic model of the self, there follows a simple yet complete outline of the self's emergence, development, sustenance, and growth toward its highest potential.

Leaves from a Sufi Journal
A unique collection of articles presenting an outstanding introduction to the areas of Sufi sm and original Islamic teachings.

The Sufi Way to Self-Unfoldment
Unfolding inner meanings of the Islamic ritual practices towards the intended ultimate purpose to live a life honorable and fearless, with no darkness, ignorance or abuse.

Witnessing Perfection
Delves into the universal question of Deity and the purpose of life. Durable contentment is a result of 'perfected vision'.

Practices & Teachings of Islam
Calling Allah by His Most Beautiful Names
Attributes or Qualities resonate from their Majestic and Beautiful Higher Realm into the heart of the active seeker, and through it back into the world.

Fasting in Islam
This is a comprehensive guide to fasting in all its aspects, with

and rituals of Islam the way to equilibrium in the most inspired and tawhidi way.

Talks & Courses
Ask Course 1 – The Sufi Map of the Self
This workbook explores the entire cosmology of the self through time, and maps the evolution of the self from before birth through life, death and beyond.

Ask Course 2 – The Prophetic Way of Life
This workbook explores how the code of ethics that govern religious practice and the Prophetic ways are in fact transformational tools to enlightened awakening.

Friday Discourses – Volume 1
The Shaykh addresses many topics that influence Muslims at the core of what it means to be a Muslim in today's global village.

Songs of Imān on the Roads of Pakistan
A series of talks given on the divergence between 'faith' and 'unbelief' during a tour of the country in 1982 which becomes a reflection of the condition occurring in the rest of the world today.

Poetry & Aphorisms
Sound Waves
A collection of aphorisms that help us reflect and discover the intricate connection between self and soul.

Beyond Windows
Offering moving and profound insights of compassion and spirituality through these anthologies of connections between slave self and Eternal Lord.

101 Helpful Illusions
Everything in creation has a purpose relevant to ultimate spiritual Truth. This book highlights natural veils to be transcended by

disciplined courage, wisdom and insight.

Bursts of Silence
Inspired aphorisms provide keys to doors of inner knowledge, as well as antidotes to distraction and confusion.

Ripples of Light
Inspired aphorisms which become remedies for hearts that seek the truth.

Pointers to Presence
A collection of aphorisms providing insights into consciousness and are pointers to spiritual awakening.

Autobiography
Son of Karbala
The atmosphere of an Iraq in transition is brought to life and used as a backdrop for the Shaykh's own personal quest for self-discovery and spiritual truth. To obtain these titles in ebook or hard copy, please visit www.zahrapublications.com and www.sfhfoundation.com.

www.ingramcontent.com/pod-product-compliance
Lightning Source LLC
Chambersburg PA
CBHW022057150426
43195CB00008B/177